A TRAILS BOOKS GUIDE

# GREAT
# WISCONSIN
# ROMANTIC WEEKENDS

CHRISTINE DES GARENNES

TRAILS BOOKS
Black Earth, Wisconsin

Library of Congress Control Number: 2004104307
ISBN: 1-931599-37-8

Editor: Stan Stoga
Photos: Christine des Garennes, except where noted
Design: Jennifer Walde
Cover Photo: Darryl R. Beers


Printed in the United States of America.

09  08  07  06  05  04          6  5  4  3  2  1


TRAILS BOOKS
A division of Trails Media Group, Inc.
P.O. Box 317  •  Black Earth, WI  53515
(800) 236-8088  •  e-mail: books@wistrails.com
www.trailsbooks.com

# Contents

# Introduction

When I first told people I was working on a guidebook to romantic getaways in Wisconsin, some of them scrunched their eyebrows and took on a perplexed look. The reaction wasn't surprising because many of these folks (some residents, some not) had a slightly different view of the state. After all, they had spent many vacations in Wisconsin at lakeside resorts, the kind with cottages furnished with bunk beds, a multipurpose room stocked with Candyland board games, and a beach house equipped with stacks of inner tubes depicting cartoon characters. There is no doubt that this kind of resort can be fun—usually when you come with a van loaded with children or grandchildren. But a weekend there may not be pleasant when you're looking for peace and privacy—when you and your sweetheart are spending your first weekend together or when you and your spouse want to reignite those romantic flames.

I hope this guide will help you discover intimate, exclusive, adults-only resorts in Wisconsin, as well as more conventional establishments that appeal to romantically inclined couples. The state is home to a surprising number of luxurious spas, carriage ride companies, hot-air balloon businesses, and fine restaurants. In addition to those in this book, I'm sure you'll discover others that you'll want to keep secret. Some destinations are well known, such as the American Club in Kohler. Others are relatively new and tucked away in more remote areas of the state, such as Percheron Paradise Romantic Hideaway, located south of Sparta. Many are just perfect for romantic couples of any age.

In researching romantic spots for this book, I scoured the state's restaurants, steering away from the ones where booster seats are available. I made a beeline toward places where couples could gaze longingly into each other's eyes while enjoying a top-notch meal with great wine. And I toured a number of inns, resorts, and bed and breakfasts. The places highlighted in the book are ones with romantic features like double whirlpool bathtubs and fireplaces. Many are open only to adults or children above a certain age.

Because not everyone defines romance in the same way, I tried to include a variety of itineraries. For some travelers, a romantic getaway might entail browsing antiques shops and walking through parks. For others, it might include snoozing on a beach for much of the afternoon. On some getaways you'll find yourselves participating in quiet, leisurely activities that I think are ideal for couples, such as getting massages, riding horses, canoeing, or bicycling. Of course, some of the suggested activities can be altered according to your fitness levels and your preferences. You may opt to take a pontoon cruise of Horicon Marsh rather than kayak or canoe through it.

On a practical note, be sure to call to verify the hours and rates of the places the two of you will be visiting. Some hours change depending on the season. Even though some restaurants don't require reservations, always make one just in case. The last thing you'll want is to be stuck driving around at night and pulling into a restaurant only to find it closed for the season or to be faced with an hour wait. Many getaways suggest the two of you spend your lunch hour picnicking in a park or on a beach. You can't beat a quiet picnic on a sunshiny day under a tree or in a meadow. So before you depart for any romantic getaway, be sure to pack a picnic basket, two wineglasses, and a corkscrew.

Keep in mind that the itineraries in this guide are one person's suggestions for three-day-weekend getaways. It may have been a while since the two of you have spent some time together. So, you may want to deviate from the suggested itinerary by skipping the visit to the museum or the park and wiling away the afternoon lounging together on the private porch of your hotel room or within your cozy bed-and-breakfast room. Don't feel as if you need to pack in all your activities in three days. Most of these destinations are so inviting, you'll want to extend your trip by a few days or plan to return in the future. And don't feel guilty about sleeping in. After all, this is about indulging yourself and your sweetie—and spending a marvelously romantic couple of days together.

With that said, happy traveling.

# Acknowledgments

❧ Thanks to all staff and volunteers with the local visitor bureaus and chambers of commerce who guided me to the most romantic hotels, bed and breakfasts, and restaurants in their towns, particularly the staff at the Saint Germain Chamber of Commerce and Gary Knowles with the Heidel House Resort. Thanks to all the owners and managers who welcomed me and provided me with tours of their great places, especially the Angel Inn in Green Lake and Percheron Paradise Romantic Hideaway in Norwalk. Thanks to my editor, Stan Stoga, and the rest of the staff at Trails Media for further crafting and fine-tuning this book. Thanks to a devoted couple, Dave and Marianne, for their suggestions; Geoff and our splendid autumn days in Mineral Point and the Old Lumberyard Inn; and Maxwell, our newest traveling partner.

# CHAPTER ONE

# Living It Up (and Loving It) in
# Lake Geneva

If you're looking to impress a companion, Lake Geneva is the place to bring him or her. For about 125 years, the southeast Wisconsin town of Lake Geneva has been a summer playground of sorts for wealthy Milwaukee and Chicago couples and families. They retreat to their sprawling estates lining Geneva Lake or to one of the many upscale lakeshore hotels and inns. Lake Geneva has a festive, joie de vivre feel to it, with cheery people shopping for pottery during an art festival and milling about on the beach, black luxury SUVs cruising the streets, and sailboats gliding across the lake, carrying one gorgeous couple after another.

Drive along the rambling lakeshore roads in a vintage Packard, driven by a chauffeur. See the sights from above during a private hot-air balloon ride. Hit the links on a championship course, and follow that with a massage for two. Dine at a table for two in a restored mansion.

Don't forget that Lake Geneva is not the only quaint town along the lakeshore. Take a short drive to the other appealing towns of Fontana and Williams Bay, where sandy beaches and lakeshore paths invite couples to laze in the sun or go for long walks together. At the end of your vacation, your checking account may be drained (or for some, it may barely have a dent in it), but you'll leave knowing that while in town you took advantage of the finer things in life.

## Day One

### ☞ MORNING

Perhaps a good way to start the weekend is with a round of golf at one of the area's finest courses. At the **Grand Geneva Resort and Spa**, two courses will challenge you: the Highlands and the Brute. The Highlands is a Scottish-style, par-71 course set amid rolling hills, originally designed by Pete Dye and Jack Nicklaus and renovated by Robert Cupp. The Brute is a par-72, 7,258-yard-long course with large greens and wide fairways. **Geneva National Golf Club**, located west of Lake Geneva on Lake Como, consists of three courses designed by Arnold Palmer, Lee Trevino, and Gary Player. All three are par-72 courses with 5,200 to 7,200 yardages. The Player and Palmer courses offer golfers views of Lake Como, while the Trevino course is set amid oak and hickory woods.

## NAME DROPPING

According to local lore, William Bell and Lee Phillips developed the soap opera *The Young and the Restless* while living in Lake Geneva and set the popular daytime drama in the nearby town of Genoa City. Paul Newman acted in summer theater here. J. D. Salinger wrote *Catcher in the Rye* here during one summer. Other famous residents? The Wrigley family of Wrigley chewing gum fame.

After your quiet morning of playing golf together, drive into town and relax over a brunch or lunch at the **Grandview Restaurant and Lounge** in the Geneva Inn. As the name implies, wherever you choose to sit in this restaurant, you'll both be able to see the blue waters of Geneva Lake outside the wall of windows. Take in the splendor as you dine at a table for two. The brunch menu varies according to the season, but you will choose from the three-course brunch menu (with items like blintzes, crab cakes, and raspberry roulade) or off the à la carte menu (which features entrées such as seared tuna with mixed greens and vegetables served in a ginger wasabi vinaigrette). Don't forget to order sparkling champagne or cider. If you visit during a weekday, you'll find the lunch menu equally impressive, with a variety of fare such as spinach *gâteau* (that's "cake" in French) and Caesar salad with fried calamari, or peppercorn-crusted Angus tenderloin of beef.

Following your meal, walk hand in hand through the gardens and to the inn's pier to watch boats go by for a while.

## AFTERNOON

Next, sign up for a massage for two at the Grand Geneva Resort and Spa. For approximately 50 minutes the two of you will relax in a private room while two separate massage therapists rub away any stress or aches you've had. Follow this treatment with a 20-minute soak in a botanical bath, a private whirlpool bath with bath oils that aim to loosen muscles and soothe minds, putting both of you in better frame of mind and body for your getaway.

Now that you and your companion are totally relaxed, check in to your room for the next two nights. A legion of bed and breakfasts and inns surround

Taking in the view at Riviera Dock in downtown Lake Geneva. Photo courtesy of the Lake Geneva Area Convention and Visitors bureau.

the Geneva Lake area, many of them providing quality accommodations. Two options stand out for couples: Lazy Cloud and the French Country Inn.

The atmosphere at the **Lazy Cloud Lodge Bed and Breakfast** is definitely romantic, from the hammocks and benches for two arranged in the courtyard to the special packages available to couples, including boxes of chocolates and bouquets of flowers delivered to the rooms. Lazy Cloud is located on three acres in Fontana, minutes from the beach and far from the crowds of downtown Lake Geneva. Each room has a whirlpool bathtub and fireplace and comes with complimentary bottles of sparkling wine, candles, and loveseats. Choose among rooms such as the cozy log cabin suite, beachcomber room, enchanted treehouse suite (which has its own private deck), and Paul Newman Suite. (Yes, he stayed here while performing summer stock in 1950.) They are all designed for couples, so pick one according to your style, whether you prefer Victorian, rustic, or nautical decor.

Order the Enchanted Evening Sweetheart Special, which includes a bouquet of flowers, the Enchanted Evening board game, the book *Love, Laughter, and Romance,* and a box of chocolates. (If you really want to splurge, you can even order private massages for two in your room from the Grand Geneva Resort.)

After you settle into your love nest, walk out to the gardens and sink into a hammock.

Part B&B, part inn, and part boutique hotel, the **French Country Inn** is three miles west of Lake Geneva on Como Lake. A former speakeasy and casino, the renovated inn contains 34 rooms. The most romantic rooms can be found in the new buildings, L'Auberge and Petite Auberge. In the Auberge building, book a two-story lakefront loft suite, which boasts a whirlpool bathtub on the loft level. The Petite Auberge is a detached cottage with two suites. Each comes with a private patio, large bedroom, and two-sided fireplace. All are decorated in light and airy colors such as cream and beige.

After you check in to the French Country Inn, unpack your bags, stop by the parlor, and pour yourselves some complimentary tea. Unwind together by walking out to the deck, soaking in the sun, and watching the boaters crisscross Lake Como.

## EVENING

This evening the two of you will spend time on the lake. Reserve seats on a dinner cruise with **Lake Geneva Cruise Line**. Depending on what day you visit, you can take a ride on the mellow sunset dinner cruise or the Dixieland cruise, which features a live band. Both cruises debark from the historic Riviera Dock in downtown Lake Geneva. Board the *Grand Belle*, a steamerlike vessel that seats up to 100 people. On the main deck, dine on entrées like prime rib or orange roughy, vegetables, and salad. The dinner cruises include light narration on the history of some of the lake's estates, such as the Wrigley and Maytag homes. Walk upstairs to the outside deck for fresh air and maybe a twirl around the deck.

If you are looking for a more private cruise (and money is not an issue), charter a 41-foot cabin cruiser, the *Lorelei* from the Lake Geneva Cruise Line. Arrange a picnic dinner of goodies from **The Cheese Box** in Lake Geneva. You can also purchase a bottle of wine and a plate of cheese at the shop. As you nibble on summer sausage and sip a microbrew or glass of wine, put your arm around your date and watch the sunset from the boat's teakwood deck.

Depending on what time you return from your cruise, listen to some music under the stars at Aurora University's **Music of the Lake Series**. Visiting artists and groups such as the Glenn Miller Orchestra set up under a tent outside.

## Day Two

## MORNING

If you are staying at Lazy Cloud, opt to have breakfast delivered to your room, allowing you to lounge in bed in your robes or in the garden with plates of pecan rolls and bowls of fruit.

Otherwise, consider dropping by the kitschy but friendly **Daddy Maxwell's Arctic Circle Diner** in Williams Bay, a popular joint with locals and regular visitors to the lake area. Cozy up together at a table in the sunny, round dining

Enjoying the footpath encircling Geneva Lake. Photo courtesy of the Lake Geneva Area Convention and Visitors bureau.

room, and order traditional comfort food such as homemade doughnuts and milkshakes.

After breakfast, the two of you should be ready for the day, a day that includes plenty of opportunities for strolling and hand-holding. Start with a short hike through the **Kishwauketoe Conservancy**, just down the street from the diner. Four miles of nature trails wind through this 230-acre preserve. Spend about 45 minutes here, and head to the observatory tower to take in views of the wetland wildflowers and plants.

Next pick up *Walk, Talk, and Gawk*, a booklet that maps out the 21-mile walk around the lake and sites and restaurants along the way. (Purchase the booklet at downtown Lake Geneva shops or at the Lake Geneva Cruise Line office at Riviera Dock.) You can access the footpath from any public park along the lake. Consider launching your walk from downtown Lake Geneva's Library or Flatiron Parks and continue southeast to view a number of grand mansions.

After you've both worked up appetites, walk over to Scuttlebutts in downtown Lake Geneva. **Scuttlebutts** is a lively restaurant that serves a wide variety of salads—like the awesome Copenhagen salad with avocado, chicken, almonds, asparagus, and tomatoes—plus burgers, deli sandwiches, stir-fried veggies, and Wisconsin cheese soup.

## ↪ AFTERNOON

Considering you spent most of the morning walking and exploring, this afternoon will be devoted to lounging on the beach and taking a peaceful parasail ride. If you are visiting on a summer weekend and want to steer clear of crowds, avoid camping out on the beach near Riviera Dock and by Big Foot State Park. Instead, lay your towel at Reid Beach in Fontana or Edgewater Park in Williams Bay. Here you will be able to read, snooze, or day dream side-by-side.

---

### SURPRISE, HONEY! I GOT YOU A HOUSE!

↪ Also according to the local historical society, Lake Geneva resident A. C. Bartlett wanted to build a summer home for his wife. In order to surprise her on her birthday in April, he erected a tent from a circus company to hide the work being done.

---

When you need a little break, call **Jerry's Marine** to find out what time they are offering parasail rides that day, or call in advance to reserve two spots. Ride tandem to enjoy the experience together. Although it may look frightening to people who are afraid of heights, parasailing is actually a gentle experience almost any couple will love. You will have a bird's-eye view of the lake and the surrounding towns for about 15 minutes.

Next, roll up your beach towels and stop by **Kilwin's Chocolate and Ice Cream Shoppe** in Lake Geneva for mega-creamy ice cream. If you're visiting on a steamy Saturday afternoon, you'll have to stand in line for a few moments, but the ice cream is well worth the wait. Choose from a dizzying array of flavors such as classic vanilla or mint chocolate chip. Don't forget to pick up a box of chocolates for your lover with the sweet tooth. Cordial cherries perhaps?

## ↪ EVENING

If the weather is warm and the wind just right, knock the socks off your companion by planning a private hot-air balloon ride above the Lake Geneva region. Here's your chance to propose, guys. You'll depart about an hour and a half before sunset and drive out to the launch site where you'll meet the crew from **A Lighter than Air Affair Hot Air Ballooning** and help prepare the balloon for its launch (or you can watch). The captain will alternate between flying high above the region's rolling hills and drifting closer to the earth, sweeping the treetops and allowing you to talk with people on the ground. On a clear day you can rise 1,000 feet in the air and view the Chicago skyline and Lake Michigan. Once you land (where you land depends on the wind patterns), you will celebrate with champagne and hors d'oeuvres.

After your awesome evening in the sky, dine in a renovated Hawaiian plantation mansion in Lake Geneva. In **Gilbert's Restaurant**, tables are set up in various rooms throughout the house, overlooking the gardens, in front of fireplaces, and under glass chandeliers, making your dining experience intimate and quiet. Try to reserve a table in the enclosed glass porch, where you will be able to gaze not only at each other but at Geneva Lake. The food served here is described as contemporary American with European and Pacific Rim influences. Dishes are prepared using free-range meat and line-caught fish. Lounge over a degustation or multicourse menu that may include entrées such as a grilled pork chop with red cabbage and pear reduction or chicken with gnocchi. Ask about Gilbert's private wine dinners and special dining events held throughout the year.

If the two of you are not in the mood to leave your room at Lazy Cloud, order the Enchanted Evening Picnic Basket. Your innkeeper will prepare a basket full of goodies like shrimp cocktail, crackers, cheese, turkey, and ham with bread, salads, fruits, and cheesecake.

After dinner take a moonlight trail ride at **Fantasy Hills Ranch**, about five miles from Lazy Cloud and the French Country Inn in the town of Delavan. For about an hour you'll ride horses over the ranch's 70 acres, through woods and fields.

If horseback riding is not your bag, Fantasy Hills also offers carriage rides off-site that can pick you up from Gilbert's and take you through downtown Lake Geneva.

## Day Three
### ❧ MORNING

After you've leisured over a light breakfast at the inn or B&B and checked out of your room, load the bags in your car and arrange to have an antique car and driver pick you up for a scenic drive in a 1937 silver Packard around the region. Call **AA Antique Limousine Service**, and a driver will greet you with a classic car. Have him or her whisk you down Snake Road, past sprawling estates and horse farms bordered by split rail fences and around Geneva Lake and nearby Lake Como and Delavan Lake.

Visit downtown Lake Geneva where you can take a walk together through Flatiron Park on the lakefront and Seminary Park. Next, if you'd like to spend more money, there are plenty of shops in downtown Lake Geneva where you can purchase gifts for each other. Starfire Custom Designed Jewelry specializes in engagement and wedding rings. Overland Sheepskin Co. stocks shearling coats, mittens, and hats. At The Tin Tub and Scents and Sensibilities you can pick up bubble bath products. Sample a variety of wine and cheeses from The Cheese Box and Global Gourmet.

Now that you have teased your taste buds, head to one of the best brunches in the region at **Kirsch's** in the French Country Inn. Try to secure a seat outside while chefs whip up a New Orleans-style brunch with homemade

View of Geneva Lake from Kirsch's restaurant.

beignets, corn bread, andouille sausages, and grilled catfish. Entrées include the Zydeco scramble, which involves poached eggs placed on top of lobster crab cakes and English muffins and doused with a hollandaise sauce.

### FOR MORE INFORMATION

**Lake Geneva Area Convention and Visitor bureau**
201 Wrigley Drive, Lake Geneva
(262) 248-4416 or (800) 345-1020
www.lakegenevawi.com

**Walworth County Visitor Bureau**
P.O. Box 1015, Elkhorn
(262) 723-3980 or (800) 395-8687
www.walworthcountytourism.com

### ATTRACTIONS AND RECREATION

**AA Antique Limousine Service**
P.O. Box 445, Fontana
(262) 245-6715 or (262) 949-5570

**Fantasy Hills Ranch**
4978 Town Hall Road, Delavan
(262) 728-1773
www.fantasyhillsranch.com

**Geneva National Golf Club**
1221 Geneva National Avenue,
Lake Geneva
(Four miles west of Lake Geneva
on Highway 50)
(262) 245-7000
www.genevanationalresort.com

**Grand Geneva Resort and Spa**
7036 Grand Geneva Way (Highways 50
and 12), Lake Geneva
(262) 248-8811 or (800) 558-3417
www.grandgeneva.com

**Jerry's Marine**
(For boat rentals and parasail rides)
At Fontana's Lakefront,
The Abbey Resort,
Lake Lawn Resort,
and Interlaken Resort
(262) 275-5222

**Kishwauketoe Conservancy**
Highway 67, Williams Bay
www.genevalakeconservancy.org

**Lake Geneva Cruise Line**
Belle of the Lake Sundowner Cruises
Riviera Dock, Wrigley Drive,
Lake Geneva
(262) 248-6206 or (800) 558-5911
www.cruiselakegeneva.com
Cruises run mid-April to late October.

**A Lighter than Air Affair**
**Hot Air Ballooning**
P.O. Box 382, Lake Geneva
(262) 249-1564
www.weflyballoons.com
Reserving the balloon for just the two of
you will cost extra.

**Music of the Lake Series**
**at Aurora University**
350 Constance Boulevard,
Williams Bay
(866) 843-5200, www.aurora.edu

## ⌖ LODGING

**French Country Inn**
W4190 West End Road, Lake Geneva
(262) 245-5220
www.frenchcountryinn.com
Rooms are from $135 in the summer.
Call for spring, fall, and winter rates.

**Lazy Cloud Lodge Bed and Breakfast**
N2025 N. Lake Shore Drive, Fontana
(262) 275-3322
www.lazycloud.com

Rooms are from $130 in the summer.
Call for spring, fall, and winter rates.

## ⌖ DINING AND NIGHTLIFE

**The Cheese Box**
801 S. Wells Street, Lake Geneva
(262) 248-3440 or (800) 345-6105
www.cheesebox.com
Open 9:00 a.m. to 5:00 p.m.
Monday through Saturday and
11:00 a.m. to 5:00 p.m. on Sunday.

**Daddy Maxwell's Arctic Circle Diner**
150 Elkhorn Road, Williams Bay
(262) 245-5757
Open for breakfast and lunch
Saturday through Thursday and
for breakfast, lunch, and dinner
on Friday.

**Gilbert's Restaurant**
327 Wrigley Drive, Lake Geneva
(262) 248-6680
www.gilbertsrestaurant.com
Open for lunch and dinner Tuesday
through Sunday during the summer.
Call for winter hours.

**Grandview Restaurant and Lounge**
In the Geneva Inn
N2009 Highway 120,
Lake Geneva
(800) 441-5881
www.genevainn.com
Open for lunch Monday through
Saturday, for dinner daily,
and for brunch on Saturday
and Sunday.

**Kilwin's Chocolate and Ice Cream**
**Shoppe**
772 Main Street, Lake Geneva
(262) 248-4400
Open 10:00 a.m. until 10:00 p.m. on
weekdays and until 10:30 p.m. on
weekends. Call for winter hours.

**Kirsch's**
At the French Country Inn
W4190 West End Road, Lake Geneva
(262) 245-5756
www.kirschs.com
Open for dinner daily and for brunch
on Sunday.

**Scuttlebutts**
831 Wrigley Drive, Lake Geneva
(262) 248-1111
Open for breakfast, lunch, and dinner
daily from spring to fall.
Call for winter hours.

# CHAPTER TWO

# Courting, Cosmopolitan Style, in
## *Milwaukee*

Known by many for its breweries, motorcycles, and meatpacking plants, Milwaukee may not seem like the most romantic city in the Midwest. But here couples can hobnob over cocktails in a piano bar, stroll through an Italianate garden, and admire first-rate artwork. During this getaway you'll find yourselves swimming atop one of the grandest hotels in the afternoon and cruising through the downtown in a horse-drawn carriage in the evening.

In the 1800s Milwaukee thrived with industry—farm machinery factories, grain mills, and elevators—and the owners of these companies, such as the beer barons, left a legacy of impressive mansions, hotels, and theaters. Although it has a grand history, the city is not languishing in its past; it has embraced a future. One recognizable sign is the sweeping building addition to the Milwaukee Art Museum, unveiled in 2001. This getaway highlights some of the city's greatest and most romantic buildings. Art and architecture aficionados will enjoy visits to the Art Museum and Pabst Theatre. As the city evolves into the twenty-first century, entrepreneurs and residents are rediscovering the wealth of historic buildings throughout the neighborhood districts. In addition to world-class museums and mansions, you'll find plenty of historic renovated buildings throughout Milwaukee that house boutiques, sleek taverns, and restaurants that serve innovative and enticing cuisine.

You'll be kept busy on this trip, but keep in mind that in Milwaukee, you're never too far from a cool tavern where you can order brews, rest your feet, and snuggle up close to one another in a booth. Though it encompasses 96 square miles and is home to about 600,000 people, Milwaukee is a city of neighborhoods. Most visitors feel welcome in this decidedly Midwestern city.

Base your vacation in a downtown hotel where you'll be able to walk or hop the bus to most of the recommended destinations. Milwaukee is a surprisingly accessible city for visitors. Unless you tour the town during the popular Summerfest music festival or during a Milwaukee Brewers baseball game, traffic is manageable and parking spots are easy to locate, keeping quarrels to a minimum. With festivals held throughout the year, opportunities for lakeshore lounging in the summer, or a horse-drawn carriage ride during the chilly winter months, Milwaukee can be romantic any time of year.

## *Day One*

### ✐ MORNING

Begin your getaway to Milwaukee by visiting one of the city's newest architectural showpieces, the **Milwaukee Art Museum**. Put your arm around your sweetheart and walk across the 250-foot-long pedestrian bridge, which rises above Lincoln Memorial Drive, toward the Quadracci Pavilion addition, which opened in 2001. Designed by Spanish architect Santiago Calatrava, the nautical-evoking addition features a 200-foot, angled mast and a movable screen dubbed the Burke Brise Soleil. The sunscreen, which sits on top of the glass welcome hall, can be raised or lowered to control the room's temperature and the amount of sunlight that spills in. Before touring the museum, walk around the building and admire the curves of the building as well as the views of the lake.

Within its walls, the museum showcases decorative arts by Frank Lloyd Wright and members of the Prairie school of architecture, Asian and African art, work by folk and self-taught artists, pop art, and German expressionism. There's a fair amount of nineteenth- and twentieth-century art, including pieces by well-known artists such as Henri de Toulouse-Lautrec, Pablo Picasso, Joan Miró, and Winslow Homer. You'll be surprised how much there is to see. (The museum contains about 20,000 pieces.) To keep your energy level up, head to the museum's café on the lower level and locate a table for two. Here you'll find even more views of the lake through the room's floor-to-ceiling windows, and treats and coffee for sale.

From the art museum, drive north on Lincoln Memorial Drive toward **Lake Park**, a county park located on a scenic bluff overlooking Lake Michigan. Here you will have some time to yourselves, away from crowds and car traffic. Take a little stroll, then rest your feet at one of the many benches perched atop the bluff. Watch a game of lawn bowling near the pavilion. Then, walk behind the pavilion and take a look at a spectacular view of the lake below and of the sailboats. Continue toward the south end of the park to check out the **North Point Lighthouse**, a Romanesque light station built in 1855 and rebuilt in 1912. Like many buildings in Milwaukee, the lighthouse was constructed with cream city brick, a light-yellow-colored brick made from clay found the region. The lighthouse rises approximately 74 feet. Depending on how hungry you are (and what kind of shoes you are wearing), consider extending your walk through the somewhat secluded, wooded ravine path in Lake Park. You'll see it below the bridge on your way to the lighthouse.

The exuberant and ultra-sleek architecture of the Milwaukee Art Museum.

For lunch, you won't have to go far. **Bartolotta's Lake Park Bistro**, located on the second floor of the Lake Park pavilion (near the lawn bowling grounds), serves dishes in a bright, romantic setting with plenty of tables positioned in front of the windows allowing you to gaze not only at each other but at the lake. The sunny dining room, with its high, white ceilings and walls, is a place where the two of you will find yourselves lingering over your meals. The Lake Park Bistro prepares a number of refreshing and tantalizing items for lunch, such as crepes, sandwiches, and salads. Picture a Niçoise salad with grilled tuna, tomatoes, olives, and potatoes. Or, you can't go wrong with the *croque monsieur,* a grilled ham and Gruyère cheese sandwich. A popular spot for weddings is the ground floor of the pavilion, and it is not uncommon to run into a bride and groom posing on the lawn or terrace behind the pavilion during your spring or summer visit.

## ⌘ AFTERNOON

After lunch, walk or drive to the **Villa Terrace Decorative Arts Museum**, just south of Lake Park on Terrace Avenue. This is yet another idyllic place for couples to spend the afternoon. Built to resemble a sixteenth-century Tuscan villa, the Italian Renaissance mansion is a stunning place to spend an hour or two, to propose, or to tie the knot. Promenade through the courtyard and gardens, by the fish ponds, and under citrus trees. The house contains collections of artwork from the fifteenth to the twentieth centuries and rotating exhibits, such as botanical prints. Before heading back to your hotel, you may want to take a quick stroll around the well-to-do neighborhood surrounding the villa admiring the exteriors of the many mansions near Villa Terrace.

## GAY-FRIENDLY MILWAUKEE

Like any cosmopolitan city, Milwaukee has a number of restaurants, coffee houses, and bars that cater to gay couples. Call or stop by the Milwaukee Lesbian Gay Bi and Transsexual Community Center, 170 South Second Street, Milwaukee, (414) 271-2656, www.mkelgbt.org The center has compiled a listing of gay-friendly organizations and businesses in the region. Whether you and your partner are in the mood for a dance club or a secluded restaurant, they can direct you to a place. During the summer be sure to stop by PrideFest, a giant gala held every year in early June. The event, the largest gay, lesbian, bisexual, and transgender festival in the state, takes place at Henry Maier Festival Park. Watch the parade, dance in the pavilion, cheer on participants in the Drag-A-Thon, compete in a volleyball match, and browse the art and flower shows. During the festival the two of you can arrange a private or community wedding or renew your vows as a couple. For more information call (414) 645-FEST (3378) or visit www.pridefest.com.

After basking in the sun at the Villa Terrace gardens, take the long way into downtown by driving by two more of the city's historical and architectural gems. Notice the majestic Cudahy Tower at 925 Wells Street. Built as apartment buildings in the 1900s and the 1920s, the complex consists of white towers made from marble, terra cotta, and brick. Next, drive west toward Schlitz Office Park at 205-219 West Galena Street for a glimpse of one of Milwaukee's former breweries. Once home to the Schlitz Brewery, this complex of buildings now houses offices and a bar.

Then make tracks to your hotel for a little relaxation before dinner.

Although it is one of the priciest hotels in town, **The Pfister** is a place that says romantic getaway everywhere you look. Take advantage of the hotel's B&B package, which allows you and yours to sleep in and check out of the room at 2:00 p.m. and includes breakfast in Café at the Pfister. Here you have your choice of more than 300 rooms, including heritage suites and Pfister suites in the hotel's original 1893 building or rooms in the tower addition built in the 1960s. No matter which room you pick, low end or high end, all come with fun features such as a minibar and a television in every bathroom. (Not that you'll be watching TV during this vacation, though.) Rooms tend to be decorated in rich colors of maroon and gold with Victorian-style art and contain marble sinks, huge bathrooms, and hot tubs.

If you're scoping out wedding reception or anniversary party spaces, take a peek at the Imperial Ballroom, the hotel's original dining room, with 32-foot ceilings.

For those who prefer modern decor over Victorian art and gold leaf-accented decor, book a room at the nearby **Hotel Metro**. The art deco building, built in 1937, was converted to an all-suites hotel in 1998. Decorated in a minimalist style compared to the Pfister, the Metro has rooms with down comforters, Egyptian cotton sheets, and bathrooms with slate floors. Many of the materials used in the hotel and much of the food served is natural and organic, such as the bamboo wood flooring and the handwoven carpets from Tibet. If you opt to stay here, you might want to lounge in your own private hot tub before dinner.

If you're staying at The Pfister Hotel, put on your swimsuit and plush robe and ride the elevator to the hotel swimming pool on the 23rd floor. With superior views of the city below, the two of you can recline in lounge chairs and swim a few laps.

## ⟨ EVENING

For dinner, make a reservation at the Pfister's **Celia**. Named for the wife of the Marcus Corporation's founder, the restaurant is located in the lower level of the hotel past oak cabinets stocked with more than 500 bottles of wine. In the cozy dining room pull up a high-back brown leather armchair for your sweetheart. This is yet another ideal spot to pop the question or celebrate an anniversary or Valentine's Day. Celia's serves up contemporary Continental cuisine, such as roasted monkfish with artichoke agnolotti, black trumpet mushrooms, and apples. Be sure to save room for desserts, which are absolutely divine. Share a slice of strawberry rhubarb tart with chai tea ice cream and ginger crème fraîche or a Brazil nut tart.

After dinner, surprise your companion with an hour-long horse-drawn carriage ride through downtown Milwaukee. Call **Shamrock Coach and Carriage** any time of the year to arrange this quintessentially romantic activity.

Complete the evening in **Blu**, the Pfister's cocktail bar and jazz club located on the top floor. Blu offers views of the lakefront and Milwaukee skyline that can be particularly spectacular when fireworks are ignited during the many summer festivals. Blu is yet another spot to toast to your love. Cuddle in an overstuffed sofa by the windows and try a wine flight. The two of you can sample four different varieties of, for example, European white wines or a number of Shiraz. If you're looking to relax with a martini, Blu concocts a traditional one made from gin, dry vermouth, and an olive or lemon, in addition to more exotic renditions, including a sinful version made from Godiva chocolate liqueur and vodka. Mmm.

## Day Two

### ✎ MORNING

For breakfast, snack on baked goodies and fresh fruit at the **East Town Farm Market** located in Cathedral Square at Wells Street and Kilbourn Avenue. The square is within walking distance of the Pfister and Metro hotels. Wander through the park and sample locally made cheeses, meats, fruits, and veggies. As you browse, a jazz band churns out live music on the stage. Don't forget to buy your sweetheart a bouquet of tulips or wildflowers. While you're in the park, take a peek inside the **Cathedral of Saint John the Evangelist**, on the east side of the park. The Milwaukee landmark was built in 1847 and was the state's first Roman Catholic cathedral.

Continue walking a few blocks west to another historic landmark, the **Pabst Theater**. Friendly and knowledgeable docents provide free tours of the baroque theater every Saturday at 11:30 a.m. (Private tours are available by appointment.) You will climb to the gallery and walk the historic stage where such artists as Leonard Bernstein and Irving Berlin have performed. Guides point out amazing features of the nearly 200-year-old theater, such as the one-ton Austrian crystal chandelier, the original oil lamps, and staircases made of alpine green-and-white Italian Carrara marble. While you're at the Pabst, buy tickets for a show there that evening. (Or, you may want to purchase them in advance to guarantee seats.)

For lunch, walk back toward Cathedral Square to **Louise's** restaurant, a smart, Italian restaurant overlooking the square. Pasta here is made fresh daily, so try dishes like the fettuccine with chicken, sun-dried tomatoes, and scallions in a chardonnay cream sauce, or the artichoke ravioli. Pizzas are prepared Neapolitan style, with thin crust and real mozzarella.

### ✎ AFTERNOON

After lunch, walk off some of those calories by strolling along the Milwaukee Riverfront in Pere Marquette Park, which has a gazebo and plenty of park benches for you to cuddle and rest your feet. (If you are visiting the city during the week, Marquette Park hosts musical concerts on Wednesdays. Check the local newspaper for times and bands.) From the park, head to the Old World Third Street neighborhood, which borders the west side of Marquette Park. Here you'll find a number of cultural landmarks that foodies will appreciate. Usinger's sausage company and Mader's German Restaurant have been in the neighborhood for more than 100 years (Usinger's since 1880 and Mader's since 1902). Drop by **Usinger's** to sample its famous summer sausage, then walk across the street to Knights Bar in **Mader's German Restaurant**. Have a seat at

Pere Marquette Park along the Milwaukee River.

one of the oak tables and order beers served in boot-shaped glasses. Choose from a slew of imported German beer, including Hofbrauhaus and Warsteiner.

Around the corner from Mader's is **Turner Hall**, another historic spot. Have a seat at the expansive bar or snuggle into one of the booths beneath the stained glass windows and try an appetizer such as the potato pancakes. Built in 1883, the cream brick building was home to the Milwaukee Turners, an athletic, social, and civic club. After your snack and drink, climb the stairs to the second floor to glimpse the ballroom, which is in the process of being restored. Notice the numerous oil paintings depicting scenes from American history hanging throughout the building. Music buffs or older couples will be tickled to discover that the waltz "After the Ball" was composed in this building. The story goes that Charles Harris, a frequent attendee of dances in the hall, became distraught after seeing a former girlfriend dancing with another partner, prompting him to write the song in the building's music room.

Next, drive south to the Historic Third Ward neighborhood, where a number of warehouse buildings have been converted into galleries, gift shops, and restaurants. Browse through the boutique gardening accessories at the Private Gardener and the contemporary furniture at Rubin's. Pick up some stationery and wax seals at Broadway Paper for writing your sweetheart a love letter. If you're planning a wedding or if you have recently tied the knot, you'll find plenty of invitations and photo albums available for purchase.

## ☙ EVENING

While you are in the neighborhood, have dinner at the eclectic **Sauce** in the Third Ward. You can order Asian concoctions such as pad thai and a variety of seafood dishes, not to mention wine and mixed drinks. If you're intimidated by Sauce's slightly chic atmosphere, have dinner at the **Third Ward Caffè**, a cheery restaurant serving primarily pasta dishes such as pesto lasagna. If the night is balmy, sit at one of the outdoor tables.

Tonight treat yourselves to a show at the historic **Pabst Theater**, where performers have included Native American flutist Carlos Nakai, French mime artist Marcel Marceau, Celtic music bands, blues singers, and comedy revue troupes. Arrive a bit early and grab a Milwaukee brew or glass of champagne at Cudahy's pub, located in the theater's former winter garden overlooking Water Street.

## CITY OF FESTIVALS

&❧ Residents of Milwaukee sure know how to throw a party. If you visit during the summer months, chances are that on the days you visit somewhere in town a group of people is celebrating. Perhaps the most well-known festival is Summerfest, a huge music festival usually held the week leading up to the Fourth of July and a few days afterward at Henry Maier Festival Park. But throughout the summer you'll find plenty of other music shows to swing by (many of them are free and not nearly as crowded as Summerfest).

They include the Historic Third Ward Jazz Festival, which is held in early August, and RiverSplash, held around Memorial Day weekend and including musical performances in and around Pere Marquette Park. At Westown's River Rhythms, also held in Marquette Park, musicians play for free every Wednesday evening in the summer. Over at Cathedral Square Park, a jazz band strikes it up every Thursday evening during the summer. For ethnic music and food, spend some time at Henry Maier Festival Park where there's always something going on, whether it is Irish Fest, Polish Fest, or African World Festival. For dates and time information, contact the Milwaukee Convention and Visitor bureau to receive a calendar of events.

If you were unable to get tickets to a show at the Pabst or choose to catch a performance in a smaller venue, consider a show at the **Chamber Theatre** in the Third Ward neighborhood's Broadway Theater Center, within walking distance of Sauce and the Third Ward Caffè. Past productions have included the Pulitzer Prize-winning play *Dinner with Friends* and a modern interpretation of the Greek tragedy *Medea.* Choose between a show at the Cabot Theatre, a 358-seat theater modeled after an eighteenth-century opera house, or the intimate Studio Theatre, a 96-seat black box performance space.

After the show, stop by **Centanni**, a sleek piano bar located close to the Chamber Theatre, for some live music and cocktails. The place oozes sophistication and cool, and it should put you and your companion in a romantic frame of mind, a mood that seems to be shared by the other patrons.

One of the many plant exhibits at Milwaukee's Mitchell Art Conservancy.

## Day Three

### ☙ MORNING

You may want to sleep in this morning. (After all, the two of you had a busy day yesterday.) After you've had your fill of lounging in bed, drive toward the lakefront, specifically North Harbor Drive, for brunch. **Pieces of Eight** is a lovely place for brunch, no matter what the season. Fireplaces inside the building and on the patio make the restaurant especially welcoming in the cool months. Plus, views of the lake and the city are awesome. Brunch consists of mounds of seafood, an omelet station, and sweet treats. After your meal, take a few minutes to relax on the leather couches facing the lake and the art museum or on one of the benches outside the restaurant.

### ☙ AFTERNOON

Following your meal, hop back in your car and drive west on Wisconsin Avenue, formerly known as Grand Avenue. One hundred years ago the street was lined with mansions. One of the most glorious was the **home of Captain Frederick Pabst**, one of few mansions on the street that survive today. The Flemish Renaissance-style home was built in 1892 for the Pabst Brewery founder and his family. The first social event held in the house was the wedding of Pabst's daughter Emma in the music room. (If you would like to get married here, the home does permit such events. You can also tour the home.) Eventually the house was sold to the archdiocese of Milwaukee, and it was home to Milwaukee's archbishop for decades.

Drive south past I-94 to the **Mitchell Park Horticultural Conservatory**, known locally as the Domes because of the three globelike structures that house a variety of plant species and were built between 1959 and 1967. Mitchell Park is the only type of conservatory to have these types of structures in the world. Take about 45 minutes to wander through the tropical, arid, and show domes. In the show dome have a seat at one of the numerous benches and breathe in the sweet scents of various seasonal flowers, from azaleas to cyclamen. A particularly stunning show is the annual "Fall in Love with Orchids" in September, where you can not only take in the beauty of these plants but purchase one for your sweetheart. After your visit, take a brief walk through the park behind the conservatory.

## FOR MORE INFORMATION

**East Town neighborhood**
www.easttown.com

**Greater Milwaukee Convention and Visitor bureau**
101 W. Wisconsin Avenue, Milwaukee
(800) 554-1448, www.milwaukee.org

**Historic Third Ward neighborhood**
(414) 273-1173
www.historicthirdward.org

**Midwest Express Center Visitor Information Center**
400 W. Wisconsin Avenue, Milwaukee
(414) 908-6205
Open Monday through Friday, 8:00 a.m. to 5:00 p.m.

## ATTRACTIONS

**Captain Frederick Pabst Mansion**
2000 W. Wisconsin Avenue, Milwaukee
(414) 391-0808
www.pabstmansion.com

Open Tuesday through Saturday, 10:00 a.m. to 3:00 p.m.; Sunday, noon to 3:30 p.m. Admission fee.

**Cathedral of Saint John the Evangelist**
812 N. Jackson Street, Milwaukee
(414) 276-9814
www.stjohncathedral.org
Donation.

**Chamber Theatre**
158 N. Broadway, Milwaukee
(414) 291-7800
www.chamber-theatre.com

**East Town Farm Market**
Cathedral Square, bordered by Wells Street, Kilbourn Avenue, Jackson Street, and Jefferson Street.
The market is open early June through mid-October on Saturday, 7:30 a.m. to 12:30 p.m. A jazz band plays from 10:00 a.m. to noon.

**Lake Park and North Point Lighthouse**
323 E. Kenwood Blvd, Milwaukee
(414) 962-8809
www.countyparks.com

## Milwaukee Art Museum

700 N. Art Museum Drive, Milwaukee
(414) 224-3200
www.mam.org
Open year-round Tuesday through
Sunday, 10:00 a.m. to 5:00 p.m., and
Thursday until 8:00 p.m. Admission fee.

## Mitchell Park Horticultural Conservatory

524 S. Layton Boulevard,
Milwaukee
(414) 649-9830
www.countyparks.com
Open daily 9:00 a.m. to 5:00 p.m.
Admission fee.

## Pabst Theater

144 E. Wells Street, Milwaukee
(414) 286-3665; box office
(414) 286-3663
www.pabsttheater.org

## Shamrock Coach and Carriage

Departures from the Hyatt
Regency Hotel
333 W. Kilbourn Avenue,
Milwaukee
(414) 272-6873

## Villa Terrace Decorative Arts Museum

2220 N. Terrace Avenue, Milwaukee
(414) 271-3656
www.villaterracemuseum.org
Open Wednesday, 1:00 p.m. to 9:00 p.m.
and Thursday through Sunday, 1:00 p.m.
to 5:00 p.m. Admission fee.

## ꙮ LODGING

### Hotel Metro

411 E. Mason Street, Milwaukee
(414) 272-1937 or (877) 638-7620
www.hotelmetro.com
Call for room prices.

### The Pfister

424 E. Wisconsin Avenue, Milwaukee

(414) 390-3800 or (800) 558-8222
www.thepfisterhotel.com
Call for room prices.

## ꙮ DINING AND NIGHTLIFE

### Bartolotta's Lake Park Bistro

3133 E. Newberry Blvd., Milwaukee
(414) 962-6300
www.lakeparkbistro.com
Open for lunch Monday through Friday,
for dinner daily, and for brunch Sunday.

### Blu

Located in the Pfister hotel.
Open evenings Monday through
Saturday.

### Celia

Located in the Pfister hotel
Open for dinner Monday through
Saturday.

### Centanni (piano bar)

218 N. Water Street, Milwaukee
(414) 221-6565
Live music Tuesday through Sunday
evenings.

### Louise's

801 N. Jefferson Street, Milwaukee
(414) 273-4224
Open daily for lunch and dinner.

### Mader's German Restaurant

1037 N. Old World Third Street,
Milwaukee
(414) 271-3377
www.maders.com
Open for lunch Monday through
Saturday. Dinner is served Monday
through Sunday. Brunch is served on
Sunday.

### Pieces of Eight

550 N. Harbor Drive, Milwaukee
(414) 271-0597
Open for lunch and dinner daily and for
brunch on Sunday.

**Sauce**
217 N. Broadway, Milwaukee
(414) 224-1480
www.tastesauce.com
Open for lunch Monday through Friday
and for dinner Monday through Saturday.

**Third Ward Caffè**
225 E. Saint Paul Avenue, Milwaukee
(414) 224-0895
Open for lunch Tuesday through Friday
and for dinner Tuesday through Saturday.

**Turner Hall**
1034 N. 4th Street, Milwaukee
(414) 276-4844
www.milwaukeeturners.org
Open for lunch and dinner daily.

**Usinger's Famous Sausage**
1030 N. Old World 3rd Street,
Milwaukee
(414) 276-9105
www.usinger.com

# CHAPTER THREE

Small-Town Romance:

# Cedarburg and Port Washington

You may feel as if you have stepped into a Norman Rockwell painting when you visit Cedarburg and Port Washington, two charming, nostalgic towns about 20 minutes north of Milwaukee. Set amid the rolling hills of eastern Wisconsin, both towns are home to working artists, cozy inns and restaurants, historic buildings, and vibrant downtowns.

Driving through Cedarburg, you'll quickly realize that it is a quintessential small town. Its downtown is lined with restored cream city brick buildings, a mill, waterfall, and pond, plus a covered bridge on the outskirts of town. You can spend hours touring the winery and filling your trunk with items from the many antiques and home decor shops. Or, if you base your vacation in an inn with well-appointed rooms, you might find yourselves camping out in the room for hours, lounging in front of the fireplace, or soaking in a claw-foot bathtub.

Port Washington, on the shores of Lake Michigan, is a shipping and sailing town, with a lighthouse standing guard on the hill and plenty of parks to explore, complete with a number of benches with lake views—perfect spots for dozing in each other's arms.

This getaway is easygoing, with plenty of time for strolling, browsing, dreaming, and reigniting the flames of romance. These towns make for a quiet getaway during the winter with inn rooms boasting fireplaces and armchairs and coffee shops where you may find yourselves browsing the real estate section of the local newspaper. You can visit any time of year and find that there's plenty to do. The winery, shops, and restaurants are open year-round. The parks and covered bridge are open all the time. To make your vacation more festive, plan to visit during one of Cedarburg's many community festivals held frequently throughout the year, from the Strawberry Festival in June to the Wine and Harvest Festival in September to the old-fashioned Winter Festival.

## *Day One*

### ✑ MORNING

A good way to begin your vacation in the Cedarburg area is to spend some time at **Covered Bridge Park**, located five minutes northwest of town. Built in 1876, the bridge is believed to be the last remaining covered bridge in the state. The pine bridge measures about 120 feet long and 12 feet wide. It is open only to pedestrian traffic, so feel free to walk across the bridge, admire its artistry, and steal a kiss under the rafters. The park grounds surrounding the bridge provide a nice spot for walking hand in hand, especially across the little footbridge.

The main attraction at Covered Bridge Park north of Cedarburg.

After visiting the park, stop by **Wayne's Drive In**, a genuine drive-in with carhops. You'll find it at the five corners area of Cedarburg on the way back into town from Covered Bridge Park. Couples who came of age during the 1950s will enjoy their time spent in this restaurant. The food is basic, yummy diner food: charbroiled burgers, cheese fries, flavored malts, and shakes. If you choose to dine inside, slide a few coins into the jukebox, put your arms around each other, and share a banana split. Wayne's is open seasonally, so if you're visiting during the winter, drive into town and have a seat in one of the cafés in downtown Cedarburg, such as **Tomaso's**, a fine and inexpensive Italian-American eatery.

## ⌘ AFTERNOON

Drive back into town on Washington Avenue and park your car when you come to the downtown area. Cedarburg is a walking town, and you can walk to most of the restaurants, shops, and parks from Washington Avenue. Mosey on over to **Cedar Creek Settlement**, at the corner of Washington and Bridge Streets. A hodgepodge of gift shops, artist studios, and galleries is housed in an 1864 former woolen mill overlooking Cedar Creek. You'll be impressed by the work of artisans in the mill, such as those with Cedar Creek Pottery and Bighorn Forge Ironworks. Shop for items like candleholders and fireplace accessories.

While you are in the settlement, spend some time touring **Cedar Creek Winery**. You can visit the cool, limestone cellars where the wines are aged and the tasting room to sample some of the wines, such as the Cedar Creek Vidal, a semidry white wine. When you've sampled all the wine and purchased a bottle for the evening, walk or drive to the inn where you'll stay for the next two nights.

Both the **Washington House Inn** and **Stagecoach Inn** are located in downtown Cedarburg, steps from restaurants, boutiques, and the babbling Cedar Creek. The Washington House Inn and Schroeder House, on Washington Avenue (the city's main street) has 34 rooms to choose from. A cream city brick building built in 1886, the Washington House was the town's first inn. After operating as an apartment and office building from the 1920s through the early 1980s, it reopened as a country, Victorian-style inn. Listed on the National Register of Historic Places, its rooms are tastefully decorated, some featuring four-poster beds, Jacuzzi bathtubs, large windows with shutters, antiques such as wardrobes and trunks, and walls exposing those famed cream city bricks. You can't go wrong with any of the rooms, although room 216, called the John Roth room, is particularly romantic with its subdued lighting, high ceilings, exposed beams, pine floors, and fireplace. Room 305, decorated in shades of pale green and gold, is also romantic with its west-facing windows. If the two of you are petered out from traveling, you should have no problem catching an afternoon doze in this room.

Just down the street, the **Stagecoach Inn** and **Weber House** also date back to the early days of the town. A former stagecoach inn built in 1853, the building was renovated in 1984. Some of its rooms offer features such as whirlpool bathtubs and fireplaces. The Weber House, located across the street from the Stagecoach Inn, is an 1847 building with three guest rooms. Here you'll find one of the more romantic rooms the inn offers—room 11, with its brass bed, skylight, and double whirlpool bathtub. The Weber House has a small, private garden in the rear of the house with a bench that makes for a lovely spot for the two of you to unwind.

After checking in, lounge in your room for a little while before the fireplace or on your downy bed. If you're staying at the Washington House Inn, head downstairs for the complimentary wine and cheese hour. If you're at the Stagecoach

Inn, drop by the chocolate shop located in the inn. Buy yourself and your sweetheart some chocolate-covered strawberries.

## EVENING

For dinner, walk over to **Klug's Creekside Inn**, yet another business located in a historic building. Built by two of Cedarburg's forefathers in the 1850s across the street from their gristmill, the building complex was initially a house and flour and feed store. (As its name implies, the inn is located by Cedar Creek.) In the 1940s a descendent of one of the founders moved into the building and started a restaurant there. It has been a restaurant ever since. If you're in the mood for German food or a solid Wisconsin fish fry, this is a good place to go for dinner. Plus, it offers you both a quiet, adult atmosphere for intimate conversations and a crackling fireplace during the winter. Dishes include entrées such as *Jagerschnitzel*, a pork loin with mushrooms, onions, bacon, and *spaetzle* (homemade noodles), and sandwiches such as the classic Reuben.

From the Creekside Inn, wander hand in hand along Washington Street to **Cedar Creek Park**, a picturesque park with pedestrian bridges, a band shell, and benches with views of the creek.

Back at the inn, pop open that bottle of wine from Cedar Creek Winery, draw a bath in the hot tub, or have a seat in the backyard garden at the Weber House.

## Day Two
## MORNING

Whether you stay at the Washington House Inn or Stagecoach Inn, you'll be treated to complimentary breakfasts of eggs, cinnamon rolls, coffee, and other such goodies in both of their respective dining rooms. Take your time enjoying breakfast, then head outdoors for a walk down Cedarburg's quaint Washington Avenue, right outside your doors.

Depending on how ambitious or curious you are, you could spend hours browsing the boutiques, which range from upscale home furnishing stores to sweet shops. Stop by Cleansing Waters Spa and Shoppe on Washington Avenue for some bath oils or massage oils and scented candles to place in and around the tub in your room during another relaxing soak tonight. At the Cedarburg Woolen Mill, Fabric and Yarn Shop and Textile Museum, pick up a warm scarf for your honey or a blanket to curl up with before a fire. If you're celebrating an anniversary or other special occasion, drop by one of the jewelry shops and choose from original design creations. Shops such as Ambruster Jewelers, The Gem Shop, and Jewelry Works are all located on Washington Avenue. Are your wedding bands looking a little dull? Have them polished or restored at Pagoda Fine Jewelry while you visit Cedarburg.

Wintry scene at Cedar Creek Park, Cedarburg.

While strolling through downtown Cedarburg, be sure to stop by the **Cedarburg Cultural Center**, a community space spotlighting a variety of artistic media, like woodwork and beadwork, of visiting artists. For more inspiration, walk about two blocks from Washington Avenue onto Riveredge Drive (yes, along the Cedar Creek River) to the **Ozaukee Fine Arts Center**, housed in a former brewery building. Discover the work of a variety of artists in this historic spot. Pop into the small **Cedarburg General Store Museum**, which also houses the town's visitor center. The 1860s building contains a collection of amusing vintage packaging and advertising art, such as apothecary and dry goods items.

For lunch, a good bet is **The Chocolate Factory Subs and Ice Cream**, an old-fashioned, soda fountain-type shop on Washington Avenue. Order a sub or croissant sandwich, and be sure to save room for desserts. The shop features more than 25 flavors of super-creamy ice cream. Here's another opportunity to share an ice cream treat. Try the hot fudge sundae.

## AFTERNOON

This afternoon hop into the car, roll down the windows, put your arm around your sweetheart, and continue driving through the rolling countryside, past stone houses and cream city brick farmsteads, for a leisurely driving

27

tour of the Cedarburg environs. Start with Hamilton, just south of Cedarburg. Settled in the 1840s, Hamilton is a Wisconsin State Historical Site and listed on the National Register of Historic Places. Be on the lookout for the remains of the early settlement, including limestone homes and a crumbling mill.

Next, Grafton (about a five-minute drive northeast from downtown Cedarburg) also has a quaint downtown and several parks where you can spend some time walking hand in hand. Veteran's Memorial Park, just off Highway 60, has a gazebo for you to relax in. Gazebos, as you will discover, are picturesque places to propose or smooch. If you're visiting this area during the winter, bring your ice skates. A portion of the Milwaukee River that passes through town at Veteran's Memorial Park is transformed into an ice rink. Next, explore **Lime Kiln Park**, a former limestone quarry (follow signs from downtown to Green Bay Road), where you can check out several towering lime kilns. Grafton, and Wisconsin for that matter, was a top producer of lime at the turn of the twentieth century. Take a few minutes to wander through this riverside park.

## FESTIVALS FOR ALL SEASONS

The hometown festivals held in Cedarburg are enchanting and will keep you and your lover coming back every year. A favorite is the Strawberry Festival in June, with its strawberry pancake breakfast and booths with folks selling more strawberry desserts than you can imagine. Although live music is a feature of most of Cedarburg's annual festivals, the art is celebrated specifically during the Cedarburg Music Festival in July and during the Spring Folk Heritage Concert Series. Shoppers looking for antiques, pottery, and other arts will want to visit during Cedarburg's Maxwell Street Days, held on weekends throughout May, July, and September, or the Cedarburg Woman's Club Antiques Show and Sale in October. During the Wine and Harvest Festival in September, visitors are treated to grape stomping, wine tastings, and apple bobbing. Also in the fall, visitors can take a peek inside the region's historic homes during the Stone and Century House Tour. During the chilly winter months, Cedarburg residents continue celebrating. The fun Cedarburg Winter Festival, usually held in early February, features bed racing across the frozen Mill Pond, ice sculpture carving, and live music.

Back in Cedarburg, pay a visit to one of the small-town coffee shops, such as **Cream City Coffee** on Washington Avenue, just down the street from the inns. It's a place where you can rest your feet, chat, or read the newspaper.

## ⤳ EVENING

Tonight you dine at the **Farmstead** restaurant. Although the restaurant is often crowded (this is not exactly a place to propose) and the wait for a table is long, the food is spectacular. People drive from miles around to eat a haystack of fried onions. While you wait at the bar for your table, strike up a conversation with other couples or visitors who drove two hours to eat at the restaurant. The Farmstead is particularly famous for its steaks, but it also has great chicken dishes served with ultra-fresh-tasting veggies and wild rice. The atmosphere is homey, like the food, with antique farm signs on the walls, rustic tables, and friendly waitstaff.

After dinner take in live music or a theatrical performance at the **Cedarburg Performing Arts Center**, located within walking distance of your inn. If an event is not taking place at the performing arts center, chances are a jazz trio or folk group is playing at the cultural center, just down the street.

# *Day Three*

## ⤳ MORNING

Rise early today and savor a breakfast at the inn before the two of you check out of your room. After saying good-bye to the quaint town of Cedarburg, head east toward Lake Michigan to the lakeside village of Port Washington. Take the back roads instead of I-43; follow Highway 60 east from Grafton and County Road C north into Port Washington.

Begin your tour of the town by stopping by the visitor center, housed in what is referred to locally as the pebble house. (You'll see why; it's made of cobblestones.) In this small house, pick up a brochure outlining the town's historic sites and a map of historic walking tours of the Old Town and City Center neighborhoods. Many visitors are drawn to the 1860 **Port Washington Light Station**, located on Johnson Street on Saint Mary's Hill. Climb the stairs (or drive up the hill) to check out this landmark. Inside you'll find a local history museum that is open on Sundays from May to September. The light station also served as living quarters for U.S. Coast Guard staff.

From the light station, continue driving further up the hill to the expansive **Upper Lake Park**. Find a bluff-top bench and spend some time talking or catnapping in the morning sun. This park is especially serene on a Sunday morning.

From there, drive back into town and park by the marina and pier, distinguishable by the 1930's-era art deco breakwater light at the end of it.

For lunch, walk over to the **Port Hotel** for an elegant Sunday brunch. For something more casual, try **NewPort Shores**, an American restaurant with superb views of Lake Michigan (it's just feet away). At NewPort you can dine on broiled whitefish, crab legs, or sandwiches.

## ᥰ AFTERNOON

Before leaving town, take a walk along Franklin Street in downtown Port Washington to browse local boutiques, such as Port Antiques and Wind in the Rigging for nautical-themed gifts, and Serendipity Cards and Gifts, which sells a selection of miniature lighthouses.

## ᥰ FOR MORE INFORMATION

**Cedarburg Visitor Center
and Chamber of Commerce**
Located in the Cedarburg
General Store Museum
W61 N480 Washington Avenue,
Cedarburg
(262) 375-3676 or (800) 237-2874
www.cedarburg.org or
www.cedarburgfestivals.org

**Grafton Chamber of Commerce**
1111 Broad Street, Grafton
(262) 377-1650, www.grafton-wi.org

**Port Washington Visitor Center and Chamber of Commerce**
126 E. Grand Avenue, Port Washington
(262) 284-0900 or (800) 719-4881
www.portwashingtonchamber.com

## ᥰ ATTRACTIONS AND RECREATION

**Cedar Creek Park**
Portland Road, Cedarburg
For more information call the
Cedarburg Visitor Center.

**Cedar Creek Settlement**
N70 W6340 Bridge Road, Cedarburg
(262) 377-8020 or (262) 375-9390
www.cedarcreeksettlement.com

**Cedar Creek Winery**
Cedar Creek Settlement
N70 W6340 Bridge Road, Cedarburg
(262) 377-8020 or (800) 827-8020
www.cedarcreekwinery.com

**Cedarburg Cultural Center**
W62 N546 Washington Avenue, Cedarburg
(262) 375-3676
www.cedarburgculturalcenter.org

**Cedarburg Performing Arts Center**
W68 N611 Evergreen Blvd.,
Cedarburg
(262) 376-6161
www.cedarburgpac.com

**Covered Bridge Park**
Highway 143 (Washington Avenue) and
Highway 60,
northwest of downtown Cedarburg
For more information call the
Cedarburg Visitor Center.

**Lime Kiln Park**
2020 S. Green Bay Road, Grafton
Village of Grafton: (262) 375-5300

**Ozaukee Fine Arts Center**
W62 N718 Riveredge Drive, Cedarburg
(262) 377-8230

**Port Washington Light Station and museum**
311 Johnson Street, Port Washington
For more information call the Port
Washington Visitor Center.

**Upper Lake Park**
Lake Street and Lakeview Drive,
Port Washington For more information
call the Port Washington Visitor Center.

## ☙ LODGING

**Stagecoach Inn and Weber House**
W61 N520 Washington Avenue,
Cedarburg
(262) 375-0208 or (888) 375-0208
www.stagecoach-inn-wi.com
Rooms are from $80.

**Washington House Inn
and Schroeder House**
W62 N573 Washington Avenue,
Cedarburg
(262) 375-3550 or (800) 554-4717
www.washingtonhouseinn.com
Rooms start at under $100.

## ☙ DINING AND NIGHTLIFE

**The Chocolate Factory Subs
and Ice Cream**
W62 N577 Washington Avenue,
Cedarburg
(262) 377-8877
www.subsandicecream.com
Open daily year-round.

**Cream City Coffee**
W62 N605 Washington Ave.,
Cedarburg
(262) 376-1366

**The Farmstead**
W62 N238 Washington Avenue,
Cedarburg
(262) 375-2655
Open for lunch and dinner Tuesday
through Saturday. The restaurant is
closed during the Fourth of July and
Labor Day weekends.

**Klug's Creekside Inn**
N58 W6194 Columbia Road,
Cedarburg
(262) 377-0660
Open for lunch and dinner Tuesday
through Saturday and for brunch Sunday.

**NewPort Shores**
407 E. Jackson Street, Port Washington
(262) 284-6383
Open year-round for lunch and dinner
Tuesday through Saturday and for
brunch and dinner Sunday. Call for
hours.

**Port Hotel**
101 E. Main Street, Port Washington
(262) 284-9473
www.theporthotel.com
Open for lunch and dinner Monday
through Friday. Open for dinner only on
Saturday and brunch only on Sunday.

**Tomaso's**
W63 N688 Washington Avenue,
Cedarburg
(414) 377-7630

**Wayne's Drive In**
1331 Covered Bridge Road, Cedarburg
(262) 375-9999
www.waynesdrivein.com
Open seasonally. Call for hours.

# CHAPTER FOUR

# Pamper Yourselves in
# *Kohler and Sheboygan*

Established by the Kohler Company's founder, Walter Kohler, in 1917, the town of Kohler was designed as a planned community for his factory and employees. Although behind that fence and those trees is a factory churning out engines and toilets, Kohler has the feel of a resort town. Located north of the meandering Sheboygan River, one hour north of Milwaukee, the town has a fabulous historic resort, top-notch golf courses, comfortable restaurants, a spa, shops, and a private nature preserve for hiking, fishing, and hunting. Despite steep fairway fees and prices for hotel rooms and spa services, Kohler tends to cater to plenty of folks like yourselves who are treating themselves to a weekend of pampering. Your fellow guests are not billionaire heirs and heiresses, so relax.

If the two of you have been working long hours lately and recently realized you haven't been paying much attention to each other or to yourselves, book a vacation in Kohler. This is a time for both of you to mellow out, tune out worries, and rejuvenate your body, soul, and passion for each other. (In fact, this getaway is perfect for couples who have been swamped with planning a wedding and need couple time.) When you are in Kohler, don't hold back. Take advantage of all the soothing services available, such as the nightly turn-down services and the foot massages after a game of golf. Go ahead and order a decadent dessert. Linger at the poolside. Sleep in.

Base your vacation at Kohler's American Club or in a historic inn in nearby Sheboygan, a town of 51,000 on Lake Michigan. Although much of your time will be centered in Kohler, the two of you will want to explore Sheboygan as well. Downtown Sheboygan boasts a riverfront with shops, restaurants, and lakefront parks.

The Black River Marsh Boardwalk at Michael Kohler–Terry Andrae State Park, south of Sheboygan.

## Day One

### ௮ MORNING

For a relaxing, glorious morning together take a walk along the Dunes Cordwalk at **John Michael Kohler–Terry Andrae State Park**, south of Sheboygan on the Lake Michigan shoreline. The Andrae part of the park has a heartwarming history. Elsbeth Andrae donated more than 100 acres of lakeshore property, formerly owned by herself and Terry (Frank) Andrae, to the state in honor of her husband after he died. This quiet and inviting park contains river marsh, pine and hardwood forests, dunes, and beaches, not to mention a variety of bird species, such as sandpipers and herons. Bird lovers will particularly appreciate a stop in this park because it is a migration corridor for bird species in spring and fall.

The 2.5-mile-long Dunes Cordwalk, made of boards and rope, takes you through dunes overlooking Lake Michigan and an inter-dunal marsh area (a marshy area surrounded by dunes). For a shorter walk, consider the three-quarter-mile Black River Marsh Boardwalk. Other beautiful trails include the Creeping Juniper Nature Trail, south of the nature center, which also takes you along the dunes, and the Woodland Dunes Nature Trail.

Under the lake's waters offshore lie about 50 shipping vessels that capsized and sank. Resting among them is *The Challenge*, a schooner built in Manitowoc in 1852. If you have time, stop by the park's nature center, where part of the ship's keel is displayed.

Following your peaceful morning along the lake, drive to the little company town of Kohler, about a 15-minute drive from the park. Snuggle up in a booth at **The Horse and Plow Restaurant** at the American Club, just down the block from the Kohler Design Center. Formerly the taproom for Kohler Company employees, the restaurant now serves regional fare in a comfy, publike atmosphere with architectural accents like tables made from the floors in the company's old bowling alley. If you're in the mood for a beer, this is the place to quench your thirst; the pub has more than 12 Wisconsin beers on tap. Forget about your diet for now and try the restaurant's popular three-cheese soup followed by a Wisconsin burger, topped with Wisconsin cheddar cheese and on a Sheboygan hard roll. Better yet, go for aphrodisiacs such as oysters on the half shell.

## ぐ AFTERNOON

Before checking in to your room, spend about an hour touring the **Kohler Design Center**. Located across the street from the Kohler factory, the center introduces you to the family behind the mammoth and long-running company and the many products the factory has churned out over the years. Plus it is a showcase of sorts for the faucets, toilets, and home decor furniture that Kohler and its companies create. You can tour the three floors at your own pace (and even while sipping lattes that you can order at the welcome desk area). Newlyweds and couples thinking about or in the midst of remodeling their bathrooms or kitchens should get a kick out of this visit.

Start your visit on the lower level, which presents a history of the Kohler family and company, from its beginnings as a manufacturer to its modern-day ventures of real estate development. A short film briefs you on all their activities through the years. A walk through the lower-level hallways will take you past a reproduction of a bathroom from the 1890s, brightly colored bathtubs from the 1960s, and photographs of the 1928 expedition to Antarctica, including a Kohler generator that helped power the camps. On the main level, meander around all the many showerheads (complete with water rushing out of the heads) and the bubbling whirlpool bathtubs. Walk up to the top floor and drift in and out of the designer rooms dreaming of your new bathroom or kitchen.

Now that you have sufficiently educated yourself about the town and the company, it's time to focus on the two of you.

If you really want to pamper yourselves, stay at the five-star **American Club**, perhaps the most acclaimed resort and hotel in Wisconsin. Built to house the immigrants who worked in the Kohler factory, the Tudor-style hotel now welcomes everyone from couples like yourselves seeking romantic retreats to golf professionals. Before booking your room, be sure to check with the hotel about any package deals they offer. The Club often runs specials during holidays such as Valentine's Day and its annual events such as the Taste of Kohler.

If you plan on utilizing any of the services at the Kohler Waters Spa (and I highly recommend you do), rent a room at the Carriage House, which offers free access to the spa one floor below. (If you stay at the American Club hotel, just a walkway away, you will have to pay a fee of approximately $20 each to utilize the spa.) The Bed to Bath service, which I recommend on the second night of your stay, is available only to guests in the Carriage House. Try to reserve an especially romantic second-floor suite, which features an oversized whirlpool in your very own greenhouse patio.

One of the well-appointed Heritage rooms at the American Club. Photo courtesy of the Kohler Company.

Yes, rooms here are pricey, especially during peak season. But you don't have to opt for the enormous Governor Suite or one of the slightly more modest Heritage rooms. The higher the price, the more amenities in your room, such as a heated towel holder, shower tower (imagine a miniature waterfall in your shower), and stereo systems. All rooms are outfitted with amenities that will elicit sighs, such as down comforters, plush robes, and marble-lined bathrooms. All bathrooms, of course, feature Kohler products, such as the whirlpool baths. Whichever room you choose, from the standard to a multi-floor suite, don't expect run-of-the-mill hotel rooms but beautiful cherry wood furniture, oak trim, and photographs of famous Wisconsinites from history.

The American Club has 152 guest rooms in the main hotel, plus 52 in the Carriage House. For the more inexpensive (but less romantic) option, you can stay at the Inn on Woodland Lake, also owned by the Kohler Company and located just down the road.

If you prefer to go the B&B route, stay at the 1907 **Brownstone Inn**, located a few blocks from the lakeshore in Sheboygan, about 10 minutes from Kohler. This is not your usual Victorian B&B but a stately Romanesque mansion complete with a ballroom, billiard room, sunny four-season room for breakfast, and awesome mahogany woodwork throughout the house. All rooms come with large, private bathrooms. Book a room here if you're looking for a quiet, child-free vacation. (No children are allowed in this inn.) Unless there's a private event going on, be sure to take a walk up to the ballroom and a spin around the floor.

After settling into your room, change into workout clothes and pay a visit to **Sports Core**, a Kohler-owned sports facility located by the Shops of Westlake, less than one mile north of the American Club. (You can take a complimentary shuttle to the facility from the American Club.) Depending on how much energy you want to expend, the two of you can play a game of tennis on one of the indoor or outdoor courts, swim laps in the adult lap pool, or lift weights. If you do decide to play a game of tennis during peak season, you may want to call in advance to reserve a court. Sports Core is free to guests of the American Club. After your workout, unwind in the steam room.

After working out for about an hour, stop by the **Kohler Waters Spa** for a side-by-side massage. In the "Twogether Room" both of you will lie side by side on separate massage tables while water trickles or a fire crackles and your aches are massaged away. Then, refresh in the large shower made for two.

Hint: gentlemen, surprise your wife or girlfriend by having a bouquet of flowers sent to your room. The American Club staffs a spectacular florist who can arrange a vase of tulips or bouquet of other flowers for you. Or stop by the florist, pick up a single rose, and present it to her before dinner.

## EVENING

For dinner, take a drive down Lower Falls Road to nearby Sheboygan Falls, a scenic five-minute drive from the American Club. Have a seat at one of the window tables in the intimate **Broadway Bistro**, located by the Sheboygan River. The bistro serves fresh, Italian-style dishes such as spinach and gnocchi, scallopini marsala, and prosciutto rolls. Down the street you'll find the locals gravitate to **The Villager** for its Friday fish fry featuring lake perch, walleye, and haddock. Request one of the cozy booths along the wall.

After dinner, walk down to Falls View Park to the south on Broadway Street and Settler's Park to the north to ogle at the tumbling waters of the Sheboygan River. At Settler's Park you'll find a number of benches and a

The relaxation pool at the American Club's Kohler Water Spa. Photo courtesy of the Kohler Company.

gazebo to take in the sound of the rushing waters. You can continue your walk through the Cole Historic District (opposite Falls View Park), past a Greek Revival millhouse and hotel. Developed in the 1830s and 1840s, Sheboygan Falls was primarily a mill town. Meander through the downtown for a few minutes, stopping to window shop at a few boutiques, such as Richardson's Furniture Emporium.

After your evening stroll, drive back to the American Club for a romantic walk through the hotel's courtyards. You'll find a gazebo surrounded by flower beds and a patio with wrought-iron tables and birdbaths. Take a break inside **The Greenhouse**, located inside the Fountain Courtyard by the open-air walkway. Built in England, the greenhouse was reassembled in Kohler and installed in the courtyard when the American Club opened in 1981. It's a little jewel box of a building; be sure to spend some time there before tucking in for the night. Feed each other delectable treats such as ice cream and smoothies or sip cappuccinos while sitting at one of the marble-topped tables.

For the ultimate turn-down service, order the Romantic Bath and Bed for after dinner. For this treat, a spa staff person will come to your Carriage House room in the evening with a tray of bathing supplies, draw a bath in your tub, sprinkling petals and soothing salts, light some candles, and pour two cups of tea for you.

## Day Two

### ✑ MORNING

Today will be a busy day of golfing and pampering. If you stay at the Carriage House, all you have to do is take the elevator to the first-level lobby where you'll find a continental breakfast served. If you are staying in the American Club, why not leave the Kohler complex and take breakfast at the **Bread and Bean Eatery** in charming Sheboygan Falls, a few miles west? On Saturdays the cooks "salute the skillet" with concoctions such as "Saturday Skillet," with hash browns, bacon, onions, and cheddar cheese cooked together in a skillet. There are also delicious bagels and muffins on hand if you're in a hurry. If you're staying at the Brownstone Inn, expect a hearty breakfast served in the Florida Room, a cheery four-season room.

After fueling up on breakfast, make tracks to the Kohler golf course of your choice: Blackwolf Run or Whistling Straits. Located on a two-mile stretch of land overlooking Lake Michigan, nine miles northeast of Kohler, Whistling Straits consists of two 18-hole golf courses on 560 acres. With the urging of Herb Kohler, world-famous golf course architect Pete Dye designed the layout in honor of traditional courses found in Ireland. Here you'll encounter Lake Michigan breezes, stone bridges, fescue fairways, dunes, and the occasional roaming Scottish sheep. The Straits course is a walking-only course, except for those who are physically unable to walk it. On the Irish Course, you'll play a round of challenging golf in another stunning environment, complete with streams, wooden bridges, and dunes.

Located south of Kohler, about a mile from the American Club, the 400-acre **Blackwolf Run** consists of two courses, the Meadows Valley Course and River Course, which are separated by the Sheboygan River. Also designed by Pete Dye, they offer views of the river valley landscape, especially beautiful during spring and summer when the wildflowers bloom and the prairie grasses blow in the wind. All are beautiful and challenging courses. You won't be disappointed with any.

When making your hotel room reservation, be sure to reserve a tee time as well, especially if you plan to visit during the summer season and would like to hit the greens early in the morning. If you don't stay at the American Club, you will have to reserve a tee time at least two weeks prior to the golf date. Arrive early and practice your shots on the driving range and putting green located near the clubhouse.

After your round of golf, enjoy a leisurely lunch at one of the clubhouse restaurants. Both will satisfy your appetite and need for a relaxing, inspiring environment. **The Blackwolf Run Clubhouse** is built of pine logs and fieldstones, with tables with views of the river valley. You can enjoy a meal of corn chowder or a walleye sandwich in the enclosed patio or outside on the deck. The **Whistling Straits Clubhouse** is a stone building, with views of the ninth and eighteenth greens. Cooks there serve dishes such as potato leek soup and corned beef sandwiches. Stop by the clubhouse's Irish pub on the second floor for hot toddies or pints of Guinness.

## FANTASIES FOR THE NIGHT

Who needs a private cabin in the woods or a hotel suite in flashy Las Vegas when you can check in to a room made to resemble a tree fort or a casino? Fantasy Suites operates two hotels in Wisconsin with themed rooms that are intended to transport you to faraway places and distant times (and whose fantastic decor will make you chuckle). There's the Arabian Nights room, where the two of you can nestle in the round water bed surrounded by royal blue draperies. Or how about the heart-shaped water bed in the Cupid's Corner room? In the Casino Royale room, decorated in red and black, you can soak in a whirlpool surrounded by mirrors. More information is available from Fantasy Suites' Don Q Inn, 3656 Highway 23, Dodgeville, (608) 935-2321 or (800) 666-7848; or Fantasy Suites' West Bend, 2520 West Washington Street, West Bend, (262) 338-0636 or (800) 727-9727.

Another hotel that you might find somewhat arousing or amusing is Char and Ken Knudson's Sybaris, which opened in Mequon, just north of Milwaukee, on Valentine's Day, 1991. Suites here come with lots of mood lighting, mirrors, and wet bars. One of the private pool suites features a 22-foot swimming pool, a pool slide, cascading water, and a steam room. You can book a room here for a few hours or overnight. More information is available from Sybaris, 10240 Highway 57, Mequon, (262) 242-8000, www.sybaris.com

### AFTERNOON

After your scrumptious meal, it's time for a little rest and relaxation at the Kohler Waters Spa. Take a shower in your room and head to the spa in your robes. Because both of you were on your feet for at least three hours walking the courses, order a golfer's foot-renewal massage. For about 50 minutes, a masseuse will apply marine mud to reenergize your tired feet, massage them, and give them a pedicure. (Guys, you will love a pedicure, too.)

After your foot massages, change into your swimsuits in the locker rooms and get ready for some heavy-duty relaxation in the spa. The spa has hot and cold dip pools, whirlpools, steam rooms, and saunas. Try them all. Recline in the lounge chairs and listen to water trickle down the eight-foot cascading wall of water and into the relaxation pool. Feel free to munch on the fruit and snacks placed throughout the spa or order a healthy treat such as yogurt smoothies. If either of you are up for it, exercise for a spell in the exercise room before heading to the spa, or consider splurging on yet another spa service. Another "twogether massage" perhaps?

## ᥰᑈ EVENING

Although you could spend all afternoon and evening in the tranquil spa, at some point force yourselves to return to your room and change for dinner.

Tonight you will dine at **The Immigrant Room and Winery**, the hotel's signature restaurant. Arrive about an hour or so before your dinner reservation to sample wine in the library during the evening cocktail hour and listen to a pianist entertain guests. Order a wine flight and try a variety of different wines before ordering a bottle at your dinner table. If you are unsure about what wine to order, the knowledgeable staff is always ready to recommend one for you.

Remodeled during the winter of 2002–2003, the Immigrant restaurant has six dining rooms, each with a different European theme (such as Scandinavian and English), and mostly two-top tables for couples. Although the dinner menu can vary depending on what fruits and vegetables are in season, expect impressive dishes such as Maine lobster bisque, pan-roasted black bass, and white truffle-crusted lamb loin. To ensure you dine at a time you both desire, make dinner reservations when you book your room or check in. Gentlemen, you will have to wear a coat to dinner.

Afterward, drive into Sheboygan and catch a show at the renovated **Stefanie H. Weill Center for the Performing Arts**. This 1928 theater, with its Spanish-style interior design (notice the stars painted on the ceiling), makes for a romantic spot to listen to the symphony or attend a concert by a visiting singer. The Sheboygan Symphony Orchestra frequently performs here. The venue also welcomes numerous visiting artists throughout the year. Past musicians have included Ricky Skaggs and Lori Line.

## *Day Three*
### ᥰᑈ MORNING

On your third day of this romantic getaway you should wake up feeling completely refreshed and relaxed, especially after yesterday's afternoon in the spa.

Treat yourself to a leisurely breakfast in **The Wisconsin Room** in the American Club. Set in the former dining hall for the Kohler Company's immigrant employees, this restaurant primarily serves regional fare in a dining room decorated with such antiques as an ethnographic map of Wisconsin hanging on the wall and leaded glass windows etched with labor-related axioms. Lounge over breakfast in comfy plush chairs of peach and light green colors. The traditional American Club breakfast should satisfy your appetites. It comes with juice; two eggs; Canadian bacon, applewood-smoked bacon, or Sheboygan sausage; potatoes; toast; and preserves.

A romantic way to top off at crisp winter evening at the American Club. Photo courtesy of the Kohler Company.

After a hearty Wisconsin breakfast, take the free shuttle to **River Wildlife,** a 500-acre recreational and dining club near Blackwolf Run and along the Sheboygan River. For a $12 access fee per person, you and yours will be allowed to hike the three miles of trails through the wildlife sanctuary. (The trails are open to hiking and cross-country skiing during the winter months.) Pick up a map at the lodge and take about an hour-long nature walk. You'll find plenty of spots to pause and listen to birds singing and wind rustling through the trees and meadow. (River Wildlife also offers clay and trap shooting. Beginners and seasoned gun handlers will get a kick out of shooting the targets. If you're feeling adventurous, give it a try.)

After your hike, head to the River Wildlife lodge, quite literally a log cabin in the woods. With cozy nooks for dining throughout the small lodge and dishes you don't normally find in most restaurants, the experience will be memorable. The menu frequently changes, but the chef always cooks up rustic-style meals. Examples of such entrées include roast duckling with a merlot sauce and tenderloin of elk with wild mushrooms, leeks, and a cabernet sauvignon sauce.

## AFTERNOON

For a change of pace this afternoon, drive to Sheboygan for a visit to the **John Michael Kohler Arts Center.** Housed in J. M. Kohler's former home, an 1882 Italianate structure, and adjacent modern galleries, the center's permanent collection includes an impressive amount of folk art. It also hosts a number of traveling exhibitions every year that focus on everything from contemporary photography to textiles, among other art forms. (Even the bathrooms are utilized as rotating gallery spaces.) Before leaving, give your feet a rest and have a seat in the center's Carriage House Café for coffees, glasses of juice, or pastries. And be sure to walk through the center's sculpture garden.

From the arts center, walk or drive to Sheboygan's riverfront, less than one mile south of the center. The Riverfront Boardwalk, also referred to as Fish Shanty Village, consists of former fish shanties that now house shops where you can pick up souvenirs for your children. After you ramble through this little district, drive northeast of the riverfront to Deland Park, off Broughton Drive by Lake Michigan, where you can walk along the lakefront promenade and watch fishing boats enter and leave the harbor. Kick off your shoes, dig your toes into the sand, or splash around for a bit in Lake Michigan's cool waters. In Deland Park you can also view remains of the *Lottie Cooper*, a schooner that sank in 1894 off the Sheboygan Harbor.

## FOR MORE INFORMATION

**Kohler Visitor Information Center**
444 Highland Drive, Kohler
(920) 458-3450 or (800) 344-2838, ext. 988
www.destinationkohler.com

**Sheboygan Convention and Visitor Bureau**
712 Riverfront Drive, Suite 101, Sheboygan
(920) 457-9495 or (800) 457-9497
www.sheboygan.org

**Sheboygan Falls Chamber of Commerce**
641 Monroe Street, Suite. 108, Sheboygan Falls
(920) 467-6206, www.sheboyganfalls.com

## ATTRACTIONS AND RECREATION

**John Michael Kohler Arts Center**
608 New York Avenue, Sheboygan
(920) 458-6144, www.jmkac.org
Free admission.

**John Michael Kohler–Terry Andrae State Park**
1520 Old Park Road, Sheboygan,
and 1020 Beach Park Lane, Sheboygan
(920) 451-4080
www.dnr.state.wi.us
Admission fee.

**Kohler Design Center**
101 Upper Road, Kohler
(920) 457-3699
Free admission.

**Kohler Waters Spa**
501 Highland Drive, Kohler
(920) 457-7777 or (866) WATERS-SPA
Admission fee.

**River Wildlife**
Riverside Drive, Kohler
(920) 457-0134
Admission fee.

**Sports Core**
100 Willow Creek Drive, Kohler
(920) 457-4444
www.sports-core.com
Admission free to American
Club guests.

**Stefanie H. Weill Center for the Performing Arts**
826 N. Eighth Street, Sheboygan
(920) 208-3243
www.weillcenter.com

## LODGING

**The American Club**
Highland Drive, Kohler
(920) 457-8000 or (800) 344-2838
www.americanclub.com
Rooms from $169 during the
winter season and from $269
during peak season.

**The Brownstone Inn**
1227 N. Seventh Street, Sheboygan
(920) 451-0644 or (877) 279-6786
www.brownstoneinn.com
Rooms are from $75.

## DINING AND NIGHTLIFE

**Blackwolf Run Clubhouse**
111 West Riverside Drive, Kohler
(920) 457-4448
Call for hours.

**Bread and Bean Eatery**
107 Pine Street, Sheboygan Falls
(920) 467-7257
Open for breakfast and lunch Monday
through Saturday and for dinner
Wednesday through Friday.

**Broadway Bistro**
334 Broadway, Sheboygan Falls
(920) 467-9082
Open for lunch and dinner Tuesday
through Saturday.

**The Greenhouse**
In a courtyard of the American Club,
Kohler
(920) 457-8888
Open Friday, 4:00 p.m. to 10:00 p.m.,
Saturday, 8:00 a.m. to 10:00 p.m., and
Sunday, 8:00 a.m. to 3:00 p.m.

**The Horse and Plow Restaurant**
At the American Club, Kohler
(920) 457-8888
Open for lunch and dinner daily.

**The Immigrant Room and Winery**
At the American Club, Kohler
(920) 457-8888
Open for dinner daily. Cocktails are
offered in the library outside the
Immigrant Room 5:30 p.m. to 9:30 p.m.
daily. Live music is offered Friday and
Saturday evenings and occasionally two
to three additional evenings during the
summer months.

**The Villager**
124 Pine Street, Sheboygan Falls
(920) 467-4011
Open for dinner Tuesday through Saturday and for brunch Sunday.

**Whistling Straits Clubhouse**
On the Whistling Straits golf course
N8501 County Road LS, Sheboygan
(920) 565-6080
Call for hours.

**The Wisconsin Room**
At the American Club, Kohler
(920) 457-8888
Open for breakfast Monday through
Saturday, for dinner daily, and for
brunch Sunday.

# CHAPTER FIVE

# The Quiet Side of
# *Door County*

When families and couples from Green Bay, Milwaukee, and Chicago first started visiting Door County back in the 1890s by way of steamers, the peninsula was largely populated by fruit farmers and ship builders. Even into the early 1920s, when celebrated landscape architect Jens Jensen began purchasing land in Door County for The Clearing, his retreat for artists and naturalists, Door was a largely unspoiled, agriculturally focused county, save for the busy lumber shipping ports like Jacksonport or the shipbuilding town of Sturgeon Bay. Since Jensen settled in the region, a number of artists have followed, settling in the Cape Cod-like villages of Ephraim and Fish Creek. And throughout recent decades, golf courses and lakeside lodges have sprouted up along the bay, concentrating around the outskirts of Peninsula State Park.

Even with the large number of tourists that flock to the peninsula every year to pick cherries, sample fruit wines, windsurf off Ephraim's bay, and scour the galleries, the 75-mile-long peninsula is charming and remains a beloved destination for couples (despite the sometimes grueling traffic that can back up on Highways 42 and 57 during the Fourth of July weekend and Fall Fest in late September). The county is still home to cherry and apple orchards, impressive limestone bluffs, sea caves, and sandy beaches. You'll discover forests full of birch and cedar trees through which you can hike. And there are plenty of adults-only resorts and inns (with whirlpool suites and four-poster beds) to retreat to at the end of the day.

Most of the hotels and restaurants are clustered around the bay-side villages of Egg Harbor, Ephraim, Fish Creek, and Sister Bay. These towns are buzzing with activity throughout the year. All contain a number of casual and fine-dining restaurants, gift shops, and art galleries, where you can purchase hand-crafted jewelry or hand-thrown pottery pieces.

The lake side of Door County tends to be called the quiet side; there are fewer hotels and more farms. Couples seeking privacy should consider booking a room on this side—where streetlights are few and there are plenty of opportunities for stargazing, roaming through a wooded bog, and listening to singing frogs and crickets.

## *Day One*

### ✧ MORNING

Instead of driving directly to your hotel or inn, spend about two hours at **Potawatomi State Park**, located northwest of Sturgeon Bay. During this time you can get up close and personal with the waters of Sturgeon Bay and Green Bay (and with each other). The waters in downtown Sturgeon Bay are busy with cargo ships and yachters crossing through the canal, but near Potawatomi, they are much calmer and good for a leisurely canoe ride.

After entering the park, follow Shore Road, a narrow road that winds through a forest of birch trees and along the shore of Sturgeon Bay. This road is especially stunning during the early fall when the birch leaves turn goldenrod and almost iridescent. Head to the north end of the park and rent a canoe for an hour. No, you don't have to be expert paddlers to rent one of the canoes. You don't even have to venture too far out into the bay to enjoy the scenery. Follow the shoreline and the limestone cliffs.

After your canoe ride, opt for a walk along one of the many trails through the forest and along the shore. The park does not have any sandy beaches for you to dig your toes into, but there are plenty of cuddling spots. Pick a bench near the water and spend a few minutes watching boats pass by and seagulls chase each other. If you aren't too tired from canoeing, climb the 75-foot-tall lookout tower. Open seasonally, the tower offers a spectacular view of the area, especially in the fall and winter.

After you've worked up an appetite at Potawatomi, head into downtown Sturgeon Bay on Shore Road, which becomes Duluth Road. Although it is the largest of all the towns in Door County, Sturgeon Bay is still a small town with a charming Main Street filled with coffee shops, historic inns, pubs, and restaurants. Order a sandwich at the **Inn at Cedar Crossing** in Sturgeon Bay, housed in a building that dates back to 1884. During the daytime, you'll find the Fireside Pub at the inn to be more cozy and suitable for couples. With exposed brick, an oak bar, and twig wreath decorations, the atmosphere of the Fireside Pub is earthy and wholesome. The food is scrumptious—all breads are made from scratch, on-site. On the menu you'll discover unexpected items such as a jerk pork sandwich. Have a seat at the cozy two-top table in the corner.

### ✧ AFTERNOON

Before checking in to your hotel, stop by the **Door Peninsula Winery** for a bottle of locally produced fruit wine. Feeling especially romantic? Order a heart-shaped gift basket containing a bottle of champagne to be delivered to your room, or have one assembled while you're there.

You can't miss the winery, located north of Sturgeon Bay just off Highway 42 in Carlsville. Housed in an 1868 one-room schoolhouse, known as the Old Carlsville Schoolhouse, the winery offers samples and tours of its cellars. Since

The cozy Fireside Pub at the Inn at Cedar Crossing, Sturgeon Bay. Photo courtesy of the Door County Chamber of Commerce.

moving into the schoolhouse in the mid-1970s, the winery has expanded its products, tasting room, and gift shop. Before purchasing a wine, feel free to sample a few. The winery specializes in fruit and sweet wines such as apple and cherry wines and the Razzle Dazzle Raspberry, as well as seasonal spirits like White Christmas. Note the white wedding wine, which comes in a heart-shaped bottle. If you don't have a taste for fruit wines, try the more traditional varietal wines, such as the cabernet sauvignon, chardonnay, and zinfandel.

Now that you have a basket full of wines and goodies like cheese and crackers, check in to your abode for the weekend. There are myriad lodging options in Door County. Here are two quiet and especially romantic spots.

Run by Bryan Groeschl and Darrin Day, the **Chanticleer Guest House** is located on 70 resplendent acres on Cherry Road, north of Sturgeon Bay. You can stay in a secluded cabin with a view of a pond or in a room within an impeccably and artistically restored barn. There are so many amenities, it's possible for the two of you to spend the entire vacation in your room. The 1915 cedar barn contains eight suites. All have double whirlpool tubs and private balconies. Some have fireplaces, armchairs, love seats, rocking chairs, and chaise lounges. Most are decorated in muted colors, filled with antiques, and accented with current issues of magazines like *Audubon*. Outside, you'll find a sauna, a heated pool, a garden almost an acre in size, wildflower fields, a gazebo, and baby lambs in a neighboring barn. It's perfectly bucolic. Across Cherry Road, the two cabins are hidden among 40 acres. Breakfast is delivered to your door every morning.

**The Blacksmith Inn,** a historic beachfront inn, is tucked into the fishing village of Baileys Harbor, about 30 minutes north of Sturgeon Bay. The inn, once the home to the peninsula's blacksmith, August Zahn, still has a working blacksmith shop on-site. (Pay a visit and watch horseshoes being made.) Built in 1912, the inn consists of the August Zahn house, where he and his family lived (the building is now listed on the National Register of Historic Places) and the Harbor House. Like many inns and resorts in Door County that cater to couples, all the rooms in the Blacksmith have balconies overlooking the water, fireplaces, and whirlpool bathtubs. Have your pick of brass or iron beds, four-poster or canopy. The innkeepers also offer special packages for couples; request a bottle of bubbly or a vase of roses sent to your room while you're out sightseeing.

After checking in to your room, walk around the property. If you're at Chanticleer, admire the gardens and visit the lambs. If you've rented one of the luxury cabins, explore the 40 private acres. If you are staying at the Blacksmith Inn, you may want to take a dip in the lake—the inn has 400 feet of sandy beach for its guests. Or, pop open that bottle of wine and settle into a bench in one of the gardens.

## EVENING

For dinner, head back into Sturgeon Bay if you're staying at the Chanticleer. Treat yourself to a candlelight dinner at **Sage Restaurant and Wine Bar** in Sturgeon Bay. An intimate and contemporary setting, Sage's dining room has tall ceilings, walls painted a muted green, and an impressive wine bar. Before dinner, enjoy a velvety merlot while sitting in the overstuffed armchairs that look out on Third Avenue, and listen as a jazz pianist entertains on the baby grand. On the menu you'll find entrées such as grilled beef filet and pecan-encrusted whitefish.

If you're staying at the Blacksmith and don't want to drive the approximately 30 minutes into Sturgeon Bay, reserve a table with a waterfront view at the **Harbor Fish Market and Grille** in Baileys Harbor, right down the street from the Blacksmith. Splurge on prime rib, lobster, or oysters, those aphrodisiacal mollusks. Like Sage, Harbor Fish Market and Grille has an extensive wine list and a full bar. Reservations are encouraged at both restaurants during the summer.

Don't want to leave your room? Have **Meadowcroft** cater a meal to your suite. Try tantalizing dishes such as pesto-stuffed cherry tomatoes, Napa salad, and Cornish game hens.

After dinner surprise your honey by arranging for a horse-drawn carriage to pick you up in front of the restaurant or inn. **Carriages of Door County,** located at Fifth Avenue and Kentucky Street, will take you through historic Sturgeon Bay

## TYING THE KNOT?

& Where to find a ring: J. Jeffrey Taylor, 4175 Main Street, Fish Creek, (920) 868-3033; Gold and Silver Creations, 742 Jefferson Street, Sturgeon Bay, (920) 743-2570; Carats and Karats, Shorewood Village, Ephraim, (920) 854-5334. All feature handcrafted jewelry.

Where to propose: on top of the observation tower in Potowatomi, at a candlelit dinner at White Gull Inn, on a rented sailboat, on Cana Island in view of the lighthouse, in the silo room in Cornerstone Suites, (920) 868-3005, in Bjorklunden's garden, at the scenic overlook in Ellison Bluff County Park.

Where to exchange vows: Boynton Chapel in Bjorklunden, (920) 839-2116 or www.lawrence.edu; or the Bridal Chapel on County Road C, (920) 432-0822,outside of Sturgeon Bay. There are numerous churches in the villages with clergy who will perform weddings for out-of-towners. Among them are the impressive Saint Joseph's Catholic Church in Sturgeon Bay, (920) 743-2062, and the historic Moravian Church, (920) 854-2804, in Ephraim.

The celebration: the Bay Shore has a room that holds about 100 people for wedding receptions. The Eagle Harbor Inn, (920) 854-2121, has a room for approximately 85 guests. For larger parties consider Stone Harbor Resort, (920) 746-0700, or Bridgeport Resort, (920) 746-9919, in Sturgeon Bay.

The planning: the Door County Chamber of Commerce maintains a comprehensive list of wedding planners, caterers, bakers, photographers, and musicians.

and along the waterfront. If they are booked, try **Mayberry's Carriage and Sleigh Rides** on County Road V in Egg Harbor. During the summer, Mayberry's offers rides through downtown Ephraim, about 30 minutes north of the Chanticleer Inn. During the winter, they offer sleigh rides throughout the county. If you opt for a ride in Ephraim, make sure the driver takes you down Valentine Lane.

After the dinner and carriage ride, hop back in your car and catch a late-night movie at the **Skyway Drive-In Movie Theatre** if you're visiting Door County during the summer. Located off Highway 42 between Fish Creek and Ephraim, Skyway has been around since 1951 and is one of the last remaining drive-ins in Wisconsin. A trip here will be a throwback to an earlier time. A note of caution: this is a popular spot, and if you're trying to avoid children, you may want to forego the drive-in. However, the crowd does tend to thin out later in the evenings, and because the movies run on radio sound you can roll up your windows to tune out any gabbing teenagers.

By the time the movie is over, you should both be quite relaxed and ready to head back to your room. Surprise your sweetheart by having a little basket of chocolates placed in your room. The innkeeper will be able to arrange this if you don't have time to slip the box onto the nightstand table during the day. Request hand-dipped chocolate-covered strawberries from Door County Confectionery in Sturgeon Bay.

## Day Two

### ☙ MORNING

Following a dreamy night in one of the king-size, down comforter-covered beds, force yourself to wake early and drive to Cave Point, a county park adjacent to Whitefish Dunes State Park, north of the town of Institute. Bring a blanket and climb out onto one of the limestone ledges to marvel at the sun as it rises above the lake, glimmering on the water and the waves as they crash into the sea caves beneath you. If the rocky surface is too uncomfortable, there are a few benches situated between the pine trees where you two can snuggle and greet the dawn. Be sure to bring your camera.

Afterward, drive about 10 miles north on Cave Point Drive and Highway 57 to the lakeside village of Baileys Harbor. Order a couple of blueberry muffins and cinnamon scones at **Baileys Harbor Coffee**. If you're still feeling drowsy, try an espresso or other caffeinated concoction. The shop brews a variety of flavored coffees, cappuccinos, and lattes.

Continue northward along scenic County Road Q and meander around Cana Island Road in the direction of one of the Door County's most photographed lighthouses—the **Cana Island lighthouse**. The lighthouse was built more than 150 years ago by order of Captain Justice Bailey, who is credited with discovering Baileys Harbor in 1848 when he sought shelter from a storm. He and a group of men persuaded the U.S. government to build a lighthouse at the harbor entrance in 1869. Unless the lake levels are especially high, you should be able to walk across a land bridge made of rocks. You won't find a parking lot near the lighthouse—the road simply stops at the rocky causeway—and traffic can get a little hairy in the middle of the day during midsummer. But if you arrive early enough in the day, chances are you two will be the only ones exploring the island. The keeper's house and oil house, where fuel was stored, are open daily from mid-May to mid-October. But you can always walk around the island.

On the way to Cana Island you will also pass by a smaller lighthouse known as the Range Lights, off Ridges Drive. Standing at approximately 12 feet high, the lighthouse was built in 1899. You'll find it at the edge of **Ridges Sanctuary**, a 1,000-acre wildlife preserve. If you're seeking more quiet time with nature, take about 30 minutes to walk through Ridges. The boardwalks allow you to explore the preserve without disturbing the bogs, dunes, and many wildflowers, including an amazing amount of orchids.

After wandering around Cana Island and the Ridges, retreat to a little spa on the bay side of the peninsula. Head northeast on County Road Q toward Ephraim and follow Highway 42 to **The Spa at Sacred Grounds**, just north of town. Instead of retreating to separate spa areas, sign up for a couples massage, which allows you both to enjoy a massage in the comfort of each other's company. You'll each have your own massage therapist in a room especially designed for two clients. Go for the traditional Swedish massage or try the Door County Stone Massage, which involves warm, smooth stones collected from area beaches and rolled over your muscles. A massage will feel wonderfully calming and

Enjoying the fauna and flora at Ridges Sanctuary, near Baileys Harbor. Photo courtesy of Wisconsin Department of Tourism.

at the same time invigorating, especially if your muscles are a little tender from canoeing the previous day. Massages tend to make people not only relaxed but also thirsty and a little hungry. Drive south to nearby Fish Creek for lunch.

Built in 1896, the **White Gull Inn and Restaurant** in Fish Creek set the standard for architectural style in the bay-side villages. It is a clapboard building painted white with black shutters and features an expansive front porch. A popular spot for vacationers and locals, the dining room has plenty of seats along windows that look out onto a little courtyard and the surrounding white cottages where guests can rent rooms. In the winter the dining room is especially cozy with the wood-burning fireplace.

Chef John Vreeke and his staff use local fruit and veggies in their dishes. For example, the Open Doorwich, a ham sandwich, has slices of Door County apples and Wisconsin Brie placed on rye bread. You'll also be able to sample the famous whitefish, a Door County tradition, and some more interesting entrées like asparagus (said to be an aphrodisiac) deviled chicken. If you arrive before noon, you can still order breakfast dishes like eggs Benedict or cherry pancakes with Door County maple syrup.

If you really like their fare, return for the candlelight dinners served nightly during the summer or their popular fish boils, which occur Wednesday, Friday, Saturday, and Sunday nights in the summer and Friday nights during the winter. Reservations are recommended.

## ✎ AFTERNOON

After your meal at the White Gull, ramble through downtown Fish Creek. Founded in 1854, Fish Creek was a booming lumber town prior to becoming a resort town at the turn of the twentieth century. Although they contain contemporary clothing and shoe stores, most buildings downtown date back to the 1880s. If you enjoyed the massage, stop by Bath Essentials in Founders Square and pick up a massage guidebook, candles, incense, and massage oils. Feeling especially generous? Have a heart pendant crafted for your wife or girlfriend at Gallery of Gold, a goldsmith studio and jewelry boutique housed in a century-old schoolhouse. Browse through J. Jeffrey Taylor on Main Street, a contemporary jewelry shop featuring handcrafted work created by Taylor himself and other area artists. In addition to square sapphire rings, you'll find items like glass bowls and silver pins. Splurge on a bottle of champagne at Siobhan's Wine, Cigars, and Liquor.

## ✎ EVENING

Tonight, don't worry about driving. Have a trolley swing by the inn and chauffeur the two of you to the restaurant and theater. You can either join a group of couples on a prearranged trolley ride to the restaurant and theater or shell out a few more dollars for you and your sweetheart to be the only couple aboard. **Door County Trolley**, based at Lautenbach's Orchard Country on Highway 42 south of Fish Creek, will pick you up..

Ask the trolley driver to take the scenic route, driving past bluffs and along the shoreline, to the restaurant where you will dine tonight, the **Inn at Kristofer's**. The Sister Bay restaurant is a surprising and refreshing treat. Run by Chef Terri and her husband, Kris Milligan, the Inn at Kristofer's is relatively new on the Door County dining scene. On most evenings a musician is strumming a classical guitar or a pianist is playing the grand piano. Decor is airy and light—with sunshiny yellow walls and fresh bouquets. Reserve a window table facing the harbor.

Start with a smooth maple butternut squash bisque or bread salad with walnut vinaigrette. Dishes are accented with herbs from the Milligans' garden, and plates are prettily accented with flower petals. The wines are from California, but the desserts are distinctly Door County, such as cherry tarts, cherry biscotti, and bumbleberry pies made with blueberries, raspberries, and cherries.

Boynton Chapel on the grounds of the secluded and serene Bjorklunden retreat center. Photo courtesy of Wisconsin Department of Tourism.

After dinner at Kristofer's, before boarding the trolley or limo, stroll around the marina across the street for a few minutes.

Next stop is a theatrical performance at **Bjorklunden**, a secluded, wooded lakeside estate-turned-retreat-center of more than 400 acres in Baileys Harbor, about 10 minutes from Kristofer's. **Door Shakespeare** stages plays such as Twelfth Night in the garden every summer. If the Bard isn't being performed on Bjorklunden's grounds, a chamber music concert is likely taking place in the lodge.

Arrive early to check out the tiny **Boynton Chapel**, a replica of a twelfth-century Norwegian stave church. The chapel and all of the hand-carved dragons and pew decorations were created by the former owner of the estate, Winifred Boynton, and her family in the 1930s and 1940s. Winifred was inspired to build such a church back in the late 1920s when she stumbled upon the original in Norway following the death of her husband, Carleton Vail, with whom she had purchased Bjorklunden in the 1920s. Follow the path to the little church and step inside to admire the frescos that Boynton, her second husband, and her six children painted. The chapel is open for tours on Monday and Wednesday afternoons from mid-June to late August. It may not be open before the performance, but you can certainly walk by and peer in the windows and have a seat on one of the benches in the nearby garden.

Bjorklunden is an enchanting place in the evening, with its mature pines, birch trees, and rolling meadows. You may want to return here for a weeklong visit. Run by Appleton-based Lawrence University, Bjorklunden (the estate's formal name, Björklunden vid Sjön, translates to "birch forest by the water" in Norwegian) welcomes not only university students seeking retreat but also adults interested in spiritual and intellectual enrichment. Classes and seminars such as Woods in the Morning, Wine in the Afternoon; Rocks of the Earth's Crust; and Play Better Bridge are held during the summer and fall.

## ⟡ ROMANTIC DOOR DRIVES

- Follow County Road J from Forestville and County Road U to Sturgeon Bay. County J and U bring you closer to the coastline and you can see more fruit orchards, Christmas tree farms, meadows, and wooded countryside full of birch and cedar trees. Pull off at Lower LaSalle County Park and enjoy a quiet moment on Brawnsdorf Beach.
- Drive along Shore Road in Potowatomi State Park.
- Take County Road Q from Baileys Harbor north to North Bay and west to Ephraim.
- Bay Shore Drive, north from Sturgeon Bay to Egg Harbor, takes you past the county quarry beach, new and old estates, and family fishing piers.

If the two of you are more in the mood for music or the weather is looking inclement, try **Birch Creek Music Performance Center**, located between Egg Harbor and Baileys Harbor on County Road E. During the day, renowned musicians coach budding violinists and percussion students. By night, the teachers strut their stuff in the 500-seat renovated barn. All summer long you can catch big-band shows and jazz and chamber orchestra concerts. Arrive early and picnic in the garden or sip some wine in the gazebo. The students themselves occasionally perform in the gazebo.

As if you couldn't have impressed your lover enough, arrange to have a bouquet of fresh flowers placed in your room while the two of you are out for the evening. The innkeeper will be able to do this for you, but if you want to pick some up yourself, consider **Sturgeon Bay Florist**. Then take advantage of the inn's sauna or whirlpool tub.

## *Day Three*

### ᥲ MORNING

After sleeping in, head north to Ellison Bay for a scrumptious, celebrated brunch at **T. Ashwell's**. It will be a bit of a drive to get to—about 15 miles from Baileys Harbor and 30 miles from the Chanticleer—but once you walk in the restaurant, housed in a renovated farmhouse painted white and blue, you'll want to hang around for a while. Located on the outskirts of town, T. Ashwell's gives the feel that you are at a friend or relative's house for the day. There's a lawn for you to mosey around, an inviting gazebo, and a screened-in porch that is heated during the winter. Inside, cuddle up before the crackling fireplace and sip a mimosa as a pianist performs on the grand piano.

**Mission Grille**, at Highways 42 and 57 in Sister Bay, and the **Landmark Resort** in Egg Harbor also serve up strata and pancakes at their comprehensive Sunday brunches.

Following brunch, drive a few miles south on Highway 42 to Porcupine Bay Road. Look for the Scenic Overlook sign directing you to Ellison Bluff County Park. Follow Ellison Bluff Road for a little more than a mile until you reach the escarpment—more than 200 feet high—which offers awesome views of Green Bay and Michigan's Upper Peninsula.

### ᥲ AFTERNOON

Spend the afternoon horseback riding through 500 acres at **Kurtz Corral Riding Stables** on County Road I, north of Sturgeon Bay, about a 5- to 10-minute drive from Chanticleer and 15 to 20 minutes from the Blacksmith Inn. The afternoon and evening rides—through fields and forests—are usually for people who have ridden horses before; you'll get to trot and canter. After the ride, if you're visiting during the fall, nuzzle up to each other beside a bonfire, sipping mugs of cider, before heading back into town or to your inn.

Feeling a little more daring and liberal with your money? **Wings over Door County**, at the Cherryland Airport south of Sturgeon Bay, will take the two of you 1,000 feet above the orchards and beaches in a petite, single-engine Cessna 172. During the intimate, one-hour plane ride (the Cessna seats a maximum of three people) your pilot will follow the shoreline and point out shipwrecks, lighthouses, and other historical markers.

### ᥲ EVENING

A great way to spend your final romantic evening in Door County is to watch the sun slide past Green Bay as a Dixieland band stirs it up or a brass quintet plays away. Drive to Gills Rock and board the *Island Clipper* for a **Summer Sunset Concert Cruise**. The *Clipper* takes riders from the northernmost point of Door County on an approximately three-hour cruise of the waters and offshore islands. You'll pass by lighthouses, impressive limestone bluffs, rocky shores, and the passage known as Death's Door, where many schooners met their fate. Finally, the boat will sail into the open waters of Green Bay and Lake Michigan. Once you're out on the bay, the band starts up. This is not a black-tie event; help yourself to the buffet dinner, which includes dishes like baked chicken and cucumber salad, and find a place to sit. Passengers are welcome to bring a cooler of beer or a bottle of wine.

If you are unable to make it to Gills Rock for a Summer Concert Cruise, **Door County Cruises,** which leave from the maritime museum in Sturgeon Bay, offer boat trips throughout the day aboard a vintage Chicago Fire Department boat. If you feel confident enough to charter your own boat, the **Snug Harbor Inn** in Sturgeon Bay rents all kinds of boats and sailboats.

After the cruise, take your date stargazing. Visit the **Leif Everson Astronomical Observatory**, located at Crossroads at Big Creek Historical and Environmental Learning Preserve, north of Sturgeon Bay. The Door Peninsula Astronomical Society holds observation nights on weekends throughout the year. If they are not holding an observation night while you're in town, they may be offering a class on how to purchase or work your telescope. Or, bring a blanket to the Crossroads and count the stars together.

### ⤚ FOR MORE INFORMATION
**Door County Chamber of Commerce**
1015 Green Bay Road, Sturgeon Bay
(920) 743-4456
www.doorcountyvacations.com

**Peninsula Arts and Humanities Alliance**
(For info on concerts, plays, and art shows)
www.doorcountyarts.com

### ⤚ ATTRACTIONS AND RECREATION
**Birch Creek Music Performance Center**
3821 County Road E, east of Egg Harbor
(920) 868-3763, www.birchcreek.org

**Bjorklunden**
A few miles south of Baileys Harbor off Highway 42
(920) 839-2216
www.lawrence.edu/about/bjork

**Cana Island lighthouse**
Off County Q, north of Baileys Harbor
For information call the Door County Maritime Museum & Lighthouse Preservation Society, (920) 743-5958
www.dcmm.org
The lighthouse keeper's house is open to visitors from mid-May to mid-October.

**Carriages of Door County**
Fifth Avenue and Kentucky Street, Sturgeon Bay
(920) 743-4343 or (920) 751-9197

**Door County Cruises**
120 N. Madison Ave., Sturgeon Bay
(920) 825-1112 or (920) 495-6454
www.doorcountycruises.com

**Door County Trolley**
1113 Cove Road, Sturgeon Bay
(920) 868-1100
www.doorcountytrolley.com

**Door Peninsula Winery**
5806 Highway 42, Carlsville
(920) 743-7431 or (800) 551-5049

**Door Shakespeare**
(920) 854-9641

**Kurtz Corral Riding Stables**
County I, Sturgeon Bay
(920) 743-6742 or (800) 444-0469
www.kurtzcorral.com

**Leif Everson Astronomical Observatory**
Crossroads at Big Creek,
Highway 42/57 and County Road TT,
Sturgeon Bay
(920) 746-1105

**Mayberry's Carriage and Sleigh Rides**
4404 County Road V, Egg Harbor
(920) 743-2352

**Potawatomi State Park**
3740 Park Drive, Sturgeon Bay
(920) 746-2890

**Ridges Sanctuary**
Highway Q, Baileys Harbor
(920) 839-2802
www.ridgesanctuary.org

**Skyway Drive-In Movie Theatre**
Off Highway 42 between Fish Creek
and Ephraim
(920) 854-9938

**Snug Harbor Inn Marina**
1627 Memorial Drive, Sturgeon Bay
(920) 743-2337
or (800) 231-5767
www.boatdoorcounty.com

**Spa at Sacred Grounds**
Highway 42 and Townline Road,
Ephraim
(920) 854-4733
www.sacredgroundsspa.com

**Sturgeon Bay Florist**
142 South Third Avenue, Sturgeon Bay
(920) 743-3465
www.sturgeonbayflorist.com

**Summer Sunset Concert Cruise**
Gills Rock
(920) 854-2986, www.concertcruises.com
Cruises run from June to September.

**Wings over Door County/Orion
Flight Services**
3418 Park Drive, Sturgeon Bay
(888) 743-6952
Rides are offered year-round.

## ᕗ LODGING
**Blacksmith Inn**
Highway 57, Baileys Harbor
(920) 839-9222 or (800) 769-8619
www.theblacksmithinn.com
Rooms are from $95.

**Chanticleer Guest House**
4072 Cherry Road, Sturgeon Bay
(920) 746-0334
www.chanticleerguesthouse.com
Rooms are from $96.

## ᕗ DINING AND NIGHTLIFE
**Baileys Harbor Coffee**
8078 Highway 57, Baileys Harbor
(920) 839-2115

**Harbor Fish Market and Grille**
8080 Highway 57, Baileys Harbor
(920) 839-9999
www.harborfishmarket-grille.com
Open for lunch and dinner daily.

**Inn at Cedar Crossing**
336 Louisiana Street, Sturgeon Bay
(920) 743-4249,
www.innatcedarcrossing.com
Open for breakfast, lunch, and dinner
daily.

**Inn at Kristofer's**
734 Bay Shore Drive, Sister Bay
(920) 854-9419
www.innatkristofers.com
Open for dinner Wednesday through
Monday.

**Landmark Resort Restaurant**
7643 Hillside Road, Egg Harbor
(920) 868-3205
www.thelandmarkresort.com
Open for breakfast, brunch, lunch, and
dinner. Call for hours.

**Meadowcroft Catering**
8605 County Road D, Forestville
(920) 825-7878

**Mission Grille**
Highways 42 and 57, Sister Bay
(920) 854-9070
Open for lunch and dinner. Call for
hours.

**Sage Restaurant and Wine Bar**
136 N. Third Avenue, Sturgeon Bay
(920) 746-1100
Open for dinner daily. Closed Monday
during the winter.

**T. Ashwell's Restaurant**
11976 Mink River Road, Ellison Bay
(920) 854-4306
Open for dinner Wednesday through
Sunday and for brunch Sunday.

**White Gull Inn and Restaurant**
4225 Main Street, Fish Creek
(920) 868-3517
www.whitegullinn.com
Open for breakfast, lunch, and
dinner daily.
Candlelight dinners are served Monday,
Tuesday, and Thursday, May through
October, and Saturday, November
through, April.

# CHAPTER SIX

# Whisked Away in
# *Green Lake County*

Located in central Wisconsin and somewhat removed from the main thoroughfares (about 30 miles from the nearest interstate), Green Lake is a traditional resort community. Couples and families have been spending summers here for almost 150 years. In fact, the first resort in the country west of Niagara Falls reportedly opened here back in the 1860s. But as you'll discover, Green Lake is not as plagued with crowds as some other resort areas during the summer (such as Lake Geneva to the south). Green Lake remains a charming community surrounded by quaint towns, orchards, farms, and wildlife areas, making it a great getaway for couples looking for some together time.

The focal point of Green Lake County is the lake, which at 230 feet deep is the deepest in all of Wisconsin. It's also quite large, with 27 miles of shoreline to explore. You will spot anglers trolling for bass and trout, water-skiers practicing their flips, and couples like yourselves lazing in the sun at the lakeshore or on the deck of a boat. You'll notice couples playing rounds of golf during the days and strolling through the parks in the evenings.

Although you could spend the entire weekend lounging at the lakeshore, this getaway recommends you board a yacht for an afternoon tour of the lake, climb into a wicker gondola and float above the countryside in a hot-air balloon, plus ride to dinner and attend a music concert via a horse-drawn surrey. By the end of the three days, you will find yourselves enchanted not only with the lake but with each other once again.

## *Day One*

### MORNING

Because you won't be able to check in to your hotel or bed-and-breakfast room until about 3:00 p.m. or 4:00 p.m., you and your sweetie can spend the morning of your first day exploring the region surrounding Green Lake.

First stop is the town of Princeton, a charming, refreshing community of about 1,500 residents situated near the Fox River. Princeton, which at one time boasted a large number of bars along its main drag of Water Street, now has countless boutiques lining its downtown. (The town was also known as Beantown because steamboats on the Fox stopped here to pick up and deliver lima beans and green beans that were grown in the region.) The town is a must-see for couples looking for home decor items, couples wanting to pick up gifts for friends, or couples in the mood to lounge over a cup of coffee in a storefront café.

## MODERN-DAY PASSION PITS

As the crickets hum and the stars twinkle, take in a film, arm in arm, within the comforts of your car—in the front or backseat. In addition to Door County's Skyway Drive-In and Wisconsin Dells' Big Sky Twin Drive-In (described in Chapters 5 and 12, respectively), you'll find a handful of other drive-in movie theaters throughout the state. When you're in Eau Claire, try the Gemini Drive-In at 6730 Highway 12, (715) 847-5701. On your trip through Green County, chances are you will drive by Monroe's Sky-Vu at 1936 Highway 69, (608) 328-4545. On the way Up North, there's the new Field of Scenes on Highway 55 in Freedom, just south of County Road E, (920) 788-1935, www.fieldofscenes.biz Another option is Moonlight Drive-In, 1494 East Green Bay Street, Shawano, (715) 524-3636. Check with local visitor bureaus to find other drive-ins.

Take some time to walk down Water Street, and you'll pass one intriguing shop after the other. One of the first stores to open and spark the downtown's revitalization was Tracy Porter, 544 Water Street, where you can purchase the designer's flatware, dinnerware, and other home decor products. There's also Henry's General Store, 604 Water Street, which contains wool sweaters, handmade soaps from France, fine stationery, and imported cheese and chocolates. Be sure to pick out some treats for your traveling partner. At Twister, 602 Water Street, just down the street, browse through cool home decor items such as contemporary area rugs and wooden puzzles for children. Twister also has a coffee bar.

After loading up your car with treasures, treat your date to lunch at **Mimi's**, a casual yet choice Italian restaurant right in the center of downtown. The atmosphere suits the renovated downtown with exposed brick walls, a large bar, and intimate tabletops. For lunch, Mimi's serves up pizzas made with fresh mozzarella and herbs, veggie-heavy salads, traditional sandwiches like the Reuben, and unique pastas such as the crispy spaghetti with toasted noodles tossed with bacon, tomatoes, onions, and eggs.

One of the many walkable trails at the Heidel House in Green Lake. Photo courtesy of Heidel House Resort.

## AFTERNOON

From Princeton, drive north on County Road D toward the White River Marsh Wildlife Area, where the two of you will enjoy a quiet scenic drive together. Head east on White River Road and follow the signs for Rustic Road 22, which is, for the most part, gravel road. The road will take you through the wildlife area. Continue on Big Island Road and you'll cross Sucker Creek and the White River. As you'll discover, the marsh makes for a very peaceful outing. Turn off the radio, lower the windows, and pull over occasionally to look for pheasants, red foxes, herons, and sandhill cranes. Be sure to stretch your legs, walk around the area for a bit (there are more than 11,000 acres to the wildlife area), and listen to the birdsongs.

After your jaunt through the wild, drive back south to Green Lake and check in to your hotel or B&B room. If you're looking for a resort type of accommodation, rent a room at the **Heidel House**, a grand 20-acre resort located right on the shores of Green Lake. Try to reserve a lake-view suite on the second floor of the main lodge. With these rooms, you'll have your own private balcony where you can sit outside and view the lake. Or, open the door and you can lounge on the couch and view the lake from inside. Lake-view suites also come with a king- or queen-size bed, whirlpool tub, and bathrobes. If you are traveling with another couple, rent the bungalow, where each couple will have its own area on separate floors, with a spiral staircase connecting the living quarters. The bungalow also has excellent views of the lake from the living room and the decks. In the winter, ask for the fireplace suite in the main lodge.

For a more secluded escape, stay at the **Angel Inn** on the south shore of Green Lake. Owners Kathy and Dave Greening purchased the Greek Revival structure in 1999 and opened in August 2000 after extensively renovating and updating the home, adding romantic features such as marblelike tile floors and cozy love seats. Each room is decorated differently, in rich colors such as maroon and gold. You can't go wrong with any of the rooms; all are romantic with features like four-poster or sleigh beds, whirlpool bathtubs, and fireplaces. For folks who love to soak in the tub, book the Raphael Room. While reclining in the bathtub you'll be able to view the lake.

After checking in to your room and unpacking, grab a book or magazine and head to the lake. If you're staying at the Heidel House, take a walk through the property following the stone paths and admire the blooming flower beds. You'll find a circular patio area on the hill overlooking the lake and plenty of benches by the lakeside, perfect for the two of you to take in the scene. At the Angel Inn, walk down to the boathouse perched near the shore. From here, you can also bask in the afternoon sun. In the afternoon the Angel Inn serves complimentary tea daily.

## EVENING

Relax for a spell, then drive to nearby Ripon for a sunset hot-air balloon ride with **Wisconsin's Majestic Balloons**. After being briefed on safety instructions, you will rise above the trees in a wicker basket guided by a pilot. You'll glide above the region's lakes, farmsteads, and woods as the sun begins to slide beyond the horizon. After you land, you'll be chauffeured back to where you departed on a trolley. (As if it wasn't fun enough to explore the region in a hot-air balloon, you also get to ride in a trolley.) Be sure to make a reservation in advance.

Next, relive your trip over dinner at the **Grey Rock** restaurant on the grounds of the Heidel House Resort. With wall-to-wall windows, each table in the restaurant's east and west wings affords vistas of Green Lake and the gardens outside the restaurant. Arrive 30 minutes before your dinner reservation and have a drink at the bar on the main level as a pianist plays tunes. The restaurant, remodeled in 2002, has a smart, contemporary atmosphere, with bold colors, comfortable chairs and sofas, and bookshelves stocked with not only books but also bottles of wine. Dishes can vary per season and year, but expect delectable entrées such as rack of lamb seasoned with rosemary. Because Green Lake is known for its excellent trout fishing, it's not unusual to find local fish on the menu. One example is the rainbow trout with crabmeat stuffing.

For those of you who have attained . . . let us say . . . a certain level of maturity, when was the last time the two of you boogied on a dance floor (other than at a relative's wedding)? Complete your evening by strutting your stuff on the dance floor at the **Boathouse**, the Heidel House's casual bar, a short walk from Grey Rock. This bar and restaurant, which also includes an outdoor patio during the summer, brings in local bands on the weekends. Get down to rock along with a band playing music from the 1950s or 2000s.

## Day Two

### ✍ MORNING

Arise early and savor a breakfast of fresh-squeezed orange juice, fruit, and breads at Angel Inn. If you are staying at the Heidel House, soak in the morning sun in the **Sunroom Café**, where you can expect such breakfasts as eggs Benedict and French toast (not to mention views of Green Lake).

Next, head to a local golf course to play a round of golf together. Across the street from the Heidel House Resort you'll find the oldest golf course in Wisconsin, **Tuscumbia**. Established in 1896, the 18-hole, par-71 course features 6,301 yards. Or go to the **Golf Courses of Lawsonia** on the grounds of the Green Lake Conference Center on the north side of the lake. Lawsonia offers two different courses: the Links, a Scottish-style layout with a yardage of 6,466 and par of 72, and the Woodlands, a course situated, as its name implies, in a forestlike setting with a yardage of 6,186 and par of 72.

For lunch, have a seat at one of the outdoor tables at **Norton's Marine Dining Room**, another lakeside spot with great views. As the waves sparkle from the midday sun, watch water-skiers and anglers skirt the lake. Lunches range from steak sandwiches to turkey walnut salad.

Cruising Green Lake on the Heidel House's 60-foot yacht *Escapade*. Photo courtesy of Heidel House Resort.

## AFTERNOON

This afternoon nothing is required of the two of you except to unwind, laze in the sun, and chat. First, slip into your swimsuits and head to Heidel House's outdoor pool. (If it's raining, the resort has a large indoor pool, too. Or you can nestle in the hot tub.) Pull two reclining lounge chairs together in the direction of the lake. Splash around, lather each other with suntan lotion, doze off for a while, and order some drinks from the patio bar. This is an afternoon to revel in each other's company. For some fun, walk a few yards from the pool to the bocce ball or croquet area, where the two of you can engage another couple in a game. (You can borrow the equipment for free at the hotel.)

At some point during the midafternoon, walk down to the pier and board the *Escapade*, a 60-foot catamaran-style yacht. During the weekends, the resort offers an hourlong sightseeing cruise of Green Lake in the afternoon. Order glasses of wine and have a seat. Glimpse historic homes lining the lakeshore; watch water-skiers performing feats and anglers casting their lines into the water. Reservations are not required, but the hotel recommends guests call in advance to reserve spots.

## EVENING

Pay homage to Green Lake's illustrious past—and indulge your romantic stirrings—by traveling to your destinations this evening in a Victorian-style surrey. Request the four-seater buggy from **Cedar Ridge Ranch**, an outfit in nearby Ripon that offers horse-drawn carriage rides on their farm or throughout outlying towns. Reserve the carriage in advance, and the driver and carriage will arrive at your door to shuttle you to downtown Green Lake for dinner. (Don't worry if it's raining; the carriage has a hardtop.)

Tonight impress your sweetheart by dining at **Two Chez**, a small, white-tablecloth restaurant in downtown Green Lake. A modern and graceful French bistro, Two Chez's menu is ever changing, with appetizers like lemon and garlic shrimp and entrées such as a filet of beef wrapped in bacon. At Two Chez, you can choose from the six-course menu or order à la carte appetizers and entrées. If you're celebrating an anniversary or other special event, be sure to tell your waiter or the host. Staff will be able to recommend a bottle of champagne. The owners, Paul and Michelle Molthan, are gracious hosts, eager to chat about the extensive wine collection in their cellar. Do share a dessert. If you're visiting in the fall, try the Granny Smith apple tart.

After dinner put your arm around your date's shoulders and walk across the street to the historic **Thrasher Opera House**, a venue built by local resident Charlie Thrasher in 1910 to host vaudeville theater acts and show silent movies. For decades it was used as a community center and eventually became a warehouse. Throughout the 1990s locals labored to renovate the building. Now it serves as a beloved performance venue. When you book your trip to

Green Lake, be sure to contact the opera house to inquire about shows while you are in town. The 200-seat theater has welcomed Irish singers, blues musicians, folk and bluegrass legends, and comedians. Try to visit during the annual **Green Lake Festival of Music**, which typically runs from the end of June through the end of August. Performers have included violinist Rachel Barton, the Milwaukee String Quartet, and the Bach Dancing and Dynamite Society.

When the show ends, don't go back to your hotel or inn room right away. Instead, have the carriage driver take you to nearby Deacon Mills Park at South Lawson Drive and the marina for a short, starlit stroll along the banks to listen to the loons and frogs singing to each other. If you're visiting Green Lake during the week, you'll find local bands performing in the band shell on Wednesday evenings.

Finally, ride back to your room cuddled inside the carriage.

## Day Three

### MORNING

Take a scenic drive through Green Lake County this morning and pay a visit to **Caron Orchard**, located between Princeton and Green Lake on County Road J. The two of you should enjoy this activity as you walk together among

A view from Green Lake's eastern shore as it stretches eight miles into the distance.

lines of fruit trees, the sun rises, and robins chirp. Depending on what month you visit Green Lake, you can pick plums, pears, raspberries, cherries, or apples at the orchard. Feed each other slices of chunky apple bread or bits of cider doughnuts while you're there. For more fresh fruit and veggies, drive to Soda's Farm Market, located on the western end of Green Lake on Highway 73 in Princeton. Stock up on berries, sweet corn, and other farm produce to take back home with you.

Next, spend about an hour walking through downtown Green Lake, which is primarily centered around Mill and Hill Streets. Buy your sweetheart a box of chocolates at Cottage Chocolates and Confections on Mill Street, a nostalgic chocolate and candy store replete with novelty and penny candy. Thinking of proposing? Gather ideas for the engagement ring or wedding bands at Wisconsin Gold and Gem Co. on Mill Street. Then, drive up to North Street, which overlooks the downtown, to Wallenfang's, a cheese and sausage store that has expanded to include gifts and woodwork items for the home. Don't forget to pick up some cheese curds and summer sausage to nibble on during the drive back home.

For lunch, stop by the **Gooseblind**, a comfy restaurant in downtown Green Lake. Order homemade pizza, pasta, or Angus burgers accompanied by glasses of iced tea or pints of beer. Couples should like the cozy booths in the bar.

## FOR MORE INFORMATION

**Green Lake Area Chamber of Commerce**
P.O. Box 337, Green Lake
The visitor information center is on Mill Street, north of Water Street.
(920) 294-3231 or (800) 253-7354
www.greenlakecc.com

**Princeton Chamber of Commerce**
708 W. Water Street, Princeton
(920) 295-3877, www.princetonwi.com

## ATTRACTIONS AND RECREATION

**Caron Orchard and Country Store**
W3649 County Road J, Princeton
(920) 295-6730
www.caronorchard.com
Call for hours.

**Cedar Ridge Ranch**
W14471 Dartford Road, Ripon
(920) 748-8405,
www.cedarridgeranch.net

**Escapade Lake Tours**
Heidel House Resort
643 Illinois Avenue, Green Lake
(920) 294-3344 or (800) 444-2812
www.heidelhouse.com

**The Golf Courses of Lawsonia**
W2615 S. Valley View Drive,
Green Lake
(920) 294-3320 or (800) 529-4453
www.lawsonia.com

**Green Lake Festival of Music**
(920) 748-9398 or (800) 662-7097
www.greenlakefestival.org

**Thrasher Opera House**
506 Mill Street, Green Lake
(920) 294-4279 or (888) 441-0140
www.thrasheroperahouse.com

**Tuscumbia Country Club**
637 Illinois Avenue, Green Lake
(920) 294-3381 or (800) 294-3381
www.tuscumbiacc.com

**Wisconsin's Majestic Balloons**
Ripon
(920) 748-3464
www.wisconsinballoon.com

## LODGING
**Angel Inn**
372 S. Lawson Drive, Green Lake
(920) 294-3087
www.angelinns.com
Rooms are from $135 in the summer
and $115 in the winter.

**Heidel House Resort**
643 Illinois Avenue, Green Lake
(920) 294-3344 or (800) 444-2812
www.heidelhouse.com
Rooms are from $79 January through April
and from $149 May through October.

## DINING AND NIGHTLIFE
**Boathouse Lounge and Eatery**
At the Heidel House Resort.
(920) 294-3344 or (800) 444-2812
Open for lunch and dinner. Call for
hours.

**Gooseblind**
512 Gold Street, Green Lake
(920) 294-6363
Open daily for lunch and dinner.

**Grey Rock**
At the Heidel House Resort
Open for dinner daily and
for brunch on Sunday.
Call for hours during the winter.

**Mimi's**
523 Water Street, Princeton
(920) 295-6775
Open Monday through Saturday for
lunch and dinner. Open on Sundays,
Memorial Day through Labor Day.
Closed in March.

**Norton's Marine Dining Room**
380 S. Lawson Drive, Green Lake

(920) 294-6577
www.nortonsmarinedining.com
Open daily for lunch and dinner.

**Sunroom Café**
At the Heidel House Resort
(920) 294-3344 or (800) 444-2812
Open for breakfast and lunch daily.
Call for hours.

**Two Chez**
509 Mill Street, Green Lake
(920) 294-0724
www.twochez.com
Open for breakfast and dinner
Wednesday through Sunday.

# CHAPTER SEVEN

For Lovebirds:

# Dodge County and Horicon Marsh

If you're looking for opportunities to walk hand in hand with your sweetie, this getaway delivers. One of the more mellow weekends in this book, this trip contains plenty of time for the two of you to stroll along a boardwalk searching for cranes and wrens, setting out on a moonlit walk to listen to herons and frogs singing, and pedaling down the Wild Goose State Trail on the lookout for Canada Geese and white-tailed deer.

The focus during these three days is on the 32,000-acre Horicon Marsh, the largest freshwater cattail marsh in the country. Every year about 200 species of birds are sighted in the marsh's wetlands, islands, woodlands, prairie, and portions of the Rock River. During the spring and fall, hundreds of thousands of geese stop by the marsh for a bit of a rest while on their migration. Other birds that can be spotted in Horicon Marsh include ring-necked pheasants, northern flickers, downy woodpeckers, marsh wrens, egrets, and herons. On this trip the two of you will cruise through the marsh in a canoe or on a pontoon boat, and you'll view it from atop a rocky ledge a few miles away. All the while you can spot a variety of wildlife.

Before starting off on your journey, you should know that the marsh the two of you are visiting has undergone a number of changes since it was created thousands of years ago as the Wisconsin glacier started retreating. In 1846, shortly after the establishment of the town of Horicon, a dam was constructed to power the industry in town creating a 50-square-mile lake. (This lake measured about nine feet higher than the water level you currently see.) The tourists came, and the wildlife started disappearing. Also, after the dam was installed, the farmland surrounding the lake became flooded. Farmers protested, and in 1869 the dam was removed. From the 1870s through the early 1900s wildlife returned, and with it came shooting clubs and hunters. Farmers tried to drain the marsh's water and transform it into farmland by building numerous drainage ditches. Their efforts proved futile, and eventually conservationists rallied to restore the marsh. In 1927 the state created the Horicon Marsh Wildlife Refuge. In 1941, the U.S. Fish and Wildlife department purchased land in the northern section of the marsh and designated it a national wildlife refuge. The northern section consists of 21,000 acres, and the southern part includes 11,000 acres. On this getaway you will visit portions of both.

## Day One

### Ꮛᎇ MORNING

Begin your trip by familiarizing yourselves with the Horicon Marsh and learning a little about bird behavior. For this, visit the **Marsh Haven Nature Center** in the northern section of the marsh near Waupon. Spend about 30 minutes touring the center. Here you can brief yourselves on bird mating rituals, migration patterns as well as learn about what birds you might see in the marsh. After your tour of the center, spend some time walking the three-quarter-mile trail surrounding it. Climb the observation tower for a view of the marsh, then settle down at one of the picnic benches or spread a blanket in the meadow for a picnic lunch. You can stock up on supplies in Waupon.

---

### MATING DANCE

Ꮛᎇ While the two of you are at Horicon Marsh, be on the lookout for the stately sandhill cranes. These tall, gray birds, distinguishable by a long neck and a red forehead, conduct spectacular mating dances. A pair of courting cranes (cranes mate for life) will stand in front of each other and dance. They will spring up into the air with their wings extended and bow. All the while they call (more like croak) to each other and toss clumps of grass into the air. It's a sight to behold.

---

### Ꮛᎇ AFTERNOON

After lunch, take each other's hands and explore the northern section of the marsh. Access the interpretive auto route dubbed the Horicon Tern Pike (named after the white, gray, and black seabird) from Highway 49, near the nature center. The road winds through the marsh for 3.2 miles, so set aside at least an hour to explore this area. You and your sweetheart will find a few spots to turn off the road and view birds and go for hikes. Continue through the loop, stopping occasionally at the interpretive signs that point out the importance of the wetlands and explain the history of the marsh. Head to the Egret Trail, a stunning, floating boardwalk adventure that literally takes you through the marsh. Take a few minutes to relax on one of the benches of the observation deck and listen to the birdcalls.

Although the types of species that visit and nest in this part of the marsh vary every year, you can typically view egrets (not surprisingly) as well as American white pelicans, Forster's terns, and marsh wrens. Don't look only for birds. You might also spy river otters and painted turtles. In spring, you will hear the mating calls of hundreds of frogs. For even more peace and privacy, extend your exploration of this area by hiking the Redhead Hiking Trail, which winds for 2.5 miles through the marsh, a portion of which is by the Rock River.

Next, check into your accommodations. Consider the Audubon Inn in Mayville and the Honeybee Inn Bed and Breakfast in Horicon. Both are

The boardwalk along the Egret Trail in the Horicon Marsh Wildlife Area.

located within a few minutes' drive of the marsh in small but bustling and quaint communities.

If you prefer the B&B experience, book a whirlpool and fireplace room at the romantic **Honeybee Inn Bed and Breakfast**. Choose from five rooms, all of which include two-person whirlpools and cushy robes. Try the Queen Bee Victorian room, which boasts a fireplace, king canopy bed, and balcony. (You can practice the famous balcony scene from Romeo and Juliet.) And be sure to order a gift basket when you book your room. The "Run Away from Home" basket, which includes bath salts, soaps, massage lotions, a candle, and chocolates, will enhance your romantic feelings on both nights after two long days of outdoor activities.

The **Audubon Inn**, as you might expect, is named in honor of the ornithologist. No, John James Audubon did not sleep here, nor was he born here, but throughout the inn you'll notice a number of reproductions of his bird drawings. Built in 1896 as the Beaumont Hotel, the Queen Anne-style building contains architectural features such as a turret and numerous decorative moldings. Decorated in earthy tones such as pine green and navy blue, all 17 rooms feature romantic four-poster beds, pine wardrobes, Shaker country quilts, and small, double whirlpool tubs. The Audubon Inn is located in downtown Mayville, steps from other restaurants and shops and a short distance from the east branch of the Rock River.

### ও EVENING

For cocktails and dinner, head to the Audubon Inn's bar and dining room, where the adult atmosphere is quiet and unassuming. Order some cocktails in the bar and perhaps an appetizer such as crab cakes with a caper sauce. Toast to your love as Frank Sinatra and Ella Fitzgerald tunes play through the hotel's sound system. Then, move into the dining room, where you'll take your seats at a table in a room decorated with more reproductions of John James Audubon's bird drawings. Sample one of the daily specials, which can range from tender moonfish to tasty chicken almondine. Share a dessert, then slip

An egret takes wing at the Horicon Marsh. Photo courtesy of Wisconsin Department of Tourism.

back to your room to change into some comfortable shoes. Before leaving, grab a light jacket and a flashlight.

Drive approximately five miles to the **Wisconsin Department of Natural Resources Flyway Center** for an evening stroll in the marsh. (You'll find the DNR center off Highway 28, halfway between Mayville and Horicon.) The four to five miles of trails wind through field, forest, and wetland. Don't worry about bringing boots; the trails that extend into the flowage are located on a dike and on the uplands surrounding the marsh.

To complete your evening, surprise your traveling partner by having a bouquet of wildflowers delivered to the inn or B&B. Call the **Village Flower Shop**, just north of Mayville, and have the innkeeper place the bouquet in your room.

## Day Two

### MORNING

Lounge over the four-course breakfast in the Honeybee Inn's dining room, or order breakfast to be delivered to your room. At the Audubon pick out a few breakfast treats at the continental breakfast, then head to **Blue Heron Landing** in Horicon for a canoe or pontoon-boat tour of the marsh.

---

## MARSH MELODIES

Birding enthusiasts should book their trip to the Horicon area around Marsh Melodies, a series of weekend birding events in April and May. They include Marshland Night Sounds, an evening walk in the dark; bird identification hikes; bird-banding demonstrations; and presentations on wetland plants. For more information call the Wisconsin Department of Natural Resources, the National Wildlife Refuge Visitor Center, or the local chambers of commerce.

---

Perhaps the most intimate and quiet way to voyage through the marsh is in a canoe. Blue Heron rents canoes for the entire day, so there's no rush to return within an hour or two. Take it slow and easy and don't forget your binoculars. From Heron Landing enter the marsh through the Rock River. Continue paddling past Fourmile and Cotton Island Heron Rookery, where the birds raise their young. If you don't mind being accompanied by others, Blue Heron also offers guided canoe tours if you are hesitant about exploring the marsh on your own. If you're not up to a canoe adventure, sign up for a cruise on one of the pontoon cruises. If you are touring with another couple, charter the pontoon boat for a private cruise of the marsh.

Following your water adventure, stop by one of the Dodge County farmers' markets in Mayville or Juneau. Stock up on meats, cheeses, and baked goods for another private picnic lunch together. Spread out your goods at one of the picnic tables at the DNR's field office on Palmatory Street (follow the signs from Highway 33 in Horicon). After you've eaten your goodies, take in the beauty of the marsh at the observation deck, which provides perhaps the best overall view of the marsh. Take a peek through the telescope, then follow the trail down to the marsh. In the distance you should be able to see Fourmile Island where Great Blue Herons nest. Put your arm around your sweetheart and embark on a scenic hike through wetlands and along a path that winds through woodlands and meadows. The loop includes some interpretive signs about the wildlife you may spot, among them Canada geese, herons, grebes, and wrens.

Next, treat yourselves to some homemade ice cream at the **Ice Cream Station** in Horicon.

Then, back at the inn order massages from **Nita More Massage Therapy** in Mayville. Afterward, wile away the afternoon in your comfy room.

---

## MEAD IN WISCONSIN

The word honeymoon dates back thousands of years. Supposedly, when a newly married couple made their home together, they drank mead, which is honey wine, for the first month of their marriage. To learn more about the history of the sweet stuff, stop by A Honey of a Museum, located at Honey Acres, about 18 miles south of Horicon, N1557 Highway 67, Ashippun, (800) 557-7745, www.honeyacres.com

---

### EVENING

Although the shape of the exterior is reminiscent of an Egyptian pyramid, the food served at **The Nile Club** is strictly Wisconsin supper club fare. Diners with hefty appetites will salivate over dishes like the 22-ounce prime rib, seafood primavera, and baby back ribs. During the fall the club serves duck with wild rice.

After dinner wander down Mayville's Main Street and catch an outdoor concert. Local bands, such as Irish groups and big-band ensembles, strike up tunes at Foster Park during the summer months. Here's your chance to practice the fox-trot or show off some moves you learned in dancing classes.

Tonight arrange for another surprise treat for your sweetheart. Buy him or her a box of chocolates from **Confections for Any Occasion** in nearby Theresa. Consider a basket or box full of truffles, turtles, or Jordan almonds.

Then, if you are staying at the B&B, fill up the two-person whirlpool bath and soak for a spell before going to bed.

## Day Three

### MORNING

After your breakfast at the inn, drive to Dodge County's **Ledge Park** (between Horicon and Mayville, east of Highway 28 and north of Highway 33) for a short hike. Drive to the upper section of the park, to the 200-foot-high limestone cliff for another view of the marsh and wildlife. Walk along the ledge hiking trail, which offers you views of the marsh and nearby farm fields. You'll find a handful of spots where you can lay a blanket and look out at the countryside or into each other's eyes.

After your morning walk, take a light lunch at the **Back Street Café** in Mayville. This homey, local spot decorated similarly to your grandmother's house with plenty of knickknacks on the walls serves a variety of sandwiches, soups, and homemade pies.

## AFTERNOON

Next, escape on a quiet, romantic bicycle ride along the **Wild Goose State Trail**, a limestone trail located on a former railroad bed. The multiuse trail runs from Juneau to Fond du Lac for about 34 miles, and a good portion follows the western edge of the Horicon Marsh. Park at Juneau City Park on Lincoln Street (in Juneau), and follow the trail north or drive to Marsh Haven Nature Center or the **Horicon Marsh National Wildlife Refuge Visitor Center** parking lot and follow it south. The stretch from Juneau to Highway 49 is about 15.5 miles long, which can take about an hour or more to bicycle, depending on how many stops you make to view wildlife (or to kiss). Pick up a map of the trail from a local chamber of commerce or the Dodge County Tourism Association.

## FOR MORE INFORMATION

**Dodge County Tourism Association**
(800) 414-0101, www.dodgecounty.com

**Horicon Chamber of Commerce**
319 E. Lake Street, Horicon
(920) 485-3200
www.horiconchamber.com

**Mayville Chamber of Commerce**
200 S. Main Street, Mayville
(920) 387-5776 or (800) 256-7670
www.mayvillechamber.com

## ATTRACTIONS AND RECREATION

**Blue Heron Landing**
Highway 33, Horicon
(920) 485-4663
www.horiconmarsh.com
Canoe and kayak rentals available April through September. Guided boat tours May through September.

**Confections for Any Occasion**
101 N. Milwaukee Street, Theresa
www.confectionsbyjoel.com
(920) 488-9269 or (920) 948-4772

**Dodge County farmers' markets**
(920) 387-5776
On Mayville's Main Street: June through October, Wednesday and Friday, 7:00 a.m. to noon.
On the lawn of the Dodge County Courthouse in Juneau: June through September, Friday. Call for hours.

**Horicon Marsh National Wildlife Refuge Visitor Center**
W4279 Headquarters Road, Mayville
(920) 387-2658, www.fws.gov
Visitor center is open 7:30 a.m. to 4:00 p.m., Monday through Friday, year-round and on weekends during the fall. The "Tern Pike" is open daily, mid-April through mid-September. Most trails are open daily, year-round. Admission is free.

**Ledge Park**
N7403 Park Road, Horicon
(920) 387-5450 or (920) 386-3700

**Marsh Haven Nature Center**
W10145 Highway 49 East, Waupon
(920) 324-5818
Open mid-May to mid-November,

10:00 a.m. to 4:00 p.m. weekdays and 9:30 a.m. to 5:00 p.m. on weekends. Admission fee.

**Nita More Massage Therapy**
Mayville
(920) 387-5841

**Village Flower Shop**
Highway Y, Kekoskee
(920) 387-4540 or (800) 390-2233

**Wild Goose State Trail**
Dodge County Planning and
Development
127 E. Oak Street, Juneau
(920) 386-3700

**Wisconsin Department of Natural Resources Flyway Center**
N7725 Highway 28, Horicon
(920) 387-7860
This area is open daily, year-round, 5:00 a.m. to 10:00 p.m. Admission is free.

### LODGING
**Audubon Inn**
45 N. Main Street, Mayville
(920) 387-5858
www.auduboninn.com
Rooms from $119.50.

**Honeybee Inn Bed and Breakfast**
611 E. Walnut Street, Horicon
(920) 485-4855
www.honeybeeinn.com
Rooms are from $99.

### DINING AND NIGHTLIFE
**Audubon Inn**
See listing under Lodging.

**Back Street Café**
11 North School Street, Mayville
(920) 387-7164

Open for breakfast, lunch, and dinner Monday through Friday and for breakfast and lunch Saturday and Sunday.

**Ice Cream Station**
518 East Lake Street, Horicon
(920) 485-2311

**The Nile Club**
W6711 Highway 33 East, Juneau
(920) 885-6611
www.thenileclub.com

# CHAPTER EIGHT

# Madison

## in Bloom

Love is in the air in the state's capital city . . . especially in springtime. Madison, made up of a blend of university students and professors, government staffers, laborers, and professionals, is especially inviting during the spring (although it is certainly bustling throughout the rest of the year). The city, with its pedestrian-friendly streets and lakeshore paths, welcomes walkers and lollygaggers. Rise early and browse the farmers' market. Buy a bouquet of tulips. Lie under a magnolia tree in one of the most well-kept arboretums you'll ever see. Bicycle along the lakeshore to Picnic Point.

But don't spend all your time outdoors. A cultural hot spot, Madison is home to numerous performing arts companies and venues that will satisfy couples who are into modern or Renaissance art. During this getaway, try to take advantage of some of Madison's arts-related activities by spending an hour together admiring visual art in a museum while a string quartet plays. Listen to the symphony or attend a professional theater production.

Your options are varied and almost limitless. Just remember to stop and smell the roses (at the Centennial Gardens) as well as kiss your sweetheart.

## Day One
### MORNING

Consider renting bicycles or bringing your own for your visit to Madison. Biking is a leisurely way to explore the city. Most likely, you will avoid spats that would come while stuck in traffic during busy weekend events like the University of Wisconsin graduation or Crazy Legs five-mile run. This bike-friendly town boasts a number of trails and streets with separate bicycle lanes that wind around recommended sites and dining spots, such as the UW Arboretum, Picnic Point, and the state capitol. For information on bicycle rental, contact **Budget Bicycle Center**. Be brave and try a tandem.

A leisurely stroll through the University of Wisconsin's Arboretum. Photo courtesy of Wisconsin Department of Tourism.

After strapping on your bicycle helmets, head to the **University of Wisconsin Arboretum**. In the spring, Longenecker Horitcultural Garden, by the visitor center, is brilliant with magnolia and crab apple trees and lilac bushes, which radiate cotton white, pale pink, and lavender blooms. You'll find benches scattered throughout the garden for you and your sweetheart to sit on. After walking through the garden, head to the visitor center and relax on the observation deck that looks out onto the grounds. Don't forget to peer through the telescope set up on the deck.

At the Arboretum, you have more than 1,200 acres to explore, including prairies, woodlands, and wetlands. From the visitor center, lock arms and walk through Curtis Prairie, a 60-acre tallgrass prairie featuring the towering bluestem and Indian grasses. Before leaving, inquire if a night walk will be held while you are in town. These moonlit strolls, which can be especially romantic for couples, are held on occasional evenings throughout the year.

After your quiet morning walking in the prairie and amid flowering trees, head to nearby **Bluephies** for lunch. This modern, veggie-friendly restaurant serves food for all types of diners in a clean, light environment with plenty of booths. The lunch menu offers a variety of salads such as artichoke salad, Southwestern dishes such as quesadillas and enchiladas, and grilled eggplant and grilled portobello mushroom sandwiches. But carnivores have no need to worry. Bluephies also serves up a strong hamburger. If your companion digs chocolate, now is not the time to pass up dessert. Try the passionate Chocolate Eruption cake (with chocolate cream, chocolate chips, and nuts), the Chocolate Terrine (with praline mousse), or Chocolate Lava cake, a warm, melt-in-your-mouth kind of cake.

## ⊱ AFTERNOON

From Bluephies, bike along the Lake Monona lakeshore path to **Monona Terrace** (or drive there in your car via John Nolen Drive). Take the elevator to the top of the terrace building for a quick peek at the 68,000-square-foot rooftop garden and its blooming tulips. It's a breathtaking spot (especially for fans of Frank Lloyd Wright, who designed the terrace) and a popular venue for weddings and other galas.

Continue on to downtown Madison and the **Elvejhelm Museum of Art** on the campus of the University of Wisconsin. If you're visiting on a Sunday afternoon, chances are you'll stumble upon one of the free concerts held there throughout the year. Here you and your date can admire modern photography and photographs dating back to pre-World War II, decorative arts, European and American watercolor paintings, plus ancient and twentieth-century sculpture.

After touring the museum, give your feet a rest and check in to your room. If you're looking for a bed-and-breakfast-type accommodation, consider the Arbor House or Canterbury Inn. For a modern hotel room with a view, book at the Hilton Madison Monona Terrace. Rooms at the **Hilton Madison Monona Terrace** overlook Lake Monona or the State Capitol.

## GREAT KISSING SPOTS

⟋ Madison is home to a number of scenic parks that are especially welcoming to couples, especially during the spring. On a sunny day, you can spend hours lazing in the city's parks, under a tree, in a gazebo, or reclining on a bench. Here are some of the best places to stroll hand in hand or lay a blanket for you to rest upon: Arboretum (under a flowering tree at the Longenecker Horitcultural Garden), Picnic Point (along the north side walking path or at the tip of the point), Olbrich Gardens (at the Thai Pavilion), Tenney Park (kiss under the bridge while ice skating on the pond in the winter), Hoyt Park (watch the sunset here).

The **Arbor House** is a top choice for environmentally conscious folks. (For example, floor tiles and porch railings are made from recycled glass and wood.) Plus, it's located right by the Arboretum. Although completely renovated and containing thoroughly modern amenities such as double-person whirlpool bathtubs, the Arbor House actually dates back to the 1850s when it was known as The Plough Inn, a stagecoach stop. Couples will find the Aldo Leopold room in the annex especially inviting with its poster bed and chapel ceiling. The John Nolen room, also in the annex, has a light and sunny feel to it and features an iron bed and private patio—an intimate spot for sharing a bottle of wine in the evening or drinking mugs of coffee in the morning while dressed in your robes.

If you prefer to stay within walking distance of the state capitol and the university campus, reserve a room at the **Canterbury Inn**, located above a charming bookstore just off State Street. You have six rooms to choose from. The Knight's Room appeals to couples (and British literature buffs) with its mural depicting two knights when they first spotted the woman whom they would eventually fight over. The Wife of Bath Room, with its king-size bed and double-whirlpool bathtub with skylight, is also great for couples.

After checking in to the Arbor House, unwind on the patio by sipping some tea and listening to the water trickling in the garden.

At the Canterbury Inn, curl up on the couch together. Pick up one of the books from the shelf or engage your lover in a game of chess.

## EVENING

Tonight you will indulge in an intense Italian meal at **Porta Bella Restaurant and Wine Cellar**. Prior to dinner, walk through the garden and head downstairs into the cool, cavernlike Wine Cellar bar. Find a table tucked into one of the many nooks and crannies of the establishment. Order a bottle of red wine and a plate of cheeses. Swirl the wine in your glasses and toast to your love.

Upstairs, dine at an intimate two-top table or plush booth. (Perhaps one with red velvet curtains in the Rose Room?) Entrées run the gamut, from

Lake Mendota from the Memorial Union terrace: a great place to hold hands and relish the view. Photo courtesy of Wisconsin Department of Tourism.

chicken marsala to homemade pasta with a tomato sauce, goat cheese, and mushrooms. And even if you savored dessert after lunch, don't think of skimping on dessert here. Share some passionberry mousse or a slice of heavenly tiramisu cheesecake.

If you can drag yourselves out of Porta Bella, mosey on down State Street to the **Memorial Union Terrace** where the two of you can have a seat on the terrace overlooking Lake Mendota and listen to music under the stars. Depending on the night, you could sway to the dance tunes of a swing band, folk group, jazz trio, or modern rock band. Take a walk down to the water, watch the ducks, and see if you can spot the Big Dipper.

Surprise your sweetheart with a carriage ride back to your room. Arrange to have the carriage from **Cornerstone Carriages** pick you both up outside the Union. Take a ride down bustling State Street and around the lit capitol. Or, call up **Gallant Knight** and order a sleek stretch limousine.

## Day Two

### ❧ MORNING

If the two of you are staying at the Arbor House during the weekend you will be served a scrumptious breakfast in the sunroom. Your hosts will whip up anything from Grand Marnier-stuffed French toast to zucchini and potato pancakes.

Don't load up on too much at breakfast though, because you can plan on nibbling on treats purchased at the **Dane County Farmers' Market** at the state capitol square. This annual open-air market, held on Saturday mornings beginning the last Saturday in April, brings in regional organic and independent farmers selling everything from fresh asparagus to bouquets of zinnias. Take about an hour to stroll around the square. Sample cinnamon rolls and coffee. Pick up a bouquet of cut flowers or a hanging basket of fuchsias (the delicate flowers are often called lady's eardrops).

Continue south on State Street on foot for about two blocks. Pop into the **Madison Art Center** for a look at contemporary and modern art from around the globe. Peruse mixed-media presentations, photographs, and paintings.

After wandering around this venue, head back to the capitol square for lunch at the **Great Dane Pub and Brewing Company**. If it's a sunny day, retreat to a table in the secluded courtyard patio. Entrées include buffalo and walnut burgers and chicken or tofu wraps. The smooth beer on tap is made on-site. Try the Emerald Isle Stout, Devil's Lake Red Lager, or Potters Run India Pale Ale.

### ❧ AFTERNOON

After lunch bicycle back down State Street to the Lake Mendota lakeshore path. You and your sweetheart can walk this path as well. When you reach Babcock Drive, take a short detour from the path to the **Allen Centennial Gardens** at Babcock and Observatory Drives. Managed by the UW Horticultural Department, this small garden is a quiet spot to rest for a little while. Cuddle under the shade of a pergola or take photographs of the daffodils. Stroll among a Victorian, English, or French garden, or find shade in a gazebo.

Continue southward to Picnic Point, a narrow peninsula that juts out into Lake Mendota. Follow the dirt path for a while and the sandy trail on the northwest side, which winds right along the lake. You'll find plenty of benches to rest your legs. At the end you'll be rewarded with views of the lake and of the city to the southeast.

On the way back into town, stop by **Babcock Hall Dairy Store,** run by the College of Agricultural Services, for ice cream cones. (Doesn't it feel as if you are a student again?) New flavors are featured every month, such as Blue Moon, as are favorites like chocolate chip.

Before dinner, relax and cleanse your bodies with a quick eucalyptus steam shower at **Kneaded Relief Day Spa**. This detoxification treatment will cleanse your pores and relieve those leg muscles you have been flexing during this getaway. Kneaded Relief also offers a variety of massage and body services for men and women, so if the steam shower doesn't appeal to you, consider another service. If you are staying at the Arbor House, the owners have a list of massage therapists that are available to perform massages in the privacy of your own room. After receiving these relaxing treatments at the Arbor House, take advantage of the inn's on-site sauna.

## EVENING

Force yourselves to get out of those robes and change into evening clothes. Tonight you will dine at the acclaimed **L'Etoile** restaurant at the capitol square. In a warm dining room with awesome views of the capitol, you'll be served artistic dishes in an unpretentious atmosphere. The menu changes frequently depending on the season, but the staff strives to whip up dishes featuring ingredients purchased from local, organic farms. During one spring visit, entrées on the menu included sautéed artisan farm rainbow trout with parsnip gnocchi, bacon broth, seared greens, and carrot sauce; and organic beef tenderloin with red wine, caramelized onion and potato tart, and seared chard. L'Etoile also stocks a variety of champagne. Be sure to sample some of this drink that monk Dom Pérignon reportedly said tasted like stars.

Following your extraordinary dinner, stroll together down State Street to the **Madison Civic Center** where you can surround yourselves with the superb sounds of a musical performance by the Madison Symphony Orchestra or Madison Opera, which has staged such productions as *La Boheme* and *The Marriage of Figaro*. For more music, contact the **Wisconsin Chamber Orchestra**, which performs at various venues around town.

A reflecting pool at Olbrich Botanical Gardens. Photo courtesy of Wisconsin Department of Tourism.

## Day Three

### MORNING

Treat yourselves to breakfast at a local favorite, **Monty's Blue Plate Diner**, on the east side of town. Slide into a booth of this retro restaurant and order up sticky cinnamon rolls or thick milkshakes. Breakfasts here, such as huevos rancheros, are hearty.

Next, walk off that omelet at **Olbrich Botanical Gardens**, accessible via the Lake Monona bicycle path. Linger in the Thai Pavilion, an ornate, shiny structure at the south end of the gardens. Notice the lotus plants in the reflecting pools. Relax under the sun's rays in the romantic sunken garden and walk through the trails among spring flowers such as the heartleaf bergenia, whose delicate pink petals resemble a heart.

For lunch, head over to the **Orpheum Theatre**, which features a restaurant in its lobby. The atmosphere here is definitely histrionic (marble statues, people dressed in black) with the feel of a European café. Impress your companion by speaking French. Luncheon dishes include farfalle pasta, yellowfin tuna, spinach salads, and a variety of sandwiches.

## ৵ AFTERNOON

Continuing the artistic mood, devote your afternoon to attending a performance staged by a local theater company. In Madison, you have a wealth of options, including work staged by the **Madison Repertory Theatre**, which performs such plays as *The Game of Love and Chance and I Love You, You're Perfect, Now Change* in the Civic Center. Recent shows of the Madison Theatre Guild include *Lumberjacks in Love* and *Dancing at Lughnasa*. If one of you is a ballet aficionado, purchase tickets to a performance by the **Madison Ballet**, which produces shows like *A Midsummer Night's Dream*.

After the show, discuss the performances over coffee or tea and treats during a visit to one of the many cafés lining State Street.

### ৵ FOR MORE INFORMATION

**Greater Madison Convention and Visitor Bureau**
615 E. Washington Avenue,
Madison
(608) 255-2357 or (800) 373-6376
www.visitmadison.com

### ৵ ATTRACTIONS AND RECREATION

**Allen Centennial Gardens**
Babcock and Observatory Drives,
Madison
www.hort.wisc.edu
Open daily dawn to dusk.
Free admission.

**Budget Bicycle Center**
1230 Regent Street,
Madison
(608) 251-8413

**Cornerstone Carriages**
(608) 251-3030

**Dane County Farmers' Market on the Square**
At the state capitol (Pinckney, Carroll, Mifflin, and Main Streets)
(608) 424-6714
www.madfarmmkt.org
The market is held Saturday, 6:00 a.m. to 2:00 p.m., from the last Saturday in April until the first Saturday in November. The market is also held near the square Wednesday, 8:00 a.m. to 2:00 p.m., from the first Wednesday in May until the last Wednesday in October.

**Elvejhem Museum of Art**
800 University Avenue, Madison
(608) 263-2246
www.lvm.wisc.edu
Open Tuesday through Friday, 9:00 a.m. to 5:00 p.m., and Saturday and Sunday, 11:00 a.m. to 5:00 p.m. Free admission.

**Gallant Knight Limousine**
(608) 242-7000

**Kneaded Relief Day Spa**
651 S. Park Ave.,
Madison
(608) 255-0070
www.kneadedreliefdayspa.com

**Madison Art Center**
211 State Street,
Madison
(608) 257-0158
www.madisonartcenter.org
Open Tuesday, Wednesday, and Thursday, 11:00 a.m. to 5:00 p.m.; Friday, 11:00 a.m. to 9:00 p.m.; Saturday, 10:00 a.m. to 9:00 p.m.; and Sunday, 1:00 p.m. to 5:00 p.m. Free admission.

**Madison Ballet**
2822 Index Road, Madison
(608) 278-7990
www.madisonballet.org

**Madison Civic Center**
211 State Street, Madison
(608) 266-9055
www.madcivic.org

**Madison Repertory Theatre**
Isthmus Playhouse/Madison
Civic Center
211 State Street, Madison
(608) 256-0029

**Monona Terrace Community
and Convention Center**
One John Nolen Drive, Madison
(608) 261-4000
www.mononaterrace.com
Admission is free, but if you drive and
park in the garage, you will have to pay a
fee. Paid tours are available.

**Olbrich Botanical Gardens**
3330 Atwood Avenue, Madison
(608) 246-4550, www.olbrich.org
The outdoor gardens are open daily,
8:00 a.m. to 8:00 p.m., April through
September. Free admission.

**University of Wisconsin–Madison
Arboretum**
1207 Seminole Highway, Madison
(608) 263-7888
www.wisc.edu/arboretum
The trails are open daily, year-round,
from 7:00 a.m. to 10:00 p.m.
The visitor center is open Monday
through Friday, 9:30 a.m. to 4 p.m. and
on weekends, 12:30 p.m. to 4:00 p.m.
Free admission.

**University of Wisconsin
Memorial Union Terrace**
Landon and Park Streets, Madison
(608) 265-3000

**Wisconsin Chamber Orchestra**
22 N. Carroll Street, Madison
(608) 257-0638
www.wcoconcerts.com

## ⊷ LODGING

**Arbor House**
3402 Monroe Street,
Madison
(608) 238-2981
www.arbor-house.com
Rooms start at under $100.

**Canterbury Inn**
315 W. Gorham Street,
Madison
(608) 258-8899
www.madisoncanterbury.com
Rooms start from $130.

**Hilton Madison Monona Terrace**
9 E. Wilson Street, Madison
(608) 255-5100
www.hiltonmadison.com
Call for room rates.

## ⊷ DINING AND NIGHTLIFE

**Babcock Hall Dairy Store**
1605 Linden Drive, Madison
(608) 262-3045

**Bluephies**
2701 N. Monroe Street,
Madison
(608) 231-366,
www.foodfightinc.com
Open daily for breakfast, lunch,
and dinner.

**Great Dane Pub and
Brewing Company**
123 E. Doty Street,
Madison
(608) 284-0000
www.greatdanepub.com
Open daily for lunch and dinner.

**L'Etoile**
25 N. Pinckney Street,
Madison
(608) 251-0500
www.letoile-restaurant.com
Open for dinner Tuesday through
Saturday and on Monday for
private parties.

**Monty's Blue Plate Diner**
2089 Atwood Avenue, Madison
(608) 244-8505
www.foodfightinc.com
Open daily for breakfast, lunch,
and dinner.

**Orpheum Theatre Lobby Restaurant**
216 State Street, Madison
(608) 255-8755
Open for lunch and dinner Tuesday
through Saturday. Open for breakfast on
Saturday and brunch on Sunday.

**Porta Bella Restaurant and Wine Cellar**
425 N. Frances Street, Madison
(608) 256-3186
Open daily for dinner.

# CHAPTER NINE

# In the Steps of Artists and Eccentrics:
# *Mineral Point, Spring Green, Mazomanie*

Cultivate your artistic inklings. Awaken the romantic. Get inspired. The southwestern towns of Mineral Point, Spring Green, and Mazomanie and the surrounding countryside are home to many working artists and couples. During this getaway you will admire and purchase original artwork. Take in a theater or musical performance. Drive through rolling hills and green and golden valleys down a winding country road. Spend the evening sipping wine before a fireplace in a rented bungalow.

On this trip you will also spend time in historic settings, including the former home of a couple who transformed a crumbling row of miner shacks into a popular restaurant, and you'll visit a home atop a 60-foot sandstone chimney rock. You'll tour Frank Lloyd Wright's estate, Taliesin, and view some of his projects, such as the Romeo and Juliet windmill. (And you'll learn about his artistic and romantic endeavors.)

Although this part of the state is scenic any time of year, try visiting with your sweetie during early fall, when the rolling hills and woods are brilliant with flaxen, copper, and henna hues. During the Fall Art Tour, artists in Mineral Point, Spring Green, Dodgeville, and other area towns open their galleries to visitors.

## *Day One*
### ☙ MORNING

A good way to start this weekend adventure is with a quiet, easy hike along the **Merry Christmas Mine Hill**, which offers views of the region. You'll find the

Some of the shops arrayed along Commerce Street in Mineral Point.

43-acre site on the eastern edge of Mineral Point by **Pendarvis State Historic Site**. Pick up a map of the trail and follow the posts to the top. (It's not too vigorous of a climb.) Along the way, you'll pass by badger holes, where miners dug hollows into the ground for shelters and mine shafts. From the top of the hill, you'll have quite a view of Mineral Point, a village tucked into a valley with branches of Brewery Creek running through town. The town of about 2,600 was settled primarily by miners from Cornwall, England, who flocked to the area to mine lead and zinc in the 1820s and '30s. Today a growing community of artisans call it home. Potters, weavers, painters and antiques dealers have settled into the historic stock of buildings for their studios and shops. Take a few minutes to sit under a grand oak tree to take it all in.

After your walk along the hill, stop by **Brewery Pottery Studio**, just up the street from the Merry Christmas Mine Hill on Shake Rag Street. Run by potters Diana and Tom Johnston, the working studio and store is housed in an 1850 brewery building made of limestone and situated at the edge of a hill. The couple has been crafting stoneware and porcelain pitchers, bowls, and goblets for more than 20 years, and they work together on every piece. You'll find home and garden decor such as sundials and candleholders here. Feel free to ask for a tour of the building to see the pottery wheels and giant kiln.

After visiting with the Johnstons, drive to downtown Mineral Point, a few minutes from the pottery studio. Park your car (there's plenty of parking in Mineral Point) and walk the streets together. Most shops and restaurants are clustered around High and Commerce Streets. On High Street, you'll find wood carver Don Mahieu, who creates wood sculptures in his Against the Grain studio; and David L. Solheim, who builds Prairie-style tables made of wood such as walnut and accented with leaded glass and copper at his store Tablewood. Also on High Street, you'll pass by M Studio, run by photographer

Philip Mrozinski. Mrozinski produces touching black-and-white and hand-colored photographs. A few doors down is Green Lantern Studios. Browse through its collection of paintings, textile art, and handmade furniture. Mineral Point also boasts a number of independent shops, run by friendly and chatty shopkeepers. Visit Ken Wheaton's Foundry Books on Commerce Street or Lyn Anglin and Miriam Nesset's Winsor Bleu Gallery Domicile, an antiques and home decor shop, also on Commerce Street.

Continue your walking tour of Mineral Point along Jail Alley, which runs parallel to High Street past the library, courthouse, and Saint Paul's Mission Church, a stone church built 1842.

## WRIGHT AND HIS WOMEN

Ꮖ Frank Lloyd Wright was not only prolific in the field of architecture but also busy courting the ladies. Here are a few of the women associated with Wright throughout his life: Catherine Tobin (first wife), Miriam Noel (second wife), Mamah Borthwick Cheney (mistress), and Olgivanna Lazovich (third wife).

Take a break from walking and order sandwiches from **Gundry and Gray**, a café in the center of the High Street, marked by the zinc statue of a pointer dog. Once a dry goods store, the building now houses a deli and food shop with yummy salads, sandwiches, and wine for sale. Order your lunch to go and wander over to **Orchard Lawn House Museum** on Madison Street. Have a seat in the gazebo on the lawn looking onto the impressive sandstone Italianate home. It was in this home that Cornish immigrants Joseph and Sara Gundry (of the Gundry and Gray business) raised seven children throughout the late 1800s. The gazebo and the expansive lawn make for a romantic picnic and rest spot.

## Ꮖ AFTERNOON

After filling up on lunch, tour the **Pendarvis Historic Site** on Shake Rag Alley. Essentially Pendarvis is a row of limestone and log homes built by Cornish miners in the 1840s and 1850s and restored by Robert Neal and his partner Edgar Hellum from the 1930s through the 1960s. During the course of their relationship, which lasted multiple decades, Neal and Hellum restored a number of buildings (you'll tour six of them), including the Pendarvis House Restaurant. The restaurant attracted diners from throughout the Midwest for its pasties, saffron cake, and tea. It garnered praise from many publications. (The *Saturday Evening Post* named it one of the best restaurants in the United States.) During your tour you will not only get a glimpse at how miners used

One of the restored buildings at the Pendarvis Historic Site, Mineral Point.

to live but also learn about Neal and Hellum's projects. Before leaving, take your date's hand in yours and walk through the gardens surrounding Pendarvis; the trails wind around flowers such as violets and hollyhocks.

After your tour, unwind from your full day and check in to the **Old Lumberyard Inn's Garden Bluff Cottage**, a restored miner's cottage just off Commerce Street. Run by Mort and Laura Crowley, the cozy and secluded cottage is an ideal getaway for couples. Relax on the front porch looking onto the little garden or on the private deck tucked behind the cottage and abreast rock outcropping. Then, lounge in the whirlpool tub, wrap yourselves in the super fluffy towels, and nap in the sleigh bed.

If you'd like to stay in a resort-type of lodging, check into the **House on the Rock Resort**, about 20 miles from Mineral Point. It's located just south of Taliesin and near the American Players Theatre. Tucked in the hills of the Wisconsin River valley, this resort is a must-see for fans of Prairie-style decor. Compared to some resorts found in places like Wisconsin Dells, this is one with an adult atmosphere. All rooms are two-room suites with private balconies, plus there's a large lap pool and a circular pool for you to swim in, a sauna, and a large whirlpool, all with views of the hills outside. After checking in, be sure to make use of the gorgeous pools.

### EVENING

For dinner, reserve a table at **Mineral Spirits Saloon and Café**, located next door to the Old Lumberyard Inn. At this former Cornish pub and stagecoach inn, you can feed each other Mineral Spirits fondue, which is made with Wisconsin cheddar cheese. Other options include filet mignon and pork chops.

Another dining option is the **Brewery Creek Brewpub** in Mineral Point (across the street from the Old Lumberyard Inn). Like most restaurants and shops in Mineral Point, this establishment is housed in a restored, circa late 1800s building. Modeled after an English pub and restaurant, the building features oak posts and beams and a large bar. Try the traditional Cornish pasty, with beef, potato, and onions baked in pastry dough—the Sicilian rib eye. Vegetarians will salivate over the walnut burger. Wash everything down with a pint of home-brewed beer.

---

## GETTING HITCHED?

᎗ Consider scenic southwest Wisconsin as a place to tie the knot. A few suggestions in the Spring Green area are the historic Hyde Chapel in Ridgeway, (608) 753-2283; Unity Chapel, where Frank Lloyd Wright's relatives attended services, (608) 233-3776; and inside the small Chapel in the Pines or on its grounds near Spring Green, (608) 753-2271.

---

After dinner, walk hand in hand up High Street and catch a movie, play, or musical performance at the **Mineral Point Opera House**. Throughout the year, the 1914 vaudeville theater showcases art films, popular movies, and performances by the local theater group, the Shake Rag Players.

After the show, light a few candles on your private deck behind the Garden Bluff Cottage, pop open a bottle of wine, and take in the night sky while listening to water trickle down the bluff. (You can pick up a bottle of wine at Gundry and Gray, and the Crowleys can supply you with wine or champagne glasses.)

If you are at House on the Rock Resort, slip on your suits and head to the whirlpool downstairs. Because it's open until 11:00 p.m., the two of you will be able to swim or lounge as the moonlight pours in through the many windows.

## Day Two

### ᎗ MORNING

At the Old Lumberyard Inn's Garden Bluff Cottage, you can nibble on homemade pumpkin bread or French toast in the privacy of your room. (If requested, the Crowleys will deliver breakfast to your door in a picnic basket.) If you are staying at the House on the Rock Resort, feast on plates of buttermilk pancakes or steak and eggs at the Grandview.

After filling up on sweet things, drive to Spring Green, which is about 25 miles north of Mineral Point on Highway 23. Today you will tour the grounds of Frank Lloyd Wright's former home, studio, and farm, as well as wander around another artistic community, Spring Green. Before you come to County Road C, where Taliesin is located, look for the scenic overlook across Highway

23. A trail and pedestrian bridge take you across the highway to view the Wisconsin River Valley below, quite a sight to see during the fall.

Then, tour **Taliesin**, the fabled 600-acre estate of Frank Lloyd Wright. If it is a beautiful fall day, consider the two-hour walking tour. Architecture aficionados might want to take the four-hour estate tour, so you won't feel as if you missed seeing anything. If you plan to take the estate tour or house tour, call ahead to reserve spaces.

A restored miner's cottage, available for lodging, at Mineral Point's Old Lumberyard Inn.

Stroll through the grounds and walk by Taliesin, Wright's private home; the Hillside Home School; Tan-y-deri house, which Wright built for his sister in 1907 (*tan-y-deri* means "under the oaks" in Welsh); the Romeo and Juliet Windmill; and other creations. The Romeo and Juliet Windmill (what you see is a replication of the original windmill) was built to pump water to the Hillside Home School. It's a diamond-shaped structure with two pieces, a part called the male section, which contains the pumping apparatus, and the female section, complete with a little balcony, which supports the structure. Wright installed a stereo speaker by the balcony so music could be played throughout the estate grounds.

Unfortunately, a few years after Wright built Taliesin, a servant torched the place, killing Wright's mistress, Mamah Borthwick Cheney, her two children, and several others. Wright decided to rebuild Taliesin and eventually lived there again for some time with his second and third wives. (For more on Wright's busy romantic life, read the sidebar on page 89.)

For lunch, head into downtown Spring Green, about a five-minute drive from Taliesin. **The Post House Restaurant**, built in 1857 and billed as the oldest continuously operating restaurant in Wisconsin, serves comfort food such as corned beef with horseradish sauce on rye bread, baked ham, and Rueben sandwiches. Be sure to have a look at the Flying Dutchman cocktail lounge. The modern decor contrasts with the traditional look of the restaurant's dining rooms. The lounge was designed by William Wesley Peters, an associate of Wright. The outdoor garden was also designed by a student from the Frank Lloyd Wright Foundation. On sunny days, the garden makes for a quiet, romantic spot for couples to enjoy their lunches.

## ᧧ AFTERNOON

After lunch drive through Spring Green to admire all the architecturally intriguing buildings. (Wright was not the only architect who used the area as his campus.) Highlights include the mustard-colored M&I Bank, also designed by William Wesley Peters, and the salmon-colored Saint John the Evangelist Church, a structure built in 1990 that espouses Prairie-style elements of Wright's day.

Next, browse through the many artists' studios and gift shops. Buy some writing paper or wine goblets at the Wisconsin Artists Showcase, and stock up on bubble bath, massage oils, and scented candles at Panacea for a soak in the tub this evening. Unwind for a few minutes with chair massages at **Bear Creek Massage Therapy**.

## ᧧ EVENING

This evening the two of you will dine at the House on the Rock's **Grandview** restaurant, which was decorated with Frank Lloyd Wright's design principles in mind. Have a seat at a table by the window. When you are not looking longingly at each other you can admire the views of the hills.

For a more economical option, pick up picnic supplies at the **Spring Green Café and General Store**. Spread out a tablecloth and pop open a bottle of wine on the grounds of the **American Players Theatre**. If you haven't the time to pack a picnic dinner, don't worry. You can purchase delectable sandwiches from the American Players Theatre, which runs a little snack hut stocked with deli sandwiches and salads.

What could be more romantic than attending a professional theatrical performance with views of the stars and treetops? Settle into your seats to watch classical plays, such as William Shakespeare's *The Tempest* and George Bernard Shaw's *Mrs. Warren's Profession,* June through October. During the intermission, head to the snack bar and order two hot chocolates jazzed up with a little liquor.

After the show, walk hand in hand back to the parking lot down the wooded trail, and drive back to your room. Take a leisurely soak in the tub again, then tuck yourselves into bed for the night.

If you are visiting the region during the winter, skip the shopping and call up **A to Z Percherons** in Highland (about 18 miles southwest of Spring Green). Arrange for a tranquil sleigh ride through the country. Bundle up and bring a thermos of hot chocolate, cider, or spiced rum. Then, back at the cottage or hotel room, cuddle in front of the crackling fireplace.

# Day Three

## ☙ MORNING

After enjoying breakfast at the inn, drive to **The House on the Rock**, an overwhelmingly large estate sitting on sandstone chimney rock. Built by Alex Jordan, with a little help from his lady friend, this house is a little bit eerie, very

kitschy, and definitely entertaining. The tour weaves through various rooms, such as the Red Room containing flashy thrones and gilded mirrors. There are collections of dollhouses, butterflies, antique rifles, sleighs, and hundreds of musical instruments. Anyone who has an interest in music will enjoy a visit here. There are countless organs, violins, and pianos. A highlight of the tour is the "world's largest carousel" room with hundreds of horses tacked onto the walls and mannequins dressed as angels dangling from the ceiling. You can't miss the Infinity Room, a room that stretches seemingly precariously over the valley below. Be sure to allow yourself plenty of time to explore this estate (usually more than an hour), because the walkways add up to 3.5 miles.

The Infinity Room, one of many truly offbeat attractions at the House on the Rock, Spring Green.

Continue on a scenic drive toward Mazomanie, a quaint

town along the Black Earth River about 15 miles west of Spring Green. Spend about 30 minutes exploring this former railroad town. Built in the 1850s as a fueling and servicing stop for locomotives, Mazomanie is pretty sleepy now compared to its heyday, but it's rather charming. Take a peek inside the handful of antiques shops downtown, and walk by the former train depot and freight and coal buildings. Stop and smell the roses at the Heritage Gardens by the train tracks, paying close attention to the Jane Jones Lees rose, named after a woman who settled with her husband in Mineral Point in the 1840s.

Next, stop for brunch or lunch at the **Old Feed Mill**. Open since 1995, the restaurant is housed in an 1857 flour mill. The country decor of quilts hanging on the walls, mix-and-matched vintage chairs, exposed ceilings, and hardwood floors is welcoming. The Old Feed Mill's Sunday brunch comprises steaming omelets, French toast, sausages, and other staples. After your meal walk through the gift shop on the second floor, then have a seat in one of the handful of sitting areas on the porch. If you're impressed by the place and scoping out venues for a wedding or anniversary celebration, take a look at the granary room upstairs, which is available for rental.

## FOR MORE INFORMATION

**Mazomanie Community Corporation**
(608) 795-2117

**Mineral Point Chamber of Commerce**
225 High Street, Mineral Point
(888) 764-6894, www.mineralpoint.com

**Spring Green Chamber of Commerce**
E5028 Highway 14, Spring Green
(608) 588-2054 or (800) 588-2042
www.springgreen.com

## ATTRACTIONS AND RECREATION

**A to Z Percherons (sleigh rides)**
1796 Tower Road, Highland
(608) 623-2888

**American Players Theatre**
Golf Course Drive, Spring Green
(608) 588-2361, www.playinthewoods.org

**Bear Creek Massage Therapy**
132 S. Albany Street, Spring Green
(608) 588-9356

**Brewery Pottery Studio**
276 Shake Rag Street,
Mineral Point
(608) 987-3669
www.brewerypottery.com

**Foundry Books**
105 Commerce Street,
Mineral Point
(608) 987-4363
www.foundrybooks.com

**Green Lantern Studios**
261 High Street, Mineral Point
(608) 987-4718
www.greenlanternstudios.com

**The House on the Rock**
Highway 23, Spring Green
(608) 935-3639 or (800) 947-2799
www.thehouseontherock.com
Open mid-March to late October, plus on days surrounding Thanksgiving and Christmas. Closed Thanksgiving, Christmas Eve, and Christmas Day. Call for hours. Admission is charged.

**Mineral Point Opera House**
139 High Street, Mineral Point
(608) 987-2642

**Orchard Lawn House Museum**
234 Madison Street, Mineral Point
(608) 987-2884
Open May to October, Thursday
through Sunday, 1:00 p.m. to 5:00 p.m.
Admission fee.

**Pendarvis State Historic Site
and Merry Christmas Mine Hill**
114 Shake Rag Street, Mineral Point
(608) 987-2122, www.shsw.wisc.edu
The Pendarvis State Historic Site is open
seasonally. Call for hours. The interpretive
walking trails at Merry Christmas Mine
Hill are open year-round. Admission fee.

**Taliesin**
Highway 23 and County Road C,
Spring Green
(608) 588-7900
www.taliesinpreservation.org
The visitor center is open daily May 1 to
October 31 from 8:30 a.m. to 5:30 p.m. It
is open on weekends only April, November, and December from 10:00 a.m. to
4:00 p.m. Admission fees vary per tour.

**Winsor Bleu Gallery**
207 Commerce Street, Mineral Point
(608) 987-4775

### LODGING
**House on the Rock Resort**
400 Springs Drive, Spring Green
(800) 822-7774 or (608) 588-7000
www.houseontherockresort.com
Rooms are from $95.

**Old Lumberyard Inn's
Garden Bluff Cottage**
10 Commerce Street, Mineral Point
(608) 987-3896
www.oldlumberyardinn.com
Rooms from $99.

### DINING AND NIGHTLIFE
**Brewery Creek Brewpub**
23 Commerce Street, Mineral Point
(608) 987-3298
www.brewerycreek.com
Call for hours.

**Grandview**
In the House on the Rock Resort
Open daily for breakfast, lunch,
and dinner.

**Gundry and Gray**
215 High Street, Mineral Point
(608) 987-4444

**Mineral Spirits Saloon and Café**
20 Commerce Street, Mineral Point
(608) 987-3682
www.mineralspiritssaloon.com
Open for lunch and dinner Tuesday
through Saturday.

**Old Feed Mill**
114 Cramer Street, Mazomanie
(608) 795-4909 or (888) 345-4909
www.oldfeedmill.com
Open for lunch Tuesday through
Saturday, for dinner Tuesday through
Sunday, and for brunch on Sunday.

**The Post House Restaurant**
127 E. Jefferson Street, Spring Green
(608) 588-2595
Open for lunch daily and for dinner
Tuesday through Sunday. A brunch is
served on Sunday.

**Spring Green Café and General Store**
137 S. Albany Street, Spring Green
(608) 588-7070
www.springgreengeneralstore.com

# CHAPTER TEN

# A Touch of the Old World:
# Iowa and Green Counties

In Wisconsin you won't go far without encountering great restaurants, food shops, and food festivals, especially in the southwestern part of the state. Romance Wisconsin-style has to involve great food, and lots of it. Your stomachs won't stay empty for long on this getaway. The two of you will spend your time tempting each other's taste buds, exploring the region, and getting to know each other better.

For those of you who are food lovers as well as lovers, this is a trip for you. Southwest Wisconsin is home to a number of small communities with rich heritages, and many of them keep the past alive as shops and restaurants continue to cook traditional Swiss and Norwegian dishes. On this trip, as you fill your stomachs you'll learn about the various ethnic groups that have settled in this region. You'll tour Monroe and New Glarus—small, Swiss enclaves rich with dairy farms, cheese factories, and taverns—and Mount Horeb, which pays tribute to its Norwegian past with food festivals that are teeming with hot Norwegian pancakes and other goodies.

This region is gorgeous any time of the year, with plenty of festive events couples will enjoy. Mount Horeb's fall festival features a breakfast of waffles with lingonberries and horse and buggy rides through the downtown. Foodies will want to visit New Glarus during its Taste and Treasures Festival in mid-July, and they'll get a kick out of Polka Fest in early June. Hours do vary per season in these towns, so call ahead before planning your three-day love and food feast. A summer visit is a good bet because most of the shops and restaurants are open daily.

## Day One: Monroe

### ☙ MORNING

A good place to get your taste buds geared up for the weekend is Monroe, a tightly knit, unpretentious town. The county seat of Green County, a nexus for cheese making, Monroe is particularly famous for producing Limburger cheese, a funky-smelling cheese that you will not want to eat before kissing a loved one.

Although most Wisconsinites will agree that it's never too early to start eating cheese, begin your day by learning about how cheese is made, before sampling the stuff. Set aside about 30 minutes to tour the **Historic Cheesemaking Center**. No, it's not the most romantic of destinations, but a brief overview of the history of cheese making will be helpful in learning to appreciate the stuff. Housed in a former train depot, the center's exhibits explain how cheese was made more than a century ago, with items such as copper kettles and Egyptian cotton cheesecloths. If you're lucky, a local guide will be on hand to share memories of pressing cheese or wrapping the infamous Limburger cheese in waxed paper and foil.

Cheese Days in Monroe: a celebration of the town's most famous commodity. Photo courtesy of Wisconsin Department of Tourism.

After your tour of the center, drive to downtown Monroe and take a walk around the Romanesque-style courthouse square. The town has a renovated movie theater, bowling alley, arts center, and gift shops. Share a sundae at **Chocolate Temptation,** located on the east side of the square. The little shop sells creamy, hand-dipped ice cream and bonbons. Have a seat at one of the old-fashioned, heart-shaped parlor chairs. And don't forget to pick out a selection of goodies (chocolate-covered cherries?) for your companion. After you've filled yourselves up with sugar, stroll down to Luecke's Diamond Center to have a look at the estate jewelry. Then, check out the paintings at **Monroe Arts Center,** a Gothic Revival Methodist church that was converted into an art space. (Look for the church with the large rose window.) The arts center shows a number of visiting art exhibitions, such as photographs, textiles, and oil paintings, and holds performances by folk musicians and big bands.

If you are visiting on a Sunday afternoon, be sure to pop by **Turner Hall**, a Swiss-style building, for a little polka dancing.

Now that you know how curds and whey are separated, head to **Baumgartner Cheese Store and Tavern** on the square. Settle into one of the booths, order up a cheese sandwich (it's their specialty), and check out the murals of Wisconsin farm scenes on the walls. Try a pint of Blumer's root beer, made right in Monroe by **Joseph Huber Brewing Company**, another institution that dates back to the 1840s. Huber's offers tours of their plant, if you'd like to learn how they brew Berghoff beer.

---

## ROMANCE AHEAD

Wisconsin is full of thoroughfares and byways with romantic-sounding names. Here are but a few. In addition to the rather common Lover's Lanes, there are Valentine Lanes (in the towns of Eastman, Mountain, and Sister Bay), Honey Lanes (in Burlington, Ellsworth, Kewaunee, Maiden Rock, Menomonee Falls, New Berlin, and Oshkosh), Sweet Street (Oshkosh), Sweet Road (Darien and Delavan), Hug Road (Saint Germain), Sexe Road (Blair), Romance Road (Genoa), Virgin Avenue (Platteville), and Virgin Road (Woodman).

---

From there, see firsthand how the cheese making process has changed and sample more cheese at one of the many local cheese factories. (You can find out which ones are open to the public by picking up information at the cheese center.) At the beginning of the twentieth century, there were about 200 cheese factories in Green County. Now there are 16. Started in 1885, the **Chalet Cheese Co-op** is reportedly the oldest continually operating cheese co-op in the country. It is also the only cheese factory in the United States that makes Limburger cheese. (They also make baby Swiss and brick). Stop by the retail store about one mile north of Monroe on Highway N, or call to arrange a tour. **The Franklin Cheese Factory**, one of the last remaining cooperatives in the state, makes Muenster, farmer, and flavored cheeses. **Roth Kase USA** specializes in cheeses such as Gruyère, fontina, butterkase, and flavored cheeses. The company also offers tours of its facilities and has small exhibits on cheese making in the public viewing area. Stop by their gift shop. **The Deppeler Cheese Factory** also makes a variety of cheeses and offers tours. Pick up more information on local cheese factories from the visitor bureau and cheese making center.

On the way out of town, visit **Brennan's Country Farm Market**, a regional food store chain that stocks fresh fruit, wines, and cheeses. Depending on what is in season, pack a basket full of snacks for the two of you, such as Macintosh apples, string cheese, and summer sausage. Choose a bottle of imported red or white wine or a bottle from one of Wisconsin's wineries. Travel north on State Highway 69 for about 17 miles to New Glarus, passing more rolling hills and dairy farms.

Because New Glarus is centrally located for this getaway, consider staying here for your two nights. Once you arrive in town, check into **My Friends' House Bed and Breakfast**. At My Friends' House, couples will want to reserve the sunny "My Love" room for its brass bed and cozy sitting area. This 1911 Tudor home is located on a hill a short walk away from downtown New Glarus. If you prefer staying in more of a hotel setting, try **Chalet Landhaus**, a modern hotel with a sauna and hot tub for guests. In the countryside and towns surrounding New Glarus you'll find a smattering of romantic bed and breakfasts. Lounge in your own private porch off your room in the environmentally friendly **Inn Serendipity** in Browntown in western Green County. Soak in either the claw-foot tub or double whirlpool bathtub in the Grand Suite of the **Chenoweth House** in Monroe.

After the two of you have unpacked your bags, head to the streets to stroll this pretty village. Settled in the 1840s by more than 100 immigrants from the canton of Glarus in Switzerland, New Glarus teems with chatty residents of Swiss descent. You'll notice the chalet-style homes and buildings and window boxes overflowing with red geraniums. Walk by the Bank of New Glarus on First Street to take a look at the glockenspiel. Have a peek at **Ruef's Meat Market**, a local shop started in 1965 by Willy Ruef and his wife, Annette. Ruef's smokes its own meats and produces divine Swiss sausages like *kalberwurst* and *landjaegers*.

## EVENING

You won't have to travel far to enjoy a romantic dinner. Walk over to the festive **New Glarus Hotel Restaurant** and try to secure a table in the room with windows overlooking downtown New Glarus. The restaurant serves Swiss specialties like *Kaesechuechli*, a baked cheese pie served with fresh fruit. Or try the Swiss sausage platter to sample morsels of locally made sausages with sauerkraut and potatoes.

Stick around after your meal. On Friday and Saturday nights a polka band will strike up. Even if you don't know how to polka, don't worry. Take your partner's hand and skip across the floor. No one will notice.

The town shuts down fairly early. You won't find movie complexes, dance clubs, or performance halls in New Glarus. Even the bars (there are only a handful), which attract an older, local crowd, are subdued. Take advantage of the quiet and take a stroll back to your room. Hold hands and kiss under the lamplight.

Back at your room, have a surprise waiting for your companion: a bouquet of flowers from **Brenda's Blumenladen**. You can also order a gift box or bag stocked with goodies all women love—scented candles and bath salts from Brenda's.

The New Glarus Hotel, one of many Swiss-inspired attractions in New Glarus. Photo courtesy of Wisconsin Department of Tourism.

# Day Two: New Glarus

## MORNING

After your hearty, full breakfast at the B&B, walk or bike the **Sugar River State Trail**, accessible from downtown New Glarus (look for the signs by Highway 69). The asphalt and crushed limestone trail stretches for 22 miles southeast to the town of Brodhead. Follow the trail south about two miles from New Glarus to New Glarus Woods State Park. You'll find a few spots in the park to rest or picnic if you like. (Gather up picnic supplies at Brennan's.) It's another four miles along the Little Sugar River to the town of Monticello. If you're feeling ambitious, bike to the romantic Clarence Covered Bridge, which is between Albany and Brodhead, about 20 miles from New Glarus.

If you don't picnic along the way, head back into New Glarus and settle into a spot at the casual pub, **Puempel's Olde Tavern**. It's a homey kind of bar, with quite a history. Built in 1893, it was a boardinghouse run by husband and wife Joseph and Bertha Puempel, followed by their son Otto and his wife, Hazel. Get to know each other over pints of New Glarus beer (usually on tap). Food is basic here, such as a hard salami sandwich or a mug of chili. Don't forget to check out the folk murals painted on the wall.

## ᧰ AFTERNOON

Drive a short distance out of town on Highway 69 and County Road W to pay a visit to **New Glarus Brewing Company**. Owned by Deb and Daniel Carey, the company started in June 1993 after Deb raised the capital and presented it to Dan as a gift. Stop by for a guided or self-guided tour and pay a visit to the gift shop to purchase brews such as the Uffda Bock or Edil Pils.

Back in downtown New Glarus, have dessert at **New Glarus Bakery**, yet another local establishment that has been around for decades (since 1912, in fact). Have a seat in the tearoom and try some of their Swiss specialties like the sweet bread stollen. Next, sample a number of fruit wines at **Primrose Winery**, a storefront winery in New Glarus. Buy your favorite bottle, a corkscrew, and two wineglasses.

## ᧰ EVENING

The elegant **Deininger's Restaurant** makes for an ideal setting for a romantic dinner. Located in a restored Victorian home, the restaurant is run by married couple Rene and Ursula Deininger and their children. Select a table in one of the three intimate dining rooms. Order a bottle of wine and choose from a menu of mostly European and American dishes, such as Wiener schnitzel, broiled pork medallions, and poached salmon.

After your dessert (don't skip the crème brûlée), take another evening stroll through the quiet town on your way back to the room. Pop open that bottle of wine from Primrose Winery, unwind on the front porch of the B&B, and look for shooting stars.

## *Day Three: Mount Horeb*

## ᧰ MORNING

After you check out of your room, drive north from New Glarus on Highway 69 to Highway 92, which winds along Mount Vernon Creek, past farmsteads with red barns and white houses. You'll come to Mount Horeb, another small village proud of its ethnic heritage. As Swiss descendants have converged around the New Glarus area, Mount Horeb is home to many folks of Norwegian descent. Start your day with a visit to downtown Mount Horeb. Billed as the Troll Capital of the World, Mount Horeb's Main Street is dotted with trolls carved out of wood and other products. You'll find plenty of antiques shops here and spots for foodies.

Visit the **Blue Sky Café** for a cup of gourmet coffee and a muffin or a traditional breakfast dish like eggs, toast, and jam. It's a sunny, friendly spot where the two of you can review your map and itinerary. Then head across the street to Main Street Antiques and Hoff Mall Antique Center, which is located in a former department store with about 30 dealers selling furniture such as dining room tables and treasures such as silver spoons, books, and glassware. After filling your trunk, stop by the **Mount Horeb Mustard Museum** to sample mustards from all over the world. Purchase one of your favorites (there are hundreds to choose from) for your picnic lunch and head to **Schubert's Old Fashioned Café and Bakery** for snacks such as *lefse*, a Norwegian potato bread, and Swedish rye bread. Schubert's is yet another shop that has been around for decades (more than 80 years, in fact).

Scout out one of the picnic tables atop Blue Mound, the highest hill in southwestern Wisconsin, in **Blue Mound State Park**, a 10-minute drive from Mount Horeb. After your meal, walk up one of the two 40-foot-high observation towers offering views to the east and west of the Lower Wisconsin Riverway and Baraboo Bluffs. Take a few minutes here to peer out at the country-

Along downtown Mount Horeb's charming main thoroughfare. Photo courtesy of Wisconsin Department of Tourism.

side and allow your companion to rest his or her head on your shoulder.

Continue on for a lovely drive through rolling, green hills to **Botham Vineyards and Winery**, about 15 minutes southwest of Mount Horeb. The hour or two you spend here, in this postcard-perfect spot a few miles from the highway, will be the perfect end to a quiet, hassle-free vacation in southwest Wisconsin. Tour the boutique winery and sample some of their wines, such as the Badger Blush, a semidry red wine, or Cupola Gold, a semidry white wine. Admire paintings in the gallery, relax in the wine garden outside, and take your final stroll of the weekend through the vineyards.

## FOR MORE INFORMATION

**Monroe Chamber of Commerce**
Ludlow Memorial Library
1505 Ninth Street, Monroe
(608) 325-7648

**Mount Horeb Area
Chamber of Commerce**
100 S. First Street (P.O. Box 84),
Mount Horeb
(608) 437-5914 or (888) 765-5929
www.trollway.com

**New Glarus Chamber of Commerce**
Information Center at Fifth Avenue and
Railroad Street
(608) 527-6838 or (800) 527-6838
www.swisstown.com

## ATTRACTIONS AND RECREATION

**Blue Mound State Park**
4350 Mounds Park Road, Blue Mounds
(608) 437-5711
www.dnr.state.wi.us
Admission fee.

**Botham Vineyards and Winery**
8180 Langberry Drive, Barneveld
(608) 924-1412
www.bothamvineyards.com

**Brenda's Blumenladen**
17 Sixth Avenue, New Glarus
(608) 527-2230 or (800) 383-2586
www.brendasblumenladen.com

**Chalet Cheese Co-Op**
N4858 County N, Monroe
(608) 325-4343

**Historic Cheesemaking Center**
2108 Seventh Avenue (Highway 69),
Monroe
(608) 325-4636
Hours vary per season.

**Joseph Huber Brewing Company**
1208 14th Avenue, Monroe
(608) 325-3191
www.berghoffbeer.com
Tours are available year-round,
Thursday, Friday, and Saturday at 11:00
a.m., 1:00 p.m., and 3:00 p.m.

**Monroe Arts Center**
1315 11th Street, Monroe
(608) 325-5700
www.monroeartscenter.com

**Mount Horeb Mustard Museum**
100 West Main Street, Mount Horeb
(800) 438-6878
www.mustardmuseum.com

**New Glarus Brewing Company**
Highway 69 and County Road W,
New Glarus
(608) 527-5850
www.newglarusbrewing.com
Guided tours are offered on Saturday,
June through August. Self-guided tours
are available Monday through Friday,
10:30 a.m. to 4:30 p.m.

**Primrose Winery**
226 Second Street, New Glarus
(608) 527-5053

**Sugar River State Trail**
W5446 County Road NN, New Glarus
(608) 527-2334, www.wiparks.net

**Turner Hall**
11208 14th Avenue, Monroe
For information call the Monroe Chamber of Commerce at (608) 325-7648.

## LODGING

**Chalet Landhaus Inn**
801 Highway 69, New Glarus
(608) 527-5234 or (800) 944-1716
www.chaletlandhaus.com
Rooms are from $89.

**Chenoweth House Bed and Breakfast**
2004 10th Street, Monroe
(608) 325-5064
www.chenowethhouse.com
Rooms are from $94.

**Inn Serendipity**
7843 County Road P, Browntown
(608) 329-7056
www.innserendipity.com
Rooms are from $50.

**My Friends' House Bed and Breakfast**
513 Sixth Avenue, New Glarus
(608) 527-3511
www.myfriendshousewi.net
Rooms are from $75.

## ↪ DINING AND NIGHTLIFE
**Baumgartner Cheese Store and Tavern**
1023 16th Street, Monroe
(608) 325-6157
Call for hours.

**Blue Sky Café**
114 E. Main Street, Mount Horeb
(608) 437-6100
Call for hours.

**Brennan's Country Farm Market**
Highways 11 and 69, Monroe
(608) 325-4433
Open daily.

**Chocolate Temptation**
1004 17th Avenue, Monroe
(608) 328-2462
Call for hours.

**Deininger's Restaurant**
119 Fifth Avenue, New Glarus
(608) 527-2012, www.deiningers.com
Open for lunch and dinner. Closed
Wednesday.

**The Deppeler Cheese Factory**
W6805 Deppeler Road, Monroe

(608) 325-6311
Tours are offered Monday through
Saturday.

**Franklin Cheese Factory**
W7256 Franklin Road, Monroe
(608) 325-3725
Tours are offered Monday through
Saturday.

**New Glarus Bakery**
534 First Street, New Glarus
(608) 527-2916
www.newglarusbakery.com
Closed Monday.

**New Glarus Hotel Restaurant**
100 Sixth Avenue, New Glarus
(608) 527-5244 or (800) 727-9477
www.newglarushotel.com
Call for hours.

**Puempels Olde Tavern**
18 Sixth Avenue, New Glarus
(608) 527-2045
www.puempels.com
Call for hours.

**Roth Kase USA**
461 17th Avenue, Monroe
(608) 328-2122
Open Monday through Friday,
8:00 a.m. to 1:00 p.m.

**Ruef's Meat Market**
538 First Street, New Glarus
(608) 527-2554
www.ruefsmeatmarket.com
Closed Sunday.

**Schubert's Old Fashioned
Café and Bakery**
126 E. Main Street, Mount Horeb
(608) 437-3393
Open for breakfast, lunch, and dinner.
Call for hours.

# CHAPTER ELEVEN

# Along the Great River and the
# *Great River Road*

Whether renting a houseboat for a few days or settling into a historic inn or bed and breakfast, couples can expect to get up close and personal with the Mississippi River this trip. Bicycle along the river. Take a sailboat cruise through Lake Pepin, a lake created by the Mississippi. Watch eagles soar along the coastline and tundra swans fly on their migration paths. Walk through a quaint riverside village, share a slice of cheesecake, and sample Napa wine.

Couples have many options for exploring the Mississippi River and the towns along its shores. You can rent a houseboat and spend most of your trip on water, docking at a beach and dozing on the deck together. You can follow the Great River Road, driving through quiet, historic towns and staying in cozy riverfront inns. Or you can reserve a room on the paddleboat *Julia Belle Swain* in La Crosse, which takes passengers on overnight tours of the river. Whether you tour the region via houseboat or car, you should be able to stop at all the recommended attractions, romantic restaurants, and scenic overlooks along the way.

This getaway covers the section of the Mississippi from La Crosse to the south and Maiden Rock to the north, about 90 miles. Keep in mind that you could spend weeks floating down or driving along the Mississippi River. The river winds for another approximately 20 miles south of La Crosse along the Wisconsin border and about 30 miles north of Pepin. You'll find that there are many more towns and parks to explore, so don't rush this vacation, just plan on returning again someday.

## Day One: La Crosse to Trempealeau

### ☙ MORNING

Begin your river adventure together by renting a houseboat from **Fun 'n the Sun** at Great River Harbor, a few miles south of Alma, about 60 miles north of La Crosse. Couples will want to reserve the smallest boat, a 15-by-42-foot boat with a queen sleeper, queen caddy, bathroom, air conditioning, stereo system, tinted windows, front deck and top deck, grill, and water slide. A few other

Along the Mississippi River at La Crosse.

houseboat rental companies, including **Huck's Houseboat Vacations** and **Northport Marine**, are located along the river in and around the La Crosse area. For a listing, contact the La Crosse Area Convention and Visitor Bureau.

You don't need to be an experienced boater to rent a houseboat. All rental companies provide training and navigational maps of the river, which detail river miles and offer tips on how to pass through the various locks on the river. Most houseboat rental companies permit early boarding, allowing you to complete your training and check in to your houseboat in the evening, giving you three nights and three days rather than two nights and three days. Be sure to take advantage of this option. Most companies rent from late spring until mid-autumn. Obviously, if you plan to rent over the Fourth of July weekend, reserve your houseboat months in advance.

Consider touring the river in early summer, when the nights aren't too humid and you can sit outside together on the deck and not be overrun by mosquitoes. Also, think about renting in early fall, when most of the crowds have disappeared and the leaves on the trees have started changing colors. Imagine cruising along the river and admiring the green, gold, and crimson trees from the water.

There's just something about scenic views that attracts romantic couples. And as you'll discover during this trip, there are quite a few majestic views along the Mississippi River. Begin your getaway by taking in the glory of the river from atop an almost 600-foot-high bluff above La Crosse. To get to **Granddad Bluff** from La Crosse, drive east on Main Street, following signs to Bliss Road and Granddad Bluff Road. Take a few minutes to look out onto the town and the river. On a clear day you can see Iowa, about 30 miles away to the southwest. Nuzzle a little closer to each other (it can get breezy up here).

Next, head back into town for more views of the river. Put your arm around your date, walk over to Riverside Park and follow the path to admire the paddleboats. Lounge together at one of the many benches and watch the barges chug down the river.

Then, have an easy lunch of sandwiches and soup or salad at the downtown eatery **Doc Powell's** or **Huck Finn's on the Water**, which is located at the marina. Huck Finn's offers more views of the river and a dock for boaters. Doc Powell's offers cozy booths in a historic setting. Both serve hearty servings of fish, burgers, and pasta.

## AFTERNOON

Whether you eat lunch at Doc Powell's or Huck Finn's, be sure to save room for dessert. Stop for sweets and hand-dipped ice cream at **The Pearl**, an old-fashioned kind of soda fountain shop in downtown La Crosse. Get a little closer to each other by sitting at one of the little tables and sharing a phosphate. Next, walk over to the boutique **Wood, Wine, & Weeds** to purchase a bottle of wine, wineglasses, and a corkscrew (if you forgot to bring one along for the trip). If you have time, check out another park, **Pettibone Park**, across the river. Here you'll find a romantic pavilion and more benches and opportunities to gaze at the river and relax in each other's arms.

---

### MORE RIVER ROMANCE

For more rest and relaxation—and a bit of Mississippi River–inspired romance—follow the Great River Road about a hundred miles south to the town of Cassville and check in to the Geiger House Bed & Breakfast, 410 Denniston Street, Cassville, (608) 725-5419 or (800) 725-5439, www.geigerhouse.com. Rooms at the Geiger House contain romantic touches such as feather beds, four-poster beds, fireplaces, and in one room, a cast-iron Franklin stove. After you unpack, join other couples for wine and cheese on Friday evenings, or play a game of chess in the library by the fireplace.

---

If you decided to forego renting a houseboat, take a cruise of the river this afternoon aboard the *Island Girl* yacht for a cocktail cruise. During this one-hour cruise the two of you can sip on mixed drinks and cold brews while sitting indoors or standing out on the deck. If you are on a houseboat, take this time to dock at one of the beaches nearby. Consult your map to find the closest one.

After your cocktail cruise, head to the village of Trempealeau, about 25 miles north of La Crosse.

Enjoying a romantic and tranquil moment on the Mississippi.
Photo courtesy of Wisconsin Department of Tourism.

## ❧ EVENING

When you roll into little Trempealeau head toward the **Historic Trempealeau Hotel**, a simple yellow building on Main Street. It was the only building in town to survive a fire in 1881. If you are touring in your car, here's where you drop your bags. Although you can rent rooms above the restaurant, couples will want to request to stay in the Doc West house or Pines Cottage, which are a bit more luxurious compared to the hotel rooms and offer private bathrooms. Suites in the Doc West house, located adjacent to the hotel, are especially appealing to couples for their features such as whirlpool bathtubs and fireplaces. The Pines Cottage is charming and comes with a deck and Jacuzzi tub.

Change into some comfortable clothes, grab a blanket, and head back over to the hotel for some live music on the lawn near the Mississippi River. This place gets kicking almost every weekend in the summer, bringing in a host of bands and musicians, from Arlo Guthrie to the Nitty Gritty Dirt Band.

Have dinner here, too. Vegetarians will salivate over the walnut burger, made of ground walnuts, bread crumbs, onions, eggs, and cheese on a kaiser roll. Other delicious options include the spinach lasagna, tenderloin tips, and Cajun chicken.

## Day Two

### ❧ MORNING

Start your day by filling up with a hearty breakfast at the **Wildflower Café** in downtown Trempealeau.

Then, drive or bicycle to **Perrot State Park**, a few miles north of Trempealeau. From there launch a canoe from the landing near the nature center for a peaceful ride through Trempealeau Bay. (Perrot State Park and the Trempealeau Hotel rent canoes and bicycles.) The Long Lake Canoe Trail, as it's known, winds for 4.5 miles through the refuge, past plenty of sloughs and islands. You may encounter another couple or two canoeing, but most likely you'll spot swimming otters, jumping fish, and diving birds on this peaceful canoe ride together.

Back on your bicycles, continue north on the **Great River State Bicycle Trail** for another few miles to the 6,200-acre **Trempealeau National Wildlife Refuge**. The refuge, on the Mississippi River flyway, is a haven for migratory birds to rest, feed, and breed. Head to the visitor center and walk out onto the observation deck to watch for shorebirds, songbirds, and raptors. If you are driving, follow the four-mile wildlife drive through prairie, wetlands, and a hardwood forest. In late spring, this drive is especially stunning when the lupines bloom. If you are bicycling, pedal out through Kiep's Island dike; you'll feel as though you are riding above the river.

## 🦎 AFTERNOON

Continue north on the Great River Road for about 16 miles to another town carved out of the land between the bluffs and the river. In Fountain City you and your sweetie can stop for sandwiches and ice cream at **Bob & Julie's Soda Fountain and Gift Shop**. For a heartier meal, stop by **The Monarch Tavern**, a brewpub that serves juicy, hand-carved roast beef sandwiches, pizzas, fajitas, and lots of burgers. Try one of the local brews, such as Prairie Moon Red or Irish Valley Spring Bock. It's a cozy, dark place that has been around since 1894, formerly a general store and a meeting hall. It's a perfect detour on a rainy day. After lunch, walk down Main Street for a spell to stretch your legs, and then continue on toward Pepin, another 35 miles north.

## 🦎 EVENING

If you are houseboating, rent an overnight slip at **Dan's Pepin Marina** in Pepin by calling in advance.

If you are not staying aboard the houseboat tonight, check in to a room at the Harbor Hill Inn or A Summer Place, both quaint B&Bs with views of the river. The **Harbor Hill Inn**, a stately, 1870 Queen Anne home, has three rooms for rent, plus a sunny atrium and a second-story porch—perfect spots for cuddling. Try to reserve the Nob Hill room, which contains a private bathroom with a double whirlpool tub. **A Summer Place** also features an arbor deck, a lovely spot for gazing at the river and sipping wine. Rooms feature double whirlpool bathtubs.

After you dock or check in to the B&B, walk hand in hand over to the **Breakwater**, a wine bar and art gallery that also offers sailing cruises. Order glasses of zinfandel or chardonnay or bottles of micro-beer at this classy, breezy joint.

Then, it's on to dinner at the spectacular **Harbor View Café**. You may have to wait a while for a table if you are visiting on a warm summer evening. But not to worry. Put your name on the list and have a seat at the bar or walk down to the river for a stroll. The wait is worth it. This place, decorated with stacks of books and blue and white check tablecloths, is a favorite of locals and visitors. You won't be disappointed. The menu, listed on a blackboard, changes daily. But you can expect mouthwatering entrées such as coq au vin and roasted pork loin.

After your meal, mosey on down Second Street to the Allen/Hovde Theater to see if the **Lake Pepin Players** are presenting a show. This professional theater stages such plays as Neil Simon's *Last of the Red Hot Lovers* and *The Fantasticks* from the late spring to fall.

Before tucking in for the night with your sweetheart, share a glass of wine on the deck of your B&B or your houseboat.

## Day Three

### ⮞ MORNING

After your breakfast, arrange for a private couple's sailboat cruise of the Mississippi River. You'll be the only people, other than the captain, aboard the *Messenger*, a 31-foot sailboat. Arrange for this relaxing two-hour tour at the Breakwater in downtown Pepin.

If you are houseboating and choose not to take the sailboat cruise, spend this time strolling through Pepin's downtown and browsing through some of its shops and galleries. Buy your sweetheart a string of Mississippi River pearls

Legendary Maiden Rock, situated on the Great River Road.

High above the Mississippi at Buena Vista Park in Alma.

at BNOX Gold & Iron. Treat yourselves to truffles at Something Special, a candy and gift shop where you can also purchase wedding accessories. Browse the many tin, wood, and weaving creations at T. & C. Latané's blacksmith shop.

After your sailboat cruise, continue north on the Great River Road, stopping at the tiny but cute town of Stockholm, about six miles north of Pepin. Have lunch at either the **Bogus Creek Café & Bakery** or the **Star Diner**. Both are sunny restaurants that serve homemade sandwiches and pies. It's easy to pass the afternoon dozing in the Bogus Creek Café's garden.

A few miles north of Stockholm, before the town of Maiden Rock, take note of a steep cliff on the Wisconsin side of the river called Maiden Rock. The story behind it is sadly romantic. Legend has it that a young and beautiful Sioux Indian girl was forced to marry a man she didn't love after her family sent away her one true love. Shortly after the ceremony, she disappeared from her lodge and was assumed to have jumped off the cliff. They found her body the next morning.

### ᧠ AFTERNOON

Drive south, back to Alma, a scenic town tucked between towering bluffs and the lazy river. To view the river and surrounding region for one last time, drive or hike to **Buena Vista Park**, an impressive city park atop a 500-foot bluff. To get to the park via car follow County Road E, or hike up the bluff on the trail from Second and Elm Streets (just follow the signs). From here you're given sweeping views of the Mississippi River, the barges locking through Lock and

Dam No. 4, and birds such as bald eagles, peregrine falcons, and turkey vultures. Walk to the observation area to take it all in. Then have a seat at one of the benches or picnic tables. You can camp out together here for as long as you like.

If you are passing through Alma in late October through November, watch for tundra swans as they migrate from the Arctic to Virginia and North Carolina. Your best bet to see the swans is at the observation platform in Rieck's Lake Park, off Highway 35. Eagles are often sighted in the Alma vicinity, too.

## FOR MORE INFORMATION

**Alma Area Chamber of Commerce**
P.O. Box 202, Alma
(608) 685-4442
www.almawisconsin.com

**Great River Road National Scenic Byway**
(800) 658-9480
www.wigreatriverroad.org

**La Crosse Area Convention and Visitor Bureau**
410 Veterans Memorial Drive,
La Crosse
(800) 658-9424
www.explorelacrosse.com

**Mississippi River Valley Partners**
(In Wisconsin: Alma, Bay City, Maiden Rock, Nelson, Pepin, Stockholm)
(888) 999-2619
www.mississippi-river.org

**Pepin County Visitor Information**
(715) 442-3011
www.pepinwisconsin.com

**Trempealeau Chamber of Commerce**
P.O. Box 212, Trempealeau
(608) 534-6780
www.trempealeau.net

**Trempealeau County Tourism Council**
P.O. Box 21, Arcadia
(715) 538-2311, ext. 205,
or (800) 927-5339
www.trempealeaucountytourism.com

## ATTRACTIONS AND RECREATION

**Buena Vista Park**
County Road H and Buena Vista Road,
Alma

**Granddad Bluff Park**
West on Main Street to Bliss Road
and Granddad Bluff Road,
LaCrosse

**Great River State Bicycle Trail**
For more information, contact the Trempealeau Chamber of Commerce or the Onalaska Center for Commerce and Tourism at (608) 781-9570 or (800) 873-9570.

**Island Girl boat tours**
Departs from Bikini Yacht Club,
deck 621, Park Plaza Drive
(next to Skipperliner Marine,
Highway 14/61), La Crosse
(608) 784-0556
www.islandgirlcruises.com

**Julia Belle Swain boat tours**
Riverside Park, La Crosse
(608) 784-4882
or (800) 815-1005
www.juliabelle.com

**Lake Pepin Players**
Allen/Hovde Theater
417 Second Street, Pepin
(877) 823-3500
www.lakepepinplayers.com

**Perrot State Park**
North on Sullivan Road from
downtown Trempealeau or Highway 35,
Trempealeau
(608) 534-6409
www.dnr.state.wi.us

**Pettibone Park**
Highways 14/16/61 and Park Plaza,
La Crosse

**Trempealeau National Wildlife Refuge**
W28488 Refuge Road, Trempealeau
(608) 539-2311
http://midwest.fws.gov/trempealeau
Open year-round, dawn to dusk.
Free admission.

**Wood, Wine, & Weeds**
200 Main Street, La Crosse
(608) 784-3005

## LODGING
**Dan's Pepin Marina**
First and Lake Streets, Pepin
(715) 442-4900

**Fun 'n the Sun Houseboat Vacations**
S2221 Highway 35,
Alma
(608) 248-3501 or (888) 343-5670
www.funsun.com
Houseboat rentals are available from
mid-May to mid-October. Rates are
from $850 for a three-day rental.

**Harbor Hill Inn**
310 Second Street, Pepin
(715) 442-2002
Rooms are from $15.

**The Historic Trempealeau Hotel**
150 Main Street, Trempealeau
(608) 534-6898
www.trempealeauhotel.com
Rooms are from $30; suites are from $100.

**Huck's Houseboat Vacations**
Docked at La Crosse Municipal Harbor
(920) 625-3142 or (800) 359-3035
www.hucks.com

**Northport Marine houseboat rentals**
Alma Marina, Alma
(608) 685-3333 or (800) 982-8410
www.northportmarine.com

**A Summer Place**
106 Main Street, Pepin
(715) 442-2132
Rooms are from $115.

## DINING AND NIGHTLIFE
**Bob & Julie's Soda Fountain
and Gift Shop**
2 S. Main Street, Fountain City
(608) 687-4182

**Bogus Creek Café and Bakery**
114 Spring Street, Stockholm
(715) 442-5017
Open for breakfast and lunch April
through December.

**Breakwater Wine Bar and Gallery**
400 First Street, Pepin
(715) 442-4424
www.pepinbreakwater.com
Open Friday and Saturday, 11:00 a.m.
to 11:00 p.m., and Sunday, 11:00 a.m.
to 9:00 p.m.

**Doc Powell's**
200 Main Street, La Crosse
(608) 785-7026
www.docpowells.com
Open for lunch and dinner Monday
through Saturday.

**Harbor View Café**
First and Main Streets, Pepin
(715) 442-3893
Open for lunch and dinner. Hours vary
per season.

**The Historic Trempealeau**
**Hotel Restaurant and Saloon**
150 Main Street, Trempealeau
(608) 534-6898
www.trempealeauhotel.com
Open daily for lunch and dinner during
the summer. Open Thursday through
Sunday for lunch and dinner during
the winter.

**Huck Finn's**
127 Marina Drive, La Crosse
(608) 791-3595
Open for lunch, brunch and dinner.
Hours vary per season.

**The Monarch Tavern**
19 N. Main Street, Fountain City
(608) 687-4231
www.monarchtavern.com
Open for lunch and dinner daily.

**The Pearl Ice Cream Parlor and Confec-
tionery**
207 Pearl Street, La Crosse
(608) 782-6655

**Star Diner**
W12128 Highway 35, Stockholm
(715) 442-2023

**Wildflower Café**
11364 Main Street, Trempealeau
(608) 534-6866
Call for hours.

# CHAPTER TWELVE

# Wisconsin Dells
## for Adults

Surprise: Wisconsin Dells, legendary for its kid-crowded water parks and all-you-can-eat pizza buffets, is becoming an appealing destination for romantic couples. With golf courses set amid rolling hills and sandstone canyons, restaurants specializing in first-class fare (not Happy Meals), and the recent opening of a destination spa for adults, you don't have to be a munchkin to enjoy the area's many pleasures.

If you have kids, leave them at home for this vacation . . . and don't tell them where you're going. And whether or not you have them, you'll find a Wisconsin Dells getaway surprisingly relaxing and fun. The two of you will cruise the Wisconsin River at sunset on a wine and cheese cruise, soak in a hot tub, and play a round of golf on a course far from the traffic of the main drag. At the same time, don't take this getaway too seriously. Indulge your inner child and have a spin down that water tube on a double raft. Impress your companion with a little poolside karaoke. And wile away the afternoon in a spa.

## Day One
### ☙ MORNING

This morning get acquainted with the scenery of the Wisconsin Dells region by hitting the greens at one of the following golf courses: **Coldwater Canyon Golf Course** or the **Wilderness Woods Golf Club**, far from the theme parks and traffic congestion. Located behind the Wilderness Hotel and Golf Resort, the Wilderness Woods' fairways are located within view of . . . you guessed it . . . 200 acres of woodlands and sandstone canyons. Have your pick of an 18-hole, par-72, 6,137-yard course or a 6-hole, par-3, links course. (If you plan to stay at Sundara, ask about the golf and spa getaway packages.) The Coldwater Canyon link-style course is carved into the river valley and also set amid rolling hills and canyons. The 18-hole, 5,400-yard course is par 70. As with the Wilderness course, you won't hear any horns beating, go-carts rumbling, or children crying when playing at Coldwater Canyon. Remember, you're on vacation: no business talk, and no throwing clubs if you hit a bogey.

After your morning of playing golf together, drive to **The Cheese Factory Restaurant**. Housed in a former cheese factory, this restaurant serves up hearty vegetarian dishes in a sunny, nostalgic atmosphere, while the smiling soda jerk churns out scrumptious ice cream desserts. Lounge over a meal of mushroom Stroganoff or *moussaka*, a Greek casserole. But be sure to save room for a slice of carrot cake or hazelnut torte. Or, share a homemade milkshake or ice cream soda with your sweetheart before leaving.

## AFTERNOON

Before checking in to your room for the weekend, take a quick ride through cool and narrow sandstone passages with **Lost Canyon Tours**. The two of you plus a handful of other passengers will board a horse-drawn wagon or carriage and travel through the rock gorges for about 30 minutes. Take this time to learn a bit about the geology of the Dells, unwind, and cuddle. (You will find the tour especially refreshing if you are visiting the Dells on a humid summer day.)

Now, unload your bags and check in to your digs for the next few nights. Perhaps the best resort for adults to stay in the Dells is the **Kalahari**, a massive complex in Lake Delton with lavish suites, a spa for couples in need of a little pampering, and an indoor watery world with a bar, cabanas, and water activities for big kids. Because the Kalahari is also a convention center, it is not as overridden with children as some of the other resorts and water parks in the Dells. Try to reserve the King Jacuzzi Suite, which, designed for two people, has a king-size bed, sofa, Jacuzzi, and private balcony on the top (fourth) floor of the hotel. (All furniture and art you see in your room and throughout the hotel are imported from Africa.) After checking in, head to the lobby, where you can sip cocktails and listen to live music on the weekends.

A relaxing moment for two at the Sundara Inn and Spa. Photo courtesy of Sundara Inn.

If you prefer to stay in a quiet B&B, check in to the **Sherman House**, run by the **White Rose Bed and Breakfast**. Rooms in this 100-year-old, Prairie-style home are gorgeous, with some offering views of the Wisconsin River. The Newport Room, with its blues and whites, is reminiscent of a room in a seaside cottage. The Kilbourne Room, with its rich reds, has an Asian mood to it. A common area offers overstuffed armchairs and a dining room table to sip tea or coffee and browse through your itinerary for the weekend. Take advantage of the "Pamper and Refresh" service, which includes truffles, champagne, flowers, and a massage. You're bound to score points with those gifts. After you unpack, sit in the rocking chairs in the four-season room and watch the rolling river.

For the ultimate pampering experience, stay at one of the newest spots in the Dells, **Sundara Inn and Spa**, a luxurious, adults-only resort. The suites are huge (450 to 1,500 square feet), with different configura-

Witches' Gulch, another chance to view the fascinating rock formations of the Upper Dells. Photo courtesy of Dells Boat Tours.

tions to choose from. Although no two are decorated the same, they each include king beds, robes, gas fireplaces, and writing desks. Each one has been designed in earth tones by a feng shui consultant (no clutter in these rooms). You'll love the Amoda suite (*amoda* means "joy" in Sanskrit) and its screened-in, pool-view porch, whirlpool bathtub, and tower shower. After checking in to Sundara, stretch out in a lounge chair on the pool deck.

## EVENING

Late this afternoon and into the early evening, bask in the golden glow of a Wisconsin sunset on a **Dells Boat Tour** wine and cheese cruise. On this two-hour adventure you will cruise past fabled sights on the Upper Dells of the Wisconsin River. One such spot is Romance Cliff. According to a Native American legend, a couple that wished to become married stood on the top of this cliff while the tribal leader tossed a lit pine branch to the water below. If the light was extinguished before the branch hit the water, the marriage was doomed and the woman could push the man over the cliff if she so desired. On the cruise you will pass through Lover's Lane, a narrow river passage, and be asked to smooch with the person sitting next to you. You will also debark at Witches Gulch, a narrow sandstone corridor lit by tiki torches. The boat will come to a rest in a wide bay, allowing you to sip wine and nibble cheese as you watch the sun set.

Following your boat tour, dine at the classic Wisconsin Dells eatery **Wally's House of Embers**. Established by Wally and his wife Barbara Obois in 1959, the restaurant is now run by the couple's sons, chefs Michael and Mark. A rather large restaurant popular with locals, Wally's is still an intimate spot for couples because of the various dining rooms. Call ahead to reserve the exotic Humphrey Bogart or Omar Sharif rooms (booths, actually). Wally's is known for its hickory-smoked and hand-rubbed barbecue ribs, but because those are not the most delicate food to eat while on a date, try the veal, fish, or tenderloin tips. (Typhoon Tenderloin Tips are sautéed with teriyaki sauce and served with vegetables and rice.) All entrées are preceded with cinnamon rolls (the recipe was developed by Barbara and aren't so overpoweringly sweet that they will spoil your dinner). After your meal, move over to the lounge to listen to a local musician croon ballads. Sip on a Mango Tango, Horni martini, or one of the many glasses of California, Italian, or French wines available.

Then, it's on to the next activity for the evening. When was the last time the two of you went miniature golfing on a date? Junior high school or high school, perhaps? This easygoing activity is much less serious than the regular round of golf the two of you played this morning, and it affords plenty of time to chitchat while walking between the holes. Head to **Shipwreck Lagoon Adventure Golf** on the Dells Parkway, a course decorated with the hulls of ships and rope bridges. Afterward, spend a few minutes in the batting cages practicing swings and showing off for each other.

Cap off the evening by arranging to have a bottle of wine or champagne delivered to your room before the two of you return from your night on the town. Staff at Sundara, Kalahari, and the Sherman House will be able to organize this for you.

## Day Two

### ๛ MORNING

If you are staying at the Sherman House, expect a full gourmet breakfast served in the dining room with muffins, fruit, and dishes like homemade quiche. If you are staying at Kalahari or Sundara, head over to **The Secret Garden Café** for breakfast. This little restaurant is an oasis from the hustle of downtown Wisconsin Dells, a few blocks from the river district. Housed in the lower level of the White Rose B&B, the Secret Garden Café is decorated as if it were

Adults getting in a little playtime at Noah's Ark water park in Wisconsin Dells. Photo courtesy of Noah's Ark.

a Tuscan villa. As soothing jazz or world music plays in the background, the cook whips up breakfast dishes such as Belgian waffles with strawberries and whipped cream, stuffed crepes, or a bacon and egg croissant with hollandaise sauce, rosemary potatoes, and fresh fruit.

After breakfast set aside some time for water therapy. This can involve dozing poolside in a chaise lounge, floating on a lazy river, or getting in touch with your inner child and racing down slides. If it's a hot summer day, take your date's hand and make tracks to **Noah's Ark**. Although other water parks such as Family Land and Riverview offer fun rides, they mainly cater to families and children. At Noah's Ark you are more likely to run into couples like yourselves (in addition to scores of kids, of course). Go to the Bermuda Triangle area where most of the rides are for two people on double tubes. For a real thrill take a spin through one of the enclosed tubes at Black Thunder. For some R&R, loop around the Adventure or Endless Rivers. Lie out in the sun by the wave pool, then woo your companion with some karaoke singing at the Big Kahuna. Afterward, strut over to the Kahuna Triangle lounge and order some fruity cocktails.

If you are visiting Wisconsin Dells during the spring or fall, head to the Kalahari's humongous indoor water park. (Admission is free to Kalahari guests.) The 127,000-square-foot indoor park contains the Tanzanian Twister, a flume ride that propels you up to 40 miles per hour; and Master Blaster, a water roller coaster–like ride. After shooting through these rides, if you still have some energy, exercise in the 64-foot lap pool. The pool features a current channel that allows you to walk or swim against the current. If that sounds too strenuous, drift through the Torrent River, soak in one of the five whirlpool spas, then wander over to the Cabana Bar for some tropical drinks. If you are staying in one of Kalahari's lavish presidential suites, you will have your very own private cabana in the indoor and outdoor parks reserved for you.

For lunch, take a break from swimming and sliding by ordering submarine sandwiches at Noah's Ark Surfside Deli or have food delivered to you in the Kalahari water park. If you want to have a late lunch outside the water park, try **Moose Jaw Pizza and Brewing Company**. Although the rustic, North Woods decor may not be the most romantic to some folks (the chandeliers are made of antlers), you will find plenty of smaller tables upstairs, unlike the picnic table–style seating in most buffet joints in the Dells. Plus, the large fireplace makes for a cozy atmosphere and the food will definitely fill you up. The restaurant serves elk burgers, Wisconsin beer brats, pizza, and a variety of brews such as pale and raspberry ales, stouts, and pilsners.

## GOING TO THE CHAPEL

So you've proposed and she said yes. Got the license, but don't want a 350-person event? Consider exchanging vows in one of Wisconsin's quaint wedding chapels. Many of them, you will find, were shuttered country churches that have been restored to their former glory. Here are a few to consider: the Bridal Churches of Door County and Green Bay at (920) 432-8022, Touch of an Angel Wedding Chapel in Adams at (608) 339-7777, the Spring Brook Chapel in Burnett at (920) 689-2357, Cornerstone Wedding Chapel in Appleton at (920) 731-5753, and the Medina Wedding Chapel in Medina at (920) 707-6250.

### AFTERNOON

Chill out together this afternoon at the Sundara Spa's Tranquility Together series of treatments. No matter how stressed either of you were before the trip, this afternoon will surely remove any tension you were carrying around and put you in a decidedly romantic frame of mind. With the Tranquility Together series (the spa offers several), the two of you will experience oh-so-pampering treatments, including aroma and water therapy regimens and massages. Whichever series you choose (some focus on relaxation, some focus on revitalizing or energizing), all treatments start the same way. You and your sweetie will step into a shower made for two and rub each other with an exfoliating Sundara Sandstone Body Polish. This is followed by the release of eucalyptus aroma oil in the steam room, then a rinse in the rainfall shower and a soak in the hot waters of the whirlpool. Rinse in the cool pool (a shocking and invigorating experience), and chill out for a bit in the relaxation lounge. Sip on some berry juice or tea, flip through inspirational books, chat, or nap.

Next your therapist will greet and escort the two of you to a private room where, amid a backdrop of a fireplace, candles, or soft music (whatever the two of you desire), your treatments will focus on a particular theme. Try the tranquility series, which involves soaking in an oversized tub as mood lighting works to lift your spirits, an aromatherapy massage, and a sodashi facial. Guys, you will like the facial, too. If you are staying at the spa, feel free to wander back up to your room in your robes once the fabulous event has concluded.

If you have opted for the "Pamper and Refresh" package at the Sherman House, arrange for the massage therapist to arrive this afternoon. Take your turns receiving a traditional Swedish massage in the privacy of your own room. If you are staying at the Kalahari and don't want to travel to Sundara, take the elevator down to the resort's Oasis Experience Day Spa and have your pick of a variety of massages and body treatments designed to relax and rejuvenate you.

## EVENING

Tonight for dinner you will drive a few miles south of Wisconsin Dells, away from the frenzy of the main strip and down a long wooded lane to the **Ishnala Supper Club.** Before becoming a restaurant in the 1950s, the site held a private residence in the 1900s and a trading post in the mid-1800s. Try to arrive about an hour before your dinner reservation, which will allow you time to walk through the gardens, along the wooded lakeshore path, and down to the pier. Nuzzle in the lounge overlooking Mirror Lake, or sit outside on the deck and listen to the wind whirling through the towering pine trees surrounding the restaurant. In the dining room request one of the tables by a window overlooking the lake or under one of the giant Norway pine trees running straight through the restaurant's roof. Try the beef tenderloin medallions, lobster tail, or sun-dried tomato ravioli.

After dinner treat your date to a show at the **Crystal Grand Music Theatre**. Whenever a popular music group visits town, usually they play at this 2,000-seat venue, which, with its pink and purple interior, resembles a performance venue in Branson, Missouri. Past musical acts have included Peter, Paul, and Mary; Charlie Pride; and the Lettermen.

If the current show at the Crystal Grand doesn't pique your interest, how about watching a drive-in movie? Drive to the outskirts of town to **Big Sky Twin Drive-In Theatres**. Pull in, park, put your arm around your companion's shoulders, and check out a first-run movie in the privacy of your own car.

## Day Three

### ⤷ MORNING

For breakfast indulge in one of the heavenly cinnamon rolls at **Denny's Diner** (it's an independent restaurant, not affiliated with the national chain). This local hangout serves typical diner comfort food (read, not low-fat). It's a great spot to people watch, read the newspaper, and chat.

Next, take about an hour to wander through the Dells River District, a walkable shopping area. Bypass the bevy of fudge, moccasin, and T-shirt shops. Instead tour the **H. H. Bennett Studio and History Center** and see how the region looked 100 years ago. It was Bennett who is credited with capturing the natural beauty of the Dells and promoting the area to tourists from the 1860s through early 1900s. (Bennett named many of the rock formations along the river, such as Honeymoon Rock.)

Say good-bye to the Dells and take a road trip about 25 miles southeast toward Prairie du Sac and **Wollersheim Winery**. Located on 23 scenic, hilly acres above the Wisconsin River, the winery was founded by couple Bob and JoAnn Wollersheim in 1972. (The hills, however, have had grapevines growing on them at various times since the 1840s.) Tour the winery and sample some of the wines, such as the award-winning white Prairie Fumé or the red Domaine du Sac. Then, stroll along the paths and unwind on the patio.

### ⤷ AFTERNOON

After your winery tour, backtrack a bit northwest to the quaint town of Baraboo, where members of the Ringling Brothers Circus used to spend their winters. Walk around the village's courthouse square and stop for a late lunch at the **Little Village Café**. This homey restaurant has an extensive lunch menu with a bit of Southwestern flare. Slide into a cozy booth. Have your pick of pasta, burritos, tostados, and entrées such as blackened salmon Caesar salad or Jamaican jerk chicken. You can also purchase bottles of wine such as chardonnays or sauvignon blancs here.

### ⤷ FOR MORE INFORMATION

**Baraboo Chamber of Commerce**
Second Street (P.O. Box 442), Baraboo
(608) 356-8333 or (800) BARABOO
www.baraboo.com/chamber

**Wisconsin Dells Visitor and Convention Bureau**
701 Superior Street, Wisconsin Dells
(608) 254-4636 or (800) 22-DELLS
www.wisdells.com

### ⤷ ATTRACTIONS AND RECREATION

**Big Sky Twin Drive-In Theatres**
Winnebago Road, Wisconsin Dells
(follow Highway 16, 1 mile south of the Dells), (608) 254-8025
Open seasonally. Shows start at dusk.

**Coldwater Canyon Golf Course**
4052 River Road, Wisconsin Dells
(608) 254-8489, www.golfcoldwater.com

**Crystal Grand Music Theatre**
430 Munroe Street, Lake Delton
www.crystalgrand.com
(800) 696-7999

**Dells Boat Tour**
Wisconsin Dells Parkway
and Highway 13 (Broadway),
Wisconsin Dells
(608) 254-8555
www.dellsboats.com
Boats generally run mid-April
to October.

**H. H. Bennett Studio
and History Center**
215 Broadway, Wisconsin Dells
(608) 253-3523
Open daily May to September and on
weekends during fall and winter. Call for
hours. Admission fee.

**Lost Canyon Tours**
Canyon Road (P.O. Box 119),
Lake Delton
(608) 254-8757
or (608) 253-2781 (off-season)
Call for hours.

**Noah's Ark**
1410 Wisconsin Dells Parkway,
Wisconsin Dells
(608) 254-6351
www.noahsarkwaterpark.com
Call for hours.

**Shipwreck Lagoon Adventure Golf**
1470 Wisconsin Dells Parkway,
Wisconsin Dells
(608) 253-7772
Call for hours.

**Wilderness Woods Golf Club**
Wilderness Hotel and Golf Resort
511 E. Adams Street, Wisconsin Dells
(608) 253-GOLF (4653)
www.golfwildernesswoods.com

**Wollersheim Winery**
Highway 188 (P.O. Box 87),
Prairie du Sac
(608) 643-6515 or
(800) VIP-WINE (847-9463)
www.wollersheim.com

## ৬ঔ LODGING

**Kalahari Resort**
1305 Kalahari Drive, Lake Delton
(877) 253-5466
www.kalahariresort.com
Open year-round. Room rates
vary per season and weekend.

**Sherman House and White Rose
Bed and Breakfast**
910 River Road,
Wisconsin Dells
(608) 254-4724
or (800) 482-4724
www.thewhiterose.com
Rooms are from $80.

**Sundara Inn and Spa**
920 Canyon Road, Wisconsin Dells
(608) 253-9200
www.sundaraspa.com
Rooms are from $159.

## ৬ঔ DINING AND NIGHTLIFE

**The Cheese Factory Restaurant**
521 Dells Parkway,
Wisconsin Dells
(608) 253-6065
www.cookingvegetarian.com
Open for breakfast, lunch, and dinner.
Hours vary per season.

**Denny's Diner**
At the corner of Wisconsin Dells
Parkway and Highway 23
(P.O. Box 324), Lake Delton
(608) 254-7647
Open daily for breakfast, lunch,
and dinner.

**Ishnala Supper Club**
F2011 Ishnala Road, Lake Delton
(608) 253-1771
www.ishnala.com
Open for dinner daily May
through October and for lunch and
dinner on Sunday.

**Little Village Café**
146 Fourth Avenue, Baraboo
(608) 356-2800
Open for lunch and dinner Tuesday
through Saturday.

**Moose Jaw Pizza
& Brewing Company**
110 Wisconsin Dells Parkway,
Wisconsin Dells
(608) 254-1122
www.moosejawbrewpub.com
Open for lunch and dinner daily.

**The Secret Garden Café**
Located in the lower level
of the White Rose Bed and Breakfast
910 River Road, Wisconsin Dells
(608) 254-4724
www.thesecretgardencafe.com
Open for breakfast, lunch,
and dinner. Call for hours.

**Wally's House of Embers**
935 Wisconsin Dells Parkway,
Lake Delton
(608) 253-6411
www.houseofembers.com
Open for dinner daily.

# CHAPTER THIRTEEN

# Pedaling Around
# *Sparta and Warrens*

Dubbed the bicycling capital of America, Sparta sits at the northern entrance to the Elroy-Sparta State Bike Trail and the eastern entrance to the La Crosse River State Bike Trail, making it a popular launching point for cycling groups, families, and active and romantic couples like yourselves. Still, the region is not overcrowded and there are plenty of cheery folks running fruit and ice cream stands, restaurants, and resorts. You don't have to be professional cyclists to pedal your way through Wisconsin's scenic driftless area, past the cranberry bogs in Warrens, and through small towns like Wilton. The trails are easy to navigate and not very steep. And there are plenty of places to rest your legs along the way.

Your itinerary may seem ambitious—bicycling the Elroy-Sparta Trail, taking a moonlit horseback ride, canoeing the Kickapoo—but know that your stops along the way include plenty of time to gaze at each other over coffee and pie. Plus, your nights are easy: lounge over a picnic dinner in a meadow or beside a pond. For this getaway, base your vacation at a miniresort set in the countryside. Rent a secluded, scenic bungalow at Percheron Paradise or the cozy Little House on a Prairie cabin at Justin Trails Resort. Yes, it will be hard to leave your love nest. You will be tempted to spend hours soaking in the double whirlpool bathtub or chatting easily with each other while sitting out on the porch or deck.

## *Day One*

### ⌘ MORNING AND AFTERNOON

The **Elroy-Sparta State Trail** is 32 miles long and fairly easy to navigate. Because its grade is never greater than three percent, the trail will be suitable for even novice or out-of-shape bicyclists. Don't be intimidated. The limestone trail, said to be the nation's first rails-to-trails project, follows the former Chicago & Northwestern railroad bed past small farming communities, along the Kickapoo and

One of the many secluded spots, ideal for lovebirds, at Percheron Paradise Romantic Hideaway, near Sparta.

Baraboo Rivers, over trestles, and through three enormous tunnels, one of which measures three-quarters of a mile.

Devote the first day to exploring this trail and the countryside that it winds through. The two of you can access the trail in a number of towns from Sparta to Elroy. Because you will be staying closer to Sparta than Elroy, consider launching your expedition at the Sparta Depot. At the depot you can pick up maps, purchase trail passes, chat with tourism staff members, and meet other bicyclists.

Because you will want to stop at scenic spots along the way, you may not be able (or want) to bicycle the entire trail from Sparta to Elroy and back again. That's OK; you're not competing in a race, you're on a romantic getaway. Luckily, some outfitters, such as **Out Spokin' Adventures**, offer shuttle service to any point along the trail. This means the two of you can bike the 32 miles from Sparta to Elroy and not have to backtrack. Out Spokin' also offers a driver service in case you park your car and bike from one town to another and find yourselves too exhausted to bike back. A driver will pick up your car and drive it back to where you are. Reservations aren't required, but they are recommended.

If you don't feel like hitching your bicycles to your car or truck for this vacation, don't worry. The two of you can rent bicycles, including tandem bikes, at a number of outfitters in Sparta, including **Speeds Bicycle Shop**. Bikes are also available for rent at the trail headquarters in Kendall. Some businesses will even deliver the bikes to your hotel. Finally, before you set off on the trail, don't forget to purchase daily trail passes at the trail headquarters or area shops.

Whether you and your sweetie debark in Sparta or Elroy, be sure to stop in Wilton, a small town located at about the trail's halfway point. (Look for the caboose.) A great spot to stop for lunch is **Gina's Pies Are Square**. Housed in a former general store, Gina's serves a variety of sandwiches such as barbecue pork, vegetable burger, and grilled chicken. As the name implies, this place's specialty is pies—pies baked in square pans, that is. Save some room for a generous slice of peach, pecan, turtle, or one of the many other flavors Gina cooked up that morning. While you're there, share an Italian soda (cream is a local favorite) and browse the antiques for sale in the store.

## AFTERNOON

After spending most of the day on the trail, a comfortable room will be much appreciated. Although the Sparta area is home to a number of hotels and bed and breakfasts, for a more secluded and romantic getaway, rent a luxurious bungalow, cabin, or chalet for the days you will be in town. Both Justin Trails Resort and Percheron Paradise Romantic Hideaway are located on the outskirts of Sparta, not far from the Elroy-Sparta Trail, and both offer splendid getaways. You'll stay in the country but will be pampered in housing that boasts oh-so-enticing extras like double-whirlpool baths, porches with views, and fluffy robes.

## SPARTA IN THE WINTER

You may not be able to bicycle along the Elroy-Sparta Trail in January, but there are plenty of other relaxing activities for couples visiting the area in the winter (or anytime, for that matter). Reconnect with your inner child at This Old Barn in Tomah, 1605 Holiday Road, Tomah, (608) 374-3330, which offers horse-drawn bobsled rides. Treat yourselves to a pampering massage at the Little Red Hen House Massage and Retreat Center in Westby, (608) 634-3179. Finally, cuddle inside a cozy, bona fide caboose. At Caboose Cabins, 1102 S. Water Street, Sparta, (608) 269-0444, www.caboosecabins.com, you can stay in a renovated 1968 Soo Line caboose. It's located right by the start of the Elroy-Sparta Trail, so if you feel like braving the elements, you can take a winter hike there.

Perched in the hills amid birch and pine trees, **Percheron Paradise** has five cabins for rent. But to call them cabins is an understatement. All the lodgings, built of rough-cut pine, are outfitted with features romantic couples will appreciate, such as the leather love seats, double-head showers, and extra-large whirlpool baths. (Even if you and your sweetheart measure beyond six feet tall, you'll be able to comfortably recline in these tubs.)

Notice the Hershey's Kisses placed in your room? There's a story behind them. Back before they got married, when innkeepers Tracy and Karl Hackbarth were in high school, they were talking under a bridge by a waterfall. Karl asked Tracy if she wanted a kiss and handed her a piece of chocolate. Aww. The

The porch of the Little House on the Prairie at Justin Trails Resort, Sparta. Photo courtesy of Justin Trails Resort.

Hackbarths' fondness for the countryside and appreciation for romantic getaways (they spent a lot of time visiting resorts for couples before designing their own) is obvious.

Once you arrive on the 200-acre homestead, you'll drive up a hill and continue to your bungalow or chalet. (If you're staying in one of the chalets at the top of the hill, you'll be given keys to a four-wheel drive vehicle to take you there.) Once you pull into the driveway of your little abode for the weekend or week, have a seat on the deck or porch. With about a football field's length of land between each bungalow or chalet, you won't be able to see any other dwellings or couples. You won't hear any children running around (couples only, here) or maids knocking on your door at 7:00 a.m., unless you request such service. Another highlight of the bungalow and chalet are the windows on all sides of the cottages, allowing you to see the sun rise or set from your bed, love seat, or bathtub.

At **Justin Trails** choose from rooms within the renovated farmhouse or rent an entire cabin located on the farmstead. The best bet for couples is to stay in Little House on the Prairie, a log cabin made of jack pine. This one is made for two people and features modern amenities such as a double-whirlpool bathtub. Decorated with handmade quilts and heated with a gas fireplace in the winter, the cabin is situated in a charming spot near the Justin's alfalfa and cornfields. One of the best features is a private porch with chairs that face the fields, perfect for lounging in the morning and evening. If you're looking for more space, try the presidential suite in the main house. (It is reported that Martin Sheen and his wife stayed here.)

Whether you stay at Percheron or Justin Trails, score extra points with your companion and have a bouquet of fresh flowers delivered to your room. Call **Sparta Floral and Greenhouse** and have a dozen roses sent over.

Now, after oohing and aahing at what will be your love nest for the next two days, unpack your things, then grab each other's hands and explore the property. Justin Trails maintains 10 miles of trails through the woods, accessible just outside your door. (While you're wandering the property, be sure to stop by and check out the disc golf course.) At Percheron, follow the cut grass vehicle trails to the top of the hill. If you're feeling ambitious, you can forage your own trails to the top.

## EVENING

For dinner, drive to Cashton, a small, primarily Amish community about 15 minutes south of Justin Trails and Percheron Paradise. Gourmands will adore the **Back Door Café** in the Ages Past Bed and Breakfast. The café is housed in a small, five-table dining room in an 1898 white, country Victorian home. The home was built by local businessman John Cremer for his bride before it became the rectory for Cashton's Sacred Heart of Jesus parish. Dinner here is an event and typically includes several courses of European-style dishes and wine from France, Germany, or Australia. Throughout the year the café hosts a number of special events such as "Dining Around the World," which involves sampling cuisine of a particular country, such as Russia. On Valentine's Day, the café supplies roses, chocolate, wine, and dinner for couples.

After dinner, drive back to your lodging, grab a blanket, and light a few candles. Pop open a bottle of wine and lounge on your deck. (Upon your arrival at Justin Trails the innkeepers, husband and wife Don and Donna Justin, will have placed a bottle of champagne in the room, plus a set of glasses. The Hackbarths also provide sparkling grapefruit juice and wineglasses.) Gaze at the stars and each other for a while, then move inside and try out that whirlpool tub. If you're staying in the Little House on the Prairie cabin at Justin Trails, you'll notice the hot tub is situated in the loft, accessible via a ladder. At Percheron Paradise all bungalows have picture windows by the hot tubs so you should be able to continue stargazing from within the tub. Both resorts have mood lighting (twinkling white lights) hung around the rooms, so be sure to turn on those too.

If you feel like venturing out, consider attending a local theater production by the **Upstage Review Theatre Company** in Sparta, which has produced such classics as Neil Simon's *Lost in Yonkers* or William Shakespeare's *As You Like It*.

## *Day Two*

### ✑ MORNING

If you are staying at Justin Trails, order a number of breakfast treats delivered to your door. (You can join other guests in the dining room, but why not enjoy breakfast in bed?) If you are staying at Percheron Paradise, mix an omelet for your companion in the chalet's kitchen. (Don't forget to buy food in town, though.)

This morning, explore another scenic area in the region. Hitch your bikes to the car and drive to Warrens, a small town in the center of cranberry country, about 30 miles northeast of Sparta. The Warrens Business Association has mapped out various bicycle tours of the region. (You can pick up a map of the routes at the Cranberry Festival office in Warrens or the **Cranberry Country**

Checking out the cranberry harvest. Photo courtesy of Wisconsin Department of Tourism.

**Antiques Mall** in Tomah.) Take the Wetlands Bike Tour, a 22-mile loop that leads you past numerous woodlands, ponds, and marshes where cranberries and sphagnum moss are harvested. Shortly after your start your tour you'll come to the **Cranberry Expo Museum** on County Road EW, where you can take a short tour of the museum to learn about the cranberry industry in the region. And of course, don't leave without sampling some cranberry ice cream. From the expo building, continue on the bicycle tour (just follow the signs). It's a quiet tour—chances are only a few cars will pass you by—allowing you plenty of time to talk and gaze at the scenery. Depending on your pace and how often you pause to take photos of the marshes or the occasional heron swooping by, the loop can take you two to three hours to complete.

By the time you have completed the tour, both of you should have worked up an appetite. You won't find a four-star restaurant in Warrens, but you will find the quaint, comfy **Cranberry Cabin Café**, a local restaurant that serves soups and sandwiches during the lunch hour.

## Ꮽ AFTERNOON

After lunch, stop by **Grant Moseley's Fruit and Vegetable Farm** south of County Road E in Warrens. Here, buy an abundance of fruit such as strawberries and apples for sale. Pick your own or purchase some already picked and cleaned. You'll nibble on these this evening. Also, stop at **Natural Scentsations** in Sparta to purchase supplies for the evening: bubble bath (almond- or musk-scented, perhaps?), candles, perfume, and soap scented with rose hips.

Back at the resort, have your legs and other muscles massaged so you're not too tired to enjoy the rest of the getaway. The former chicken coop at Justin Trails has been remodeled into what they now call the "comfort coop." This is where a massage therapist will meet you both to deliver Swedish massages. While one of you is receiving a massage, the other can be resting in the sauna in the same building.

## Ꮽ EVENING

Tonight you don't have to go far to savor a fresh, delicious, homemade meal. At Justin Trails the innkeepers will prepare a dinner for the two of you and deliver it to your door. Dishes are made using produce from area farmers' markets, plus homemade breads and pies. Justin Trails has a number of spots for you to enjoy your picnic, such as under the mammoth silver maple tree (it's 125 years old) in front of the farmhouse and on your porch overlooking the fields. For a more private getaway, hike about a half mile on the trail and pick a spot near the pond.

At Percheron Paradise, each cabin comes with a large grill on the deck. Drive into Cashton or Sparta to one of the supermarkets and stock up on fresh vegetables, steak, chicken, or fish. For dessert, feed each other those juicy strawberries you picked up at Moseley's. The bungalow and chalets are also stocked with real dishes; you won't have to serve your partner on Styrofoam or paper. Dine on your deck or porch or spread a blanket in a nearby field. Watch the sun set over the hills.

The best part about this evening's dinner? It's just the two of you among nature—no chatty strangers next to your table and no waitstaff cutting in on your private conversations.

Try to tear yourselves away from your evening picnic and drive about five minutes away to **Red Rock Trail Rides** for a moonlit horseback ride through the countryside. Red Rock is located on a 365-acre working dairy farm on top of a ridge. Tonight you will ride through woods, over meadows, and on ridgetops on

A jug of wine . . . a loaf of bread . . . part of a picnic for two at Justin Trails Resort. Photo courtesy of Justin Trails Resort.

one of several three-mile trails. (Which one you take will depend on your skill level.) When you reach Red Rock, a rock ledge for which the farm is named, you'll dismount for a few moments to stretch your legs and view the valleys below. The entire trip will take about an hour and a half. Red Rock offers evening rides all the time; however, it is especially beautiful to ride by the moonlight on the evenings leading up to a full moon. Be sure to make your reservations for the evening and moonlit rides by 5:30 p.m. on the day of the ride.

## Day Three

### ୧ MORNING

After lounging through breakfast and checking out of your cottage, drive about 20 miles south to the small town of Ontario, a popular canoe-launching site on the Kickapoo River. Take a leisurely canoe ride on a stretch of this scenic, twisty river. Depending on where you choose to launch, your trip can last anywhere from one hour and 40 minutes to almost six hours. Relax in the sunshine. Float past sandstone cliffs, listen for the Kentucky warbler, watch a trout jump, and try to spot wildflowers such as marsh marigolds and bloodroot. The river tends to be safe for novice canoe enthusiasts to navigate.

A number of canoe rental businesses are based in Ontario, among them the **Kickapoo Paddle Inn**, **Titanic Canoe Rental**, and **Mr. Duck's Canoe Rental**. Most are clustered around Highways 33 and 133. If you brought along your own canoe, launch it at **Wildcat Mountain State Park**, just south of Ontario off Highway 33.

After your trip downriver you should have worked up two hearty appetites. Complete your trip with a meal at **Badger Crossing Pub and Eatery in Cashton**, west of Ontario. This casual, railroad-themed restaurant cooks up burgers such as the olive and Swiss burger and sandwiches such as the turkey Swiss Reuben. Locals love it for pizzas like Northern Express, which is topped with pepperoni, Canadian bacon, and mozzarella.

## FOR MORE INFORMATION

**Elroy-Sparta State Trail**
(608) 463-7109
www.elroy-sparta-trail.org

**Greater Tomah Area Chamber of Commerce and Convention and Visitor Bureau**
805 Superior Avenue, Tomah
(608) 372-2166 or (800) 94-TOMAH
www.tomahwisconsin.com

**Sparta Area Chamber of Commerce and Sparta Depot**
111 Milwaukee Avenue, Sparta
(608) 269-4123 or (888) 540-8434

**Sparta Convention and Visitor Bureau**
201 W. Oak Street, Sparta
(608) 269-2453 or (800) 354-2453
www.bike-me.com

**Warrens Cranberry Festival**
402 Pine Street, Warrens
(608) 378-4200

## ATTRACTIONS AND RECREATION

**Cranberry Country Antiques Mall**
I-94 and Highway 21, Tomah
(608) 372-7853
or (888) 757-0044
Pick up a bicycle map of Warrens here.

**Cranberry Expo Museum**
28388 County Road EW, Warrens

(608) 378-4878
www.cranberryexpo.com

**Kickapoo Paddle Inn Restaurant and Canoe Rental**
Highway 33, Ontario
(608) 337-4726

**Mr. Duck's Canoe Rental**
Highways 133 and 31, Ontario
(608) 337-4711

**Natural Scentsations**
123 N. Water Street, Sparta
(877) 970-3636

**Out Spokin' Adventures**
409 N. Court Street, Sparta
(800) 493-2453
www.outspokinadventures.com

**Red Rock Trail Rides**
13597 Katydid Avenue, Sparta
(608) 823-7865
Open daily year-round. Horseback riding is offered spring through fall, and horse-drawn bobsled rides are offered in the winter.

**Rex Moseley's Fruit and Vegetable Farm**
23933 Cortland Avenue, Warrens
(608) 378-4543

**Sparta Floral and Greenhouse**
636 E. Montgomery Street, Sparta
(608) 269-4141

**Speeds Bicycle Shop**
1126 John Street, Sparta
(608) 269-2315
www.speedsbike.com

**Titanic Canoe Rental**
Highway 131, Ontario
(608) 337-4551
www.titaniccanoerental.com

**Upstage Review Theatre Company**
Jackson Chevrolet Building
518 E. Wisconsin Street, Sparta
(608) 269-7247
www.upstagereview.org

**Wildcat Mountain State Park**
E13660 Highway 33, Ontario
(608) 337-4775
www.dnr.state.wi.us

## LODGING

**Justin Trails Resort**
7452 Kathryn Avenue, Sparta
(608) 269-4522 or (800) 488-4521
www.justintrails.com
Rooms are from $85.

**Percheron Paradise**
**Romantic Hideaway**
12833 County Road XX, Norwalk
(608) 366-1212
www.percheronparadise.com
Bungalows and chalets are from $175.

## DINING AND NIGHTLIFE

**Back Door Café**
1223 Front Street, Cashton
(608) 654-5950 or (888) 322-5494
www.backdoor.net
Open year-round for dinner Tuesday
through Saturday. Reservations
are required for dinner.
Call for lunch hours.

**Badger Crossing Pub and Eatery**
909 Front Street, Cashton
(608) 654-5706
Open year-round for lunch
and dinner daily.

**Cranberry Cabin Café**
212 Market Street, Warrens
(608) 378-4144
Open daily for breakfast and lunch.

**Gina's Pies Are Square**
400 Main Street, Wilton
(608) 435-6541
Hours vary per season.

# CHAPTER FOURTEEN

# Cruising the
# Saint Croix Riverway

For couples who cherish spending time surrounded by water, trees, prairie, and sky (as well as each other), a getaway to the Saint Croix River region will be the ultimate retreat. Designated a National Scenic Riverway in the late 1960s, the Saint Croix River winds through picturesque rolling hills and steep bluffs in far northwestern Wisconsin. It is home to eagles, turtles, and songbirds as well as canoeists and campers. The approximately 250-mile-long National Scenic Riverway begins with the Namekagon River north of Cable, which joins the Saint Croix River near Danbury and continues as the Saint Croix River south to Prescott, where it meets the Mississippi River. This getaway centers on the Upper Saint Croix River and the town of Saint Croix Falls to the south, a former lumber town where you can now pamper yourselves with a Swedish massage after a morning of canoeing, and Grantsburg to the south, where the expansive Crex Meadows Wildlife Area attracts birds (and birders) from all over.

Expect to spend a lot of time outdoors on this trip. Your weekend will be packed with adventures, but the two of you should be able find plenty of time for reflection and relaxation during a quiet canoe ride or early morning hike along the river. Spend an evening riding through the countryside in a 1910 piano box surrey. Take in views of the river while dining in a vintage train car. And consider roughing it in one of the national forest campsites along the river, where the two of you can fall asleep to the sounds of whippoorwills calling and wolves howling.

## Day One
### ⚘ MORNING

Begin your visit to the region with a trek through **Wisconsin Interstate State Park**, Wisconsin's first state park. With 12 trails in varying lengths from almost half a mile to 1.6 miles, the park attracts hikers from all around who make a

View of the Saint Croix River from Interstate State Park.

day of exploring the rocky ledges, canyons, creek beds, and shores of Lake O' the Dalles. Start with a walk along the popular Pothole Trail, a loop atop a bluff that affords you views of the river and rock climbers scaling cliffs across the river at Minnesota Interstate State Park. From the Pothole Trail, try the Echo Canyon Trail, which dips into an extinct riverbed and cool canyon (you'll be glad you chose this trail on a humid day), or the half-mile Summit Rock Trail, which leads you up into the high bluffs. Be careful with trekking through the park. Most trails are uneven and follow steep terrain, so leave your high heels at home. For those of you unused to climbing up stone stairs or through rocky ravines, you'll be happy to know there are plenty of benches for the two of you to catch your breath, snap photos, and rest in each other's arms.

For lunch, drive to Osceola, a few miles south of the state park, and have a seat in **Not Just a Café**, a casual place serving breakfast all day (great waffles and omelets) and soup and sandwiches, such as roast beef, during lunchtime.

### ↜ AFTERNOON

This afternoon you and your traveling partner can exercise, sightsee and share several quiet moments together surrounded by nature. From Osceola, drive north a few miles on Highway 35 to the Polk County Information Center in Saint Croix Falls where you can park your car and hop on your bicycles for a ride up the **Gandy Dancer Trail**. The crushed-limestone trail, a former railroad grade, winds for 98 miles from Saint Croix Falls to Superior, through Polk County and Burnett County, weaving past county and city parks, lake beaches, and museums. Take the afternoon to bike to and from the first town of Centuria (about 4.5 miles each way). Although the trail isn't difficult or too steep, you'll find the trip back to Saint Croix Falls fairly easy as you coast down a slight grade.

After your bicycle ride, you should be ready to spend some time resting in your love nest for the next few days. For quiet views of the river valley, book a room at the **Saint Croix River Inn** or the Croixwood, both in Osceola. For a more secluded, private hideaway, look into the Wissahickon on the outskirts of Saint Croix Falls.

The Saint Croix River Inn is located above the river within walking distance of Cascade Falls and antiques shops. Inside the 80-year-old stone home, seven guest rooms feature Jacuzzi whirlpool bathtubs. (You'll be thankful for these tubs tomorrow evening after your day of canoeing and hiking.) Two other pluses: no children will be running up and down the hallways (no kids allowed in this B&B), and the innkeepers have arranged little tables outside on the terrace creating spots to watch the sun set and the boats cruise by. Ask the innkeepers to arrange for a vase of roses, box of truffles, or bottle of champagne to be placed in your room prior to your arrival.

At the **Croixwood**, located south of downtown Osceola, the rule is couples only. This translates to suites with king beds, two-person bathtubs, private decks overlooking the river, and gas fireplaces. After you check in, your hosts will serve you appetizers such as shrimp and a cheese plate and drinks. Choose from the rich, gold-hued Moroccan suite or the cool, white Caribbean suite.

You'll have to drive a few miles north of Saint Croix Falls and down a long, sandy driveway to reach the **Wissahickon Farms Country Inn**. Here you'll camp out in a cabin built as a replica of a frontier store. It's furnished with a four-poster bed, whirlpool bathtub, and kitchen.

## EVENING

Because fine-dining options are limited in Osceola and Saint Croix Falls, you'll have to drive about 30 minutes west to the town of Amery or northwest to Balsam Lake for tonight's dinner. Both these drives are scenic and the towns inviting and quiet.

To reach Amery, meander along Rustic Road 28. (Watch for turtles crossing the road.) Amery, rightly called the "city of lakes," is surrounded by Pike, North Twin, and South Twin Lakes and the Apple River. Depending on what time you prefer to eat dinner, stop by the shores of North Twin Lake before or after your meal to watch the sunset. In Amery dine at **The Experience**, a small dining room located behind the Amery Inn, a casual bar and grill on Main Street. The Experience is a real find. The waitstaff whips up Caesar salads at your table, and cooks prepare rare entrées such as elk porterhouse. For dessert yield to your longings for chocolate and feed each other fruit dipped in white-chocolate fondue.

Your other option for dinner is driving to Balsam Lake, another small lake town. (But steer clear of the place saddled with the unfortunate name of Loveless Lake, just southwest of Balsam Lake.) In Balsam Lake, the **Indianhead Supper Club** serves refreshing entrées such as jambalaya and apple Brie chicken in a rustic, lodge setting. Have a seat near the window and lean into each other as a pianist strikes up tunes.

After dinner treat your date to a show at the **Saint Croix Art Barn** in Osceola or the **Saint Croix Festival Theatre** in Saint Croix Falls. In addition to exhibiting traveling art shows, the Saint Croix Art Barn hosts visiting bluegrass musicians, contemporary dance troupes, and community theater productions. As the name implies, the intimate theater is housed in a restored, century-old dairy barn. The Saint Croix Festival Theatre, a professional company, produces comedies, dramas, and musicals, such as the Victorian comedy *Engaged!* and Shakespeare's *Much Ado About Nothing.* Hang around after the show and share a slice of cherry pie or other sweet treat at the Mezzanine, the theater's café.

During the summer, stop by Mill Pond Park in downtown Osceola for free music concerts held Thursday evenings in June and July. Bring a blanket, lie together on the grass or kick off your shoes and ask, "May I have this dance?" Complete your day by arranging an evening surrey or Amish buggy ride through the property and nature preserve surrounding the Wissahickon Inn in Saint Croix Falls. (This service is also available to couples not staying there.) During the cool months bundle up for a ride in a 1913 cutter sleigh or bobsled.

View of the Saint Croix River from Interstate State Park.

# Day Two

## MORNING

If you stay at the Croixwood or Saint Croix River Inn, expect a full breakfast served to you. If you are staying at Wissahickon, whip up pancakes or eggs in the cabin's kitchen and deliver breakfast in bed to your sweetheart.

---

## CHARMING HUDSON

Historic Third Street in the Saint Croix River town of Hudson, 40 miles south of Saint Croix Falls, is lined with one grand home after the other. If you love Victorian architecture and antiques from that time period, check into the Phipps Inn, a grand old Queen Anne on Third Street. The master suite features a screened-in porch with a view of the Saint Croix. For another perspective of the river, try the Willow room on the third floor. You can lounge in the double-whirlpool bathtub and peer through the windows down at the river below. The Phipps is great for couples; innkeepers can honor your special requests such as providing flower bouquets or boxes of chocolate. More information is available from Phipps Inn, 1005 Third Street, Hudson, (715) 386-0800 or (888) 865-9388.

---

After you and your sweetheart have filled up on fresh berries, muffins, or eggs, drive north from Saint Croix Falls about 25 miles to Grantsburg, where you will launch your canoe or kayak trip on the Upper Saint Croix River. The Upper Saint Croix, from Saint Croix Falls to Danbury, where the river meets the Namekagon River, tends to draw more canoeists, whereas the Lower Saint Croix River, from Saint Croix Falls to Prescott, is wide and attracts boaters and anglers casting for trout and sturgeon. Although you have a number of options where you can canoe, consider a three- to four-hour trip from Nelson's Landing (located north of Grantsburg) to the landing at Highway 70. During the 13-mile river trip you'll pass over Class I rapids. You don't have to be an expert paddler to canoe the Saint Croix; however, be aware that the entire trip won't be over flat water. As you paddle past the tree-lined riverbanks, watch for bald eagles heading to their nests or otters slipping into the water. Drift along the river and let the current or your significant other do the work for a spell. **Wild River Outfitters**, based in Grantsburg, rents canoes and kayaks (tandems, too) and offers a shuttle service.

If you already own a canoe or kayak, you can still launch at Nelson's and disembark at Highway 70. Wild River will pick you up or drop you off even if you don't rent canoes or kayaks from them.

Your other option is renting canoes from **Quest Canoe Rental** in Saint Croix Falls and paddling three hours from Saint Croix Falls to Osceola or five to six hours from Saint Croix Falls to William O'Brien State Park in Marine-on-Saint Croix in Minnesota. Whichever route you choose, you will paddle your way through an unspoiled part of the state, past steep sandstone cliffs, around sandy islands, and over rapids.

When your canoeing trip comes to an end at the Highway 70 landing, look for the Sandrock Cliffs Trail on the Wisconsin side. Follow the rustic foot trail along the Saint Croix River by the riverbank and up along a sandstone ridge toward primitive campsites set among lofty pine trees. If you plan to forego staying at an inn or B&B, stake a claim on one of these scenic campsites. Otherwise, pack a picnic lunch and take in the scenery from a spot at the top of the cliff or near the riverbank. (If you choose to picnic, pick up supplies that morning at the supermarket on Highway 70 in Grantsburg, a few miles from Wild River Outfitters.)

## ᐒ AFTERNOON

After your lunch, relax behind the wheel of your car and take in the beauty of **Crex Meadows**, located on the outskirts of Grantsburg. This sprawling prairie and wetland preserve is home to trumpeter swans, sandhill cranes, Blanding's turtles, and more. The easiest and quickest way to explore the 30,000-acre state wildlife-management area is by following the self-guided auto tour. If you follow the tour for the complete 24 miles, expect it to take about an hour and a half to complete. (You'll probably drive between 15 and 20 miles per hour.) Of course this journey will take longer if you plan to stop and read the interpretive signs and look for wildlife.

Follow the auto tour around the park taking time to stop at the rest area by Reisinger Lake. Here you'll find picnic tables set up on a hill overlooking the lake. As you stretch your legs, nibble on some snacks and sip some juice, watch ducks diving into the lake, and listen for the loons calling to one another. The staff has carved a few short walking trails throughout the park, such as behind the visitor center, near Phantom Lake, the rest area, and by the North Fork Flowage. These grassy trails are not groomed regularly, so if you plan to walk them during the summer, be sure to wear pants or a lot of bug repellent. But these walks are a great way to discover a pair of fox kits playing with each other, a Karner blue butterfly in flight, or a cluster of lupine.

On your way back to the inn, pay a visit to **Majestic Falls**, a day spa housed in a Victorian home in Saint Croix Falls. If you haven't de-stressed yet already, a visit here will relax and refresh the both of you, reawaken your senses and get you in the mood for a quiet, relaxing evening together. Make appointments for a deep-tissue sports massage or traditional Swedish massage to loosen those muscles you used this morning. Although you won't be able to receive the treatments in the same room, one of you can shop for bubble bath, candles, and other romantic bath supplies to use tonight in your hot tub. While your partner is receiving his or her massage, sink into the couch before a fireplace or on a chair on the spacious porch.

Then, if you're celebrating a special occasion or want to find favor with your traveling partner, stop by **Forget Me Not Floral** in Saint Croix Falls to pick up a bouquet of flowers, then make a trip to **Loni's River Gifts and Candy Bouquet** for French truffles.

## ROMANTIC CAMPING

Make this romantic weekend a true getaway and camp out at one of the many remote, primitive campsites along the Saint Croix River. Backpackers will find Sandrock Cliffs Campground off the beaten path, miles from Highway 70 and any cars. Sites are located at the top of a ridge overlooking the river, beneath whistling pine trees. Because the sites are walk-in, with no electrical hookups, you won't hear cars pulling in and other campers setting up in the middle of the night. Instead, you'll listen to the owls and ospreys calling and the campfire crackling.

An option for those who prefer running water on-site or electrical hookups for their RVs is the Saint Croix Campground, located just south of Highway 70 at the Saint Croix River. The sites there are wooded, with a lot of space in between for privacy. A hiking trail also runs through the campground.

## EVENING

Tucked deep in the piney woods on the outskirts of a teeny town called Lewis, **Seven Pines Lodge** provides an ideal setting for romantic couples looking for a quiet place to dine. The 1903 lodge, which overlooks a babbling trout stream, is set within a 60-acre estate and surrounded by white pines that are more than three hundred years old. The former fly-fishing lodge, listed on the National Register of Historic Places, has been renovated and designed in warm arts and crafts style. But don't come here just to take a look at the estate. People, especially those romantically inclined, love Seven Pines for its four-course, candlelit dinners. The menu changes nightly, but the event (it's more than just a meal) typically includes a choice of fresh rainbow trout caught from the stream running through the property. Other dishes served may be duck cakes with shiitake cream sauce, mixed greens or vegetables grown on the estate, and desserts such as crème brûlée and chocolate truffle cheesecake. Top-shelf liquors and wines are available.

After dinner (which may last for two hours) take your sweetheart by the hand and wander through the property, stopping to kiss on the little bridge over the creek.

## *Day Three*

### 🐾 MORNING

For anyone feeling a little achy from all the canoeing, bicycling, and hiking these past two days, you will be pleased to know that your last day in the Saint Croix River region will not entail strenuous activity. After checking out of your room, stroll through downtown Osceola, pausing to browse through the Old Mill Shoppes on Main Street, which are stocked with antiques and crafts for sale. Next, check out Cascade Falls at Wilke Park, an observation deck off Main Street. If the mood strikes, follow the steps down to Osceola Creek and to the Saint Croix River. Back up, cross Cascade Street, and have a seat in the gazebo in Mill Pond Park by the creek. (Feeling romantic? Of course, you are. Then re-create the gazebo scene from *The Sound of Music* when Liesal and Rolf danced and revealed their true feelings for each other.)

View of the Saint Croix River from Interstate State Park.

Next, drive to the Osceola train depot just north of downtown for a brunch train ride with the **Osceola & Saint Croix Valley Railway** through the river valley. During the 2.5-hour trip you'll ride along the ridge above the Saint Croix River, past miniature waterfalls, through forests full of oak and pine trees and ferns, past wetlands, and through the hills. You'll cross the river and wave to anglers in their boats while you are seated in the first-class passenger car dining on eggs, potatoes, and baked goodies. If the train does not offer a brunch ride while you are in town (they are usually held the first and third Sundays in June, July, August, and September), opt for the two-hour ride from Osceola to Marine, Minnesota, which offers you similar views of the river and countryside.

## ☙ AFTERNOON

Complete your trip by spending an easy afternoon floating down the Apple River, which flows into the Saint Croix River. Rent a tube at one of several outfitters (Float-Rite Park or Apple River Camping) in Somerset, about 14 miles south of Osceola.

After your float down the river, indulge in another summertime tradition: order ice cream cones at Brown's Ice Cream or blended coffee drinks at **Zodiac Coffee** on Somerset's Main Street.

### ☙ FOR MORE INFORMATION

**Burnett County Tourism**
7410 County Road K, Siren
(715) 349-7411

**Osceola Area Chamber of Commerce**
P.O. Box 251, Osceola
(715) 755-3300 or (800) 947-0581
www.riversrailsandtrails.org

**Polk County Information Center**
710 Highway 35, St. Croix Falls
(715) 483-1410 or (800) 222-7655
www.polkcountytourism.com

**Somerset Chamber of Commerce**
(For information on inner tubing the Apple River)
(715) 247-3366

**Saint Croix Falls Chamber of Commerce**
106 S. Washington Street, St. Croix Falls
(715) 483-3580
www.stcroixfallschamber.com

**Saint Croix National Scenic Riverway**
401 N. Hamilton Street (P.O. Box 708), St. Croix Falls

(715) 483-3284
www.nps.gov/sacn

**St. Croix Valley Regional Tourism Alliance**
www.saintcroixriver.com

### ☙ ATTRACTIONS AND RECREATION

**Crex Meadows**
102 East Crex Avenue, Grantsburg
(715) 463-2896
www.crexmeadows.org
The visitor center is open year-round, 8:00 a.m. to 4:30 p.m. weekdays and 10:00 a.m. to 4:00 p.m. on weekends. You can take the auto tour through the Meadows any time. Free admission.

**Forget Me Not Floral**
133 N. Washington Street, St. Croix Falls
(715) 483-5695

**Gandy Dancer Trail**
For information call the Burnett County Tourism office or Polk County Information Center.

**Loni's River Gifts and Candy Bouquet**
125 S. Washington Street, St. Croix Falls
(715) 483-1936

**Majestic Falls Aveda Concept Day Retreat and Spa**
120 Maryland Street East, St. Croix Falls
(715) 483-3175 or (877) 232-8332

**Osceola & Saint Croix Valley Railway**
Highway 35 and Depot Road, Osceola
(715) 755-3570 or (800) 711-2591
www.trainride.org
The railroad offers Sunday morning brunch trains June through September as well as many other train rides throughout the year. Call for times.

**Quest Canoe and Bicycle Rentals and Shuttles**
Highways 8 and 35 South, Saint Croix Falls One block north of the entrance to Wisconsin Interstate State Park
(715) 483-1692

**Saint Croix Art Barn**
1040 Oak Ridge Drive, Osceola
(715) 294-ARTS (2787)
www.stcroixartbarn.com

**Saint Croix Festival Theatre**
210 N. Washington Street
(P.O. Box 801), St. Croix Falls
(715) 483-3387
www.festivaltheatre.org

**Wild River Outfitters**
15177 Highway 70, Grantsburg
(715) 463-2254
www.wildriverpaddling.com

**Wisconsin Interstate State Park**
Highway 35, St. Croix Falls
(715) 483-3747

### LODGING
**Croixwood on the Saint Croix**
421 Ridge Road, Osceola

(715) 294-2894 or (866) 670-3838
www.croixwood.net
Rooms are from $195.

**Saint Croix River Inn**
305 River Street, Osceola
(715) 294-4248 or (800) 645-8820
www.stcroixriverinn.com
Rooms are from $100.

**Wissahickon Farms Country Inn**
2263 Maple Drive, St. Croix Falls
(715) 483-3986
www.wissainn.com
The cabin rents for $125 per night.

### DINING AND NIGHTLIFE
**The Experience**
337 S. Keller Avenue, Amery
(715) 268-2637
Open for dinner Tuesday through Saturday.

**Indianhead Supper Club**
107 Indianhead Road, Balsam Lake
(715) 485-3359
Open for dinner Wednesday through Monday.

**Not Just a Café**
102 Second Street, Osceola
(715) 755-3663
Open daily for breakfast and lunch, plus occasional dinner buffets.

**Seven Pines Lodge**
1098 340th Avenue, Frederic
(715) 653-2323
www.sevenpineslodge.com
Open for dinner Tuesday through Sunday, May through October. Reservations required.

**Zodiac Coffee**
242 Main Street, Somerset
(715) 247-2477
Open Tuesday through Sunday. Call for hours.

# CHAPTER FIFTEEN

# Love Springs Eternal in
# Chippewa Falls

Located in a quiet part of the state on the Chippewa River, the town of Chippewa Falls does not have traffic jams or overpriced hotels and eateries. It's a friendly place where you can still find an ice cream parlor downtown, a café where locals meet for coffee, and old-fashioned festivals like Christmas parades and Easter egg hunts. A historic town built to serve the local lumber industry, Chippewa Falls is famous for its spring water. (Leinenkugel Brewery, which was first called Spring Brewery, used the town's spring water to make beer.) Legend has it that the Native American chieftain Hiawatha charmed his love Minnehaha after drinking the spring water here.

The pace during this getaway is slow and easy. Take plenty of time to talk and get to know each other or reacquaint yourselves. Stop and smell the roses, literally hundreds of them, near Marshall Park. Float down the Chippewa River in a canoe. See the countryside in a restored stagecoach.

An ideal spot to spend this getaway is in a romantic B&B a few miles from town on Lake Wissota, near a state bicycle trail and a state park. Here you can wake up to the sun and walk down to the dock with your cups of coffee, and lounge in the evening with glasses of wine. Although we can't guarantee that your companion will fall in love with you after drinking Chippewa water, it is likely that the two of you will come away from this getaway much more relaxed.

## Day One
### 🦎 MORNING

Because Chippewa Falls is well known for its spring water, perhaps your first stop should be at the historic spring house by the Chippewa Spring Water head-quarters. Although the site is not remarkable (it's just a little white house), the story behind the spring will interest romantics. As memorialized by poet Henry Wadsworth Longfellow, the story goes that the Native American chief Hiawatha believed the spring's water was a love potion with which he was able to woo his love, Minnehaha. Also, according to local lore, politician and businessman

A tranquil spot for lovebirds in Irvine Park, Chippewa Falls.

Thaddeus Pound swore that drinking the water restored his health. You can't actually get inside the little hut to see the spring except during special events, such as Chippewa Falls' Pure Water Days, an annual heritage festival held in August, but it makes for a nice stop on your way into town.

After your visit to the spring, drive to **Irvine Park**, a 300-acre park that feels like a county or state park because of its many features. The park boasts picnic grounds, a band shell, a pavilion, hiking trails, a pond, and a zoo. From the park's main entrance, follow the scenic drive through the woods and above Duncan Creek (away from the crowds of schoolchildren that tend to congregate around the zoo) toward the top of the park called Flag Hill. Stop by the overlook that provides views of Glen Loch, a dam built in 1875, and listen to the rushing waters of the creek for a few minutes. There's a footpath at the overlook that weaves through the woods and craggy ravine. A number of quiet hiking trails, totaling about two miles in length, wind through this part of the park. Set off on a peaceful hike through this trail. Or, access one of the trails that spark your interest along the scenic drive. You'll find occasional turnoffs for parking.

Next, walk across Bridgewater Avenue to the rose and lily gardens near Marshall Park. This may be a good spot to get down on one knee if you're thinking of proposing. It's also a nice time to give your sweetheart a squeeze and a smooch.

For lunch dine in the historic **James Sheeley House** in downtown Chippewa Falls. Listed on the National Register of Historic Places, it was built in 1884 as a boarding house, restaurant, and bar for the many loggers working in the region. Climb the stairs to the upstairs dining room where you'll find a small number of tables arranged as though you were stepping in to a private home. Find a table in the cozy alcove. The lunch menu consists mainly of sandwiches—prime rib and chicken breast—plus salads and wraps.

## AFTERNOON

After your meal, walk over to the visitor center and pick up a brochure outlining the historic sites in downtown Chippewa Falls. A number of businesses started years ago are still run by the same families, such as **Olson's Ice Cream Parlor and Deli**, a local favorite since the 1940s, and Sokup's Market, established in 1891 by Joseph Sokup. Walk through the downtown for a bit, stopping at Olson's for ice cream cones.

From downtown, walk or drive to the **Cook-Rutledge Mansion**, an Italianate and Victorian home surrounded by gardens and a spacious lawn. Built in 1873, the home was purchased in 1887 by a local lumber baron, Edward Rutledge, whose wife reportedly had always wanted to live in a castle. (Ah, to live in a time when husbands would purchase homes as gifts for their wives.) Though not a

The charming gardens at the Cook-Rutledge Mansion in Chippewa Falls.

The atrium of the Pleasant View Bed and Breakfast, with a view of Lake Wissota and, with the aid of a telescope, the stars.

castle, the mansion comes pretty close. Tour this magnificent house and all its awesome architectural features such as parquet floors, crystal chandeliers, oak staircase, and stained glass window. After your visit inside, be sure to spend plenty of time lazing in the picturesque garden.

Now, head east out of town to Lake Wissota and **Pleasant View B&B**, your haven for the next two nights. Pleasant View is a spacious, modern ranch with walk-out basement. (The owners, Jeanine and Mike Adams, live in their own apartment downstairs, and you feel as if you have the place to your selves.) After walking through the entrance, the first room you will notice is the sunny atrium, which provides a spectacular view of the lake and western sky. Be sure to try out the telescope tonight. Of the five rooms available, couples will fall in love with the Wind and Waves Room, a light, nautical-themed room with a four-poster bed, whirlpool bathtub, and an entrance to the deck, or the Hidden Harbor Room, a spacious suite with its own patio facing the lake.

After checking in, head outside to the expansive deck, which beckons for you to pull up some patio chairs and unwind together. After your break, stretch your legs and walk across the sprawling lawn and down to the dock. Nestle on the bench for more R & R.

If you choose to stay in downtown Chippewa Falls, try **McGilvray's Victorian B&B** located in a historic residential neighborhood. The 1892 house was modeled after a home exhibited during the Chicago World's Fair. It has quiet sitting areas on the wide front porch and in the cozy screened-in porch on the side of the house. Book the Rose Room, which features a private porch, clawfoot bathtub, and fainting couch. Or try the Room with a View, which also features a private porch. Innkeeper Melanie Berg adds romantic touches to the rooms, such as making sure there are fresh flowers and leaving a bottle of wine for the two of you.

After you check in, cuddle on one of McGilvray's porches with some complimentary tea.

## EVENING

Tonight take your date to the theater. Drive about 30 miles from the B&B to the outskirts of Eau Claire for dinner and a theater show at **Fanny Hill** in Eau Claire. Even if theater is not your thing, plan to have dinner at Fanny Hill. Arrive early and stay late to enjoy the landscaped grounds, which feature flower beds, walkways with benches, and views of the Chippewa River. Hang out on the deck underneath the tree lit up at night. If you decide to eat dinner and see a show, you can take your meal in the dining room overlooking the river valley or in the theater. (It's more scenic if you dine in the restaurant.) The chef cooks up all kinds of chicken, steak, pasta, and fish entrées. Two specials that are perfect for dining couples are the chateaubriand for two and the roasted rack of lamb for two. Other tantalizing options include an appetizer of prosciutto with mango and cilantro and an entrée of hazelnut-encrusted scallops.

The theater, which debuted in 1978 with, appropriately enough, Neil Simon's *Last of the Red Hot Lovers*, stages such well-known musicals as *My Fair Lady*. Visiting entertainers, such as country music singers, also perform in the space throughout the year.

If you like what you see at Fanny Hill and plan to tie the knot, or are thinking about it, the compound hosts outdoor weddings. There's also a Victorian-style inn on-site with guest rooms featuring amenities like king beds, whirlpools, and fireplaces.

After the show, stop by the atrium room in Pleasant View B&B and engage in some stargazing before you tuck in for the night.

## Day Two

## MORNING

This morning you will find a wake-up tray outside your bedroom door at Pleasant View filled with coffee, juice, and muffins. Take the tray to the patio or down to the dock and sit in the sun for a spell. Chances are you won't be awakened by WaveRunners or Sea-Doos. Lake Wissota tends to be quiet compared to other larger lakes in the state, such as Green Lake or Geneva Lake.

When you walk back to the house, Mike and Jeanine will have prepared a comprehensive breakfast in the sunny dining room, consisting of dishes such as potato quiche or strawberry-banana French toast Fill up. (You will also be served a grand breakfast at McGilvray's.)

You'll need the energy today as you bicycle the **Old Abe State Trail** and canoe or kayak the Chippewa River, which flows into Lake Wissota. The Adamses have bicycles, canoes, and kayaks available to guests. Try this: bicycle the seven miles or so north to the town of Jim Falls, then meet Mike at the landing on the Chippewa River, where he will help you launch your canoe or kayak. Spend the rest of your time paddling down the river. The bicycle ride will take about an hour; the paddle down the Chippewa will take about two and a half hours.

Even though the hearty breakfast may sustain you until dinner, you might want to pack a picnic lunch of sandwiches and fruit, water, and juice. You can pick up supplies at the supermarket in downtown Chippewa Falls.

If you choose to stay at McGilvray's, you might still be able to rent canoes from the Adamses, who also rent canoes and bicycles to visitors. You can also rent canoes at **Lake Wissota State Park** and explore the waters of Lake Wissota.

## ⤳ AFTERNOON

After your biking and canoeing trip, drive to nearby **Lake Wissota State Park**. It's just down the road from Pleasant View; if you're not too tired, you can bike there. Take a leisurely stroll along the Jack Pines or Lake Trail, which winds along Lake Wissota, through prairie and woodlands. Lounge in each other's arms on one of the many benches along the trail, or spread a blanket at the sand beach.

## ⤳ EVENING

The Adamses and the staff at **High Shores Supper Club** will arrange for a pontoon boat to pick you up from Pleasant View's boat landing to take you on

## SKIING BY CANDLELIGHT

⤳ On Valentine's Day, the staff at many state parks, trails, and forests organize candle- and torch-lit cross-country skiing evenings, complete with bonfires and thermoses of steaming hot cider waiting for you at the end of the trail. Many of the state parks mentioned in this guide, such as Interstate Park, are open in the evening for these kinds of events throughout the winter season. In fact, depending on weather conditions, more than a dozen parks will host evening skiing or similar events throughout the winter. For example, Merrick State Park in Fountain City transforms the frozen Mississippi River backwater into a rink where people can skate and ski by candlelight. For more information, contact the Wisconsin Department of Natural Resources, which compiles a calendar of events. You can reach the main office at (608) 873-9695 or www.dnr.state.wi.us

a cruise of the lake, rambling Paint Creek, and eventually to the restaurant. Sip on champagne served to you by the cruise staff. Once you arrive at High Shores, walk arm-in-arm up the hill through the manicured gardens and have a seat at a white-tablecloth, candlelit table in the lake-view dining room. Arrange to have a carafe filled with wine and a plate of shrimp cocktail waiting for you. Take your time ordering; there are more than 50 entrées to choose from, from the traditional Wisconsin entrée of fried lake perch to the more intriguing Cajun alligator served broiled or fried.

After your meal take your drinks outside to the deck and share a dessert while listening to the water rush over miniature waterfalls.

Depending on how long you relax at High Shores, try to attend a music concert or theater performance at the **Heyde Center for Arts** in Chippewa Falls. Housed in a former high school, the center showcases folk musicians, ragtime players, brass quintets, community theater productions, and art exhibits.

## Day Three

### ɚ MORNING

Greet the dawn this morning by taking your breakfast tray outside and basking in the warm sunshine for a few moments.

After you finish your superb breakfast and check out of the B&B, drive about 15 minutes to rural Cadott (east of Chippewa Falls) for a leisurely morning stagecoach ride with **Cabin Ridge Rides**. (During the winter they switch to sleigh rides.) You will traverse through 400 acres of woods and fields and along the babbling Paint Creek. Again, if you like what you see here and are engaged (or about to be), consider tying the knot here. They've got a wedding chapel and lodge available for rental.

For lunch drive to the **Bake n' Brew**, a casual café and coffee shop in downtown Chippewa Falls. Sandwiches are basic—turkey or ham—but the drink and sweets menus are extensive. Buy your sweetie a fruit smoothie or flavored coffee, and indulge in rich cheesecake or buttery chocolate chip cookies.

### ɚ AFTERNOON

On your way out of town stop by **Bushel and a Peck** on County Road OO to pick strawberries, raspberries, or apples, depending on what fruit is in season. The farm is located on a ridge overlooking the Chippewa River valley. Be sure to browse the bakery to shop for caramel apples and fruit pies to take with you. Depending on which direction you are headed, you'll find a number of other fruit stands and farm markets in the countryside surrounding Chippewa Falls and Eau Claire, among them Klinger's on 132nd Street, where you can also purchase flowers and Christmas decorations, and Carlson's Orchard and Gallery in Eau Claire, where you can also browse for furniture and home decor accessories.

## 🦎 FOR MORE INFORMATION

**Chippewa Falls Area
Chamber of Commerce**
10 S. Bridge Street, Chippewa Falls
(715) 723-0331 or (866) 723-0340
www.chippewachamber.org

**Chippewa Valley Convention
and Visitor Bureau**
3625 Gateway Drive, Suite F, Eau Claire
(715) 831-2345 or (888) 523-FUNN
www.chippewavalley.net

## 🦎 ATTRACTIONS AND RECREATION

**Bushel and a Peck**
18444 County OO, Chippewa Falls
(715) 723-0133

**Cabin Ridge Rides**
4271 220th Street, Cadott
(715) 723-9537 or (715) 723-0960
www.cabinridgerides.com

**Cook-Rutledge Mansion**
505 W. Grand Avenue, Chippewa Falls
(715) 723-7181
Open June through August, Thursday
through Sunday, with tours at 2:00 p.m.
and 3:00 p.m. Admission fee.

**Heyde Center for Arts**
3 S. High St., Chippewa Falls
(715) 726-9000

**Irvine Park**
Bridgewater and Jefferson Avenues,
Chippewa Falls
Free admission.

**Lake Wissota State Park**
18127 County Road O,
Chippewa Falls
(715) 382-4574
www.dnr.state.wi.us
Admission fee.

**Old Abe State Trail**
Trail marker and parking at 97th
Avenue, at the junction of Counties S
and O, northwest of Chippewa Falls
(800) 866-6264
Trail passes are required for bicyclists,
in-line skaters, and horseback riders and
can be purchased at the Chippewa Falls
Visitor Center.

## 🦎 LODGING

**McGilvray's Victorian B&B**
312 West Columbia Street,
Chippewa Falls
(715) 720-1600 or (888) 324-1893
www.mcgilvraysbb.com
Rooms are from $79.

**Pleasant View B&B**
16649 96th Avenue, Chippewa Falls
(715) 382-4401 or (866) WISSOTA
(947-7682)
www.pleasantviewbb.com
Rooms are from $85.

## 🦎 DINING AND NIGHTLIFE

**Bake n' Brew Café & Coffee Shop**
117 N. Bridge Street,
Chippewa Falls
(715) 720-2360
Open for breakfast, lunch, and dinner
Monday through Saturday.

**Fanny Hill restaurant,
dinner theater, and Victorian inn**
3919 Crescent Avenue, Eau Claire
(715) 836-8184 or (800) 292-8026
www.fannyhill.com
Call for hours.

**High Shores Supper Club**
17985 County Road X, Chippewa Falls
(715) 723-9854
Open year-round for dinner Monday
through Saturday and for lunch and
dinner on Sunday.

**James Sheeley House**
236 W. River Street, Chippewa Falls
(715) 726-0561
Open for lunch and dinner Tuesday
through Saturday.

**Olson's Ice Cream Parlor and Deli**
611 N. Bridge Street, Chippewa Falls
(715) 723-4331
Call for hours.

# CHAPTER SIXTEEN

Ah, Wilderness:
# Canoe Bay and the Indianhead Region

Outside their bungalows, guests of the exclusive Canoe Bay resort in north-western Wisconsin have their own private wilderness. Set deep in the woods on a private lake near Chetek, Canoe Bay makes it difficult for the guests to run into each other—except during dinnertime at the lodge. It's an idyllic place for nature lovers—and, of course, just lovers—wanting quiet time together. This getaway is all about tranquility, and the resort makes for an ideal roman-tic getaway because it caters exclusively to couples and bars children and unan-nounced visitors.

The two of you can spend most of your time in your cottage lounging in the emperor-size bed (imagine a bed larger than a king), eating gourmet dishes, and reading and sunning yourselves on your private porch together. But don't forget to picnic in the woods, take the rowboat out onto the lake, and go for a leisurely bicycle ride and scenic drive through the region. Rental rates are steep at this resort, but if the two of you need some serious together time, this is the place to go. If you want to propose, this is the place to do it. If you want to rekin-dle the flames of romance, this is the place to reignite them. If you and your se-cret lover want to run away together, you'll find the privacy you need here. And if you aren't secret lovers, here's the chance to pretend you are.

## Day One
### ◦ MORNING
Because you won't be able to check in to your lodging until later in the after-noon, spend the morning exploring the region around Rice Lake and Chetek. Sometimes called the Indianhead region, this area contains plenty of simple lake-side resorts catering to families and anglers (which is why it may be surprising to some to find the classy, some may say chichi, Canoe Bay in the region).

The Tuscobia State Trail, near Rice Lake.

Get acquainted with the topography by bicycling or walking along the **Tuscobia State Trail**. On your way to the trail, which is located on the outskirts of Rice Lake, stop by a grocery store in town for picnic supplies. Then, pop in the **Village Dell & Wine Shop**, also in Rice Lake, for wine and cheese. Once you have stocked your backpacks or picnic baskets with refreshments, drive north of town a few miles to where the Tuscobia State Trail and Wild Rivers Trail meet, at County Road SS and Highway 53. Bring your bikes or slip on some hiking boots and make your way along the Tuscobia Trail; it tends to be a bit quieter than the Wild Rivers Trail, which follows Highway 53 for quite some time.

Like many state trails, the 74-mile Tuscobia is on a former railroad bed that served the logging and farming industry. It extends from Rice Lake to Park Falls. Parts of the trail are grass-covered, so leave your road bikes at home. It is fairly flat around Rice Lake, so don't expect any hard-core challenges. You will, however, pass by farmland, creeks, and the Brill River. Relax over your picnic whenever you feel the need to rest.

### ✿ AFTERNOON

After your bicycle ride or hike, drive about 15 to 20 miles south of Rice Lake to the small resort town of Chetek where a favorite pastime of residents and visitors is boating and fishing. To get there, bypass Highway 53 and take a more scenic route to Chetek from Rice Lake on Counties SS or M. On your way there, stop by **Mommsen's Produce Patch** off County Road SS for fresh fruits and veggies, such as strawberries and squash, depending on the season. Tour the stone barn and chase each other through the nine-acre maze (during the fall). Check out the catapult that launches pumpkins hundreds of feet away.

Your home for the next few nights will be **Canoe Bay**, a private luxury resort on Lake Wahdoon. Getting there (and leaving—you'll be tempted to prolong your stay) is not easy. The resort is situated about 10 miles from Chetek, through rolling hills and built way back in the piney woods. You're miles from the nearest town and cellular tower. Don't even think about bringing your laptops to catch up on a little bit of work or to check e-mail.

Depending on how much money you want to spend (and you can spend a lot), you can rent a room in the inn; choose one of the select, deluxe, or hillside cottages (attached, duplex-style buildings); stay in one of the stand-alone dream or lakeside cottages; or splurge on one of the sprawling Rattenbury or Edgewood cottages. There are a total of seven rooms and thirteen cottages for rent. Because it's a private resort and lake (and tours are given by appointment only) you won't find tourists moseying through the property or trying to get a glimpse of your cottage. All cottages are Prairie-style design with fieldstone fireplaces, furniture such as warm brown leather couches, whirlpools, and private decks.

## KISSING BY THE CASCADES

Big Manitou Falls has the distinction of being Wisconsin's highest waterfall. Located in Douglas County in the far northwest part of the state, Big Manitou is a thundering, 165-foot waterfall on the Black River. You and your companion can get up close and personal with the cascade by hiking along the half-mile-long Big Manitou Falls Trail. A few miles south of Big Manitou is Little Manitou Falls, a 30-foot waterfall. The falls are about 10 miles south of Superior, in Pattison State Park, 6294 Highway 35, (715) 399-3111, a facility with a beach at Interfalls Lake and secluded backpack campsites located 1.5 miles from the parking lot.

Those in search of some pampering will never want to leave the Lakeside Cottage, which contains a spa room with a wet and dry sauna, steam shower, Jacuzzi whirlpool bathtub, and elliptical trainer. To get as close as possible to the lake and swim area, stay in one of the lakeside cottages. Another option is the Rattenbury, designed by John Rattenbury of Taliesin Architects, which offers perhaps the best view of Lake Wahdoon, a cantilevered deck, huge fireplace and sitting area, and wet room shower.

Check in as early as possible to take advantage of all this resort has to offer. Because the two of you spent your morning walking or bicycling, why not spend the afternoon floating in the water? You and your sweetheart can lie out on the beach, paddle out to the swim raft, and doze in the sun under the trees.

Dining in the intimate wine cellar at Canoe Bay resort, near Chetek. Photo courtesy of Canoe Bay resort.

While you are out, arrange for staff to bring in a bouquet of roses or wildflowers to your cottage as a surprise for your companion. (Be sure to ask the staff to do this about five days in advance.)

Activities for this weekend getaway assume the two of you will stay overnight at Canoe Bay. However, if you cannot afford a getaway to Canoe Bay but would still like to explore the Rice Lake region, consider the **Hemlock Hide-A-Way Resort**, located north of town on Hemlock Lake. Rent the Lakeside cabin (it's 30 feet from the shoreline), which features a whirlpool bathtub and love seat. The resort also has rowboats and paddleboats available to guests. Hemlock Lake is not private, like Lake Wahdoon, but it is a quiet, no-wake lake.

## EVENING

To maintain that wonderful ambience of privacy and intimacy, have dinner in Canoe Bay's wine cellar. Although it is called a wine cellar, you will not be eating in a basement or cave underneath the inn. The classy, private room is just down the hall from the cozy lounge and main dining room. Imagine the two of you surrounded by thousands of bottles of wine. The menu for the multicourse meal changes daily, so you may not know until that morning what concoctions the chef will prepare for you. Do count on the staff preparing food made with organic ingredients, naturally raised beef and free-range chickens, locally farmed herbs and dairy products, and hand-harvested rice. A recent menu featured such items as butternut squash soup, rainbow trout, pork chop with a merlot sauce, and fruit mousse. Don't hold back. Order the extra cheese plate and sample a selection of divine organic cheeses.

Following your scrumptious dinner, walk over to the boathouse and take a rowboat onto the lake. Watch the moon rise; listen to loons and frogs singing to each other. If you are thinking of proposing, now would be a lovely moment.

Back at the cottage, spend some time on your private deck. Pop open a bottle of wine and lounge in the Adirondack chairs. Look up. Here's why you should nest in the Wisconsin North Woods, far from large cities or towns. Through the trees the two of you should be able to see countless stars.

# Day Two

## MORNING

A continental breakfast of seasonal fruit, assorted baked goods, juice, and coffee will be delivered to your cottage. If one of you prefers a heartier breakfast, order (for a fee) items such as wild blueberry buttermilk pancakes with Wisconsin maple syrup or smoked salmon, cream cheese, and capers on a bagel.

The two of you can relax on your deck for a spell, sipping freshly squeezed orange juice or rich coffee. After you finish your breakfast, be sure to order your picnic basket for lunch. No need to hoof it to the reception desk or call in the order, just check off what you want on an order sheet and place it in the breakfast basket. (The staff will pick it up for you.)

Next, walk over to the boathouse and pick out a canoe or set of kayaks. There are no forms to fill out or deposits you need to leave for the canoe. Just grab a boat and launch it. Take as much time as you want to glide around the small lake. Explore the little island. Pull into a little bay and kiss and dream away the morning.

When you return from your canoe or kayak trip, you'll find the picnic basket waiting for you on your porch. In it you'll uncover goodies such as mixed green salads, oatmeal cookies, and sandwiches such as roasted Angus beef on a rosemary kaiser roll or grilled vegetables with sun-dried tomato tapenade (spread) on grilled panini. Want a cheese plate for the afternoon and a bottle of wine? Go ahead and order those too.

## AFTERNOON

Depending on how motivated you are after your lunch (you may be tempted to nap on one of the chaise lounges on your deck), hike over to the lodge and browse through the comprehensive library. Curl up in one of the overstuffed chairs with a romance novel, mystery, or history book. Upstairs you'll find a workout room with a view of the woods, but you may want to spend your time cuddling on the couch with your book or magazine in one hand and your other arm around your sweetheart.

Because this getaway is not about holding back or denying yourselves any possible pampering experiences, order massages. A masseuse will come to your cottage and treat you to private massages. It's best to order the massages in advance.

The Red Barn Theater, near Rice Lake.

After the massages, take advantage of every spalike feature in your cottage: the two-person shower, the whirlpool, and the wet/dry sauna.

## EVENING

If you are staying at Canoe Bay, change into evening clothes (men, jackets are required in Canoe Bay's dining room) and walk to dinner at the inn. Arrive early and take a stroll on the deck for more views of the lake or browse through the comprehensive wine list while snuggling in the cozy lounge. The impressive wine list—about 700 wines are on it—includes domestic and imported red and white wines, sparkling wines, and port wines. If you're overwhelmed, just ask the sommelier to recommend a bottle for the evening. As with the dinner in the wine cellar, the prix fixe dinner menu in the dining room varies nightly. Dishes feature regional food ingredients.

If the two of you are staying at Hemlock Hide-A-Way or want to try a restaurant outside the resort, sample the cuisine at Turtleback Restaurant, located on the grounds of Turtleback Golf Course in Rice Lake. The dining room overlooks the 18th hole. The food is traditional Wisconsin fare like slow-roasted prime rib, cod, and salmon with baked potatoes and mixed vegetables.

If you choose to leave the estate for some entertainment after dinner, consider a show at the **Red Barn Theatre**, a quaint barn on the outskirts of Rice Lake. Other alternatives include seeing a performance by the **Northern Star Theater Company**, located in downtown Rice Lake, which stages many different shows throughout the year. Plus, a variety of bands—brass, jazz, and bluegrass—take the stage Thursday evenings for **Music in the Park** in Rice

Lake's City Park band shell. The lakeside park provides a lovely setting for concerts, allowing you to walk along the shore hand in hand during intermission or after the performance.

Follow this evening's entertainment with a moonlight swim back at the resort. There's nothing quite as intimate as sharing a swim under the stars. But if the water is too chilly or the mosquitoes too plentiful, head back to the cottage and soak in the whirlpool tub.

## Day Three

After polishing off your breakfast, put on your hiking boots and walk through the wooded acres on Canoe Bay's property. The trails—easy and a few miles long—wind through the woods and along the lake.

Once you reluctantly check out from this paradise, drive into Chetek and have lunch at colorful local hot spot **Nana's Cottage**. The staff assembles yummy (and usually light) sandwiches, wraps, and salads. Share your thoughts for a while over Viennese coffee or hot white chocolate. Don't leave Nana's without trying a sweet. There's the raspberry delight—a raspberry-chocolate brownie, ice cream, raspberry puree, and whipped cream—and the sweet dream pretzel—a warm, soft pretzel filled with cream cheese. Guys, your girls will be enchanted with this place.

From Chetek drive north to Rice Lake, then west on County Road C for a leisurely scenic drive through the Blue Hills, the rolling hills west of Rice Lake. If you are visiting during the winter months, drop by **Swiss Shire Farm** for a Shire horse-drawn sleigh ride through the Chetek countryside in a three-person cutter.

### FOR MORE INFORMATION
**Chetek Online Visitors Guide**
www.chetek.com

**Rice Lake Chamber of Commerce**
37 S. Main Street, Rice Lake
(715) 234-2126 or (800) 523-6318
www.ricelaketourism.com
or www.rice-lake.com

### ATTRACTIONS AND RECREATION
**Mommsen's Produce Patch**
Hwy SS South, Rice Lake
(715) 234-6363, www.producepatch.com

**Music in the Park**
Concerts in Rice Lake's
City Park band shell
Lakeshore Drive and Eau Claire Street
Held Thursday evenings June through August.

**Northern Star Theater/ Center for the Arts**
104 S. Main Street, Rice Lake
(877) 379-7529

**Red Barn Theatre**
35 W. Evans Street, Rice Lake
(715) 234-8301
or (888) 686-3770

**Swiss Shire Farm**
626 19th Street, Chetek
(715) 837-1102

**Tuscobia State Trail**
Approximately five miles north of Rice
Lake on County Road SS, by Highway 53
(800) 269-4505, www.tuscobiatrail.com

**Village Dell & Wine Shop**
819 Hammond Avenue, Rice Lake
(715) 234-4146

## LODGING
**Canoe Bay**
Hogback Road (P.O. Box 28), Chetek
(715) 924-4594 or (800) 568-1995
www.canoebay.com
Inn rooms start at about $300;
cottages are from $340.

**Hemlock Hide-A-Way Resort
and Gift Shop**
2772 25th Avenue, Rice Lake
(715) 234-1841
www.hemlockhideawayresort.com
Cottages are from $110.

## DINING AND NIGHTLIFE
**Nana's Cottage**
529 Second Street, Chetek
(715) 924-3333
www.nanaschetek.com
Open for breakfast and lunch daily.
Closed in January.

**Turtleback Restaurant**
West Allan Road, Rice Lake
(715) 234-6607
Open for lunch Monday through Friday
and dinner Monday through Saturday.

# CHAPTER SEVENTEEN

# Falling in Love in

# *Hayward*

## …Hook, Line, and Sinker

Set amid the Chequamegon National Forest, the North Woods logging towns of Hayward and Cable have been attracting tourists for decades. Visitors, particularly anglers, keep coming to the lakes said to be teeming with walleye, pike, and muskie. Even if you aren't serious about fishing, a visit to this part of the state can be very rewarding for couples. Although you'll find seemingly countless resorts and supper clubs in the area, there are unspoiled wilderness areas open for exploring, with trails and picnic spots where the two of you can unwind and watch for herons and eagles.

Abounding in natural beauty (water, water, everywhere) the region tends to attract the most visitors during the summer months when the lakes are warmer. But consider renting a cottage or shacking up in a cozy B&B during the fall, when the hardwood forests turn a lustrous gold and crimson color and the muskies and walleyes are biting. And remember, this area does not shut down during the winter. You'll find many resorts are open, fires burning and whirlpool hot tubs bubbling during the chilly months. The area is also home to the Birkebeiner, a 51-kilometer cross-country ski race from Cable to Hayward held annually in February.

## *Day One*

### ✍ MORNING

Begin your vacation with a short walk through a quiet, remote wetland preserve, Lynch Creek Waterfowl Management Area, located about halfway between County Road M and Highway 77. If you encountered any traffic congestion on your way Up North or are bogged down with any thoughts of work or children, a walk through the wilderness will put you both at ease and in the right frame of mind for the getaway. Follow Farm Road 622 to the wildlife area.

From the parking lot, walk along the hiking trail that takes you along the north side of the creek and to the viewing platform. (It's an easy, 1,000-foot trail.) Pull out your binoculars, wait, and you should be able to spot great blue herons, ducks, and beavers. Next, follow the trail that winds around the south end of Lynch Creek for about 2,000 feet.

If you have time, drive to Ghost Lake, located about 20 miles northeast of Hayward off Highway 77, for some bank fishing. Ghost Lake is a quiet, 372-acre lake with a 10-mile-an-hour speed limit (no skiers here). It also has spruce and cedar bogs. Fish for muskie, walleye, and bass at this 12-foot-deep lake. Novices may want to arrange for fly-fishing lessons with a professional guide at Boulder Lodge, which is situated on Ghost Lake.

After your peaceful morning, have a late lunch together at **Madeline's** in downtown Hayward. The café's relaxing atmosphere—smooth jazz playing in the background—will set the tone for this getaway. Relax on the deck under a large umbrella or at one of the oak or Formica tables set up throughout the dining rooms. The café serves "simple food done well" (in other words, healthful, hearty food). Share a plate of antipasti and nibble on finger foods such as garlic basil goat cheese with focaccia fingers. Before leaving, pick up a bottle of wine for the evening. Then walk or drive over to **Tremblay's Sweet Shop** on Main Street to pick out a few treats such as pecan clusters and peanut butter balls for your honey.

## AFTERNOON

Next, check in to your room or cabin for the next few days. You'll find plenty of mom-and-pop resorts on the lakes around Hayward and Cable. One of the best is **Treeland Resort** on the Chippewa Flowage. Depending on how much money you want to spend and how long you plan on staying in the area, choose from among 27 vacation homes and motel suites. Home #8 is a one-bedroom, one-bath log cabin with a porch that is suitable for couples. Stay at Treeland if you want to be right on the flowage. At Treeland you can rent a pontoon boat, fishing boat, rowboat, paddleboat, canoe, or kayak. And with the homes clustered near the lake (some as close as 10 feet from the water), you can still hear the loons from your open windows and the water lapping against the shoreline. Being a resort, it has an outdoor swimming pool, sunning deck, swim raft, and volleyball court. But it's not a massive resort where you feel the other cottages are within arm's reach of your windows.

For a more secluded getaway check in to the **Spider Lake Lodge B&B**, a log cabin bed and breakfast found at the end of a long, winding road on the shore of Spider Lake, northwest of Hayward. All the rooms are cozy and romantic. One standout is the Moody's Camp room, where you just have to open sliding glass doors to step out onto a deck for views of the lake. Lounge in the private whirlpool bathtub amid a backdrop of exposed-log walls decorated in warm hues and accented with such items as antique fishing equipment. After check-

The Treeland Resort on the Chippewa Flowage, with lots of water toys.

ing in, have a seat in the screened-in porch, or if it's a chilly fall day, sink into the armchairs in front of the fieldstone fireplace.

## ☙ EVENING

Tonight, channel the festive mood of the Roaring Twenties by paying a visit to the lavish summer retreat of 1920s Chicago gangster Al Capone. To get to **The Hideout**, Capone's former estate that has been converted to a restaurant and 1920s museum, follow County Road CC south from Treeland. Take your time. This scenic drive takes you through the heart of the Chippewa Flowage. Created after a power company built a dam across the Chippewa River in the 1920s, the Lake Chippewa Flowage is a 17,000-acre lake, one of the largest in Wisconsin. At its deepest, the lake is 92 feet, with a mean depth of 15 feet. There are hundreds of islands and miles of undeveloped shoreline. Look for beavers building dams, otters slipping onto the shores, and anglers dozing in their boats. Eventually you will rumble down a long driveway to the Hideout. Prior to your meal, tour this rambling estate, walk through Capone's lodge, peek into a jail cell, and check out the flapper fashions in the Roaring Twenties museum.

Next, head over to the restaurant and slip into a booth for dinner, surrounded by photographs of Capone and his contemporaries hanging on the walls. The cooks here prepare plenty of steak and seafood dishes, such as New

York strip steak and broiled deep-sea scallops. As a nod to Capone, you'll find specialties such as chicken cacciatore and veal parmigiana and sandwiches with such names as "the Enforcer" and "the Boss." Head to the bar afterward for a cosmopolitan or martini.

Back at Treeland, before tucking in for the night, take a canoe or paddle-boat onto Musky Bay for a little moonlight boat cruise through the flowage. (These are free to guests.) If you've rented a rowboat for the weekend, slip out onto the lake in that. Listen to the frogs and to water lapping at the shore, and catch the moon rising above the pines. If you are at Spider Lake Lodge, walk down to the water and listen to the loons.

## ROMANTIC HEIGHTS

 Take your date's breath away by locking lips (or proposing) atop the highest geographical point in the state. Timm's Hill County Park (the hill is 1,951.5 feet above sea level) is in the northwest part of the state in woodsy Price County. Climb up the observation tower and have a look at the maple, ash, and birch trees. While you're at the park, you can mosey around the two spring-fed lakes, drop a line off the fishing pier, or picnic on the beach. The park is located east of Ogema, off Highway 86. More information is available at (715) 339-2555.

## *Day Two*

### MORNING

After the two of you have downed a hearty breakfast in the Spider Lake Lodge's lakeside dining room or in your kitchen at Treeland, spend your day fishing on Spider Lake or rent a boat from Treeland. (You don't have to be a guest to rent equipment.) Rent a 12-foot pontoon boat (ideal for one or two couples) or a fishing rig (different sizes are available) and head out onto the Chippewa Flowage for a morning of fishing.

Spend the morning sailing through the flowage exploring the many bays and islands. Turn off the motor, cast your lines, and watch for bald eagles, loons, beavers, deer, and ducks. The flowage is chock-full of muskie, northern pike, bass, crappie, and walleye. During the fall, walleye fishing tends to be good from mid-September to late October. Muskie fishing is usually at its best from the third week of September through October and early November. Fish for largemouth and smallmouth bass through September.

If you choose to explore the waters of Spider Lake and its islands, bogs, and bars, you will find the fishing is good for muskie, walleye, bass, or panfish.

For lunch, cruise into one of the secluded bays in the Chippewa Flowage, or find harbor at one of the many islands for a picnic. (You can purchase supplies in downtown Hayward.) If you're spending time on Spider Lake, make waves to Picnic Island or Bird Island. Before picking up those fishing rods again, give your companion a smooch while your boat is tucked away in a little inlet.

## ᠊ᡣᢌ AFTERNOON

Chances are you will return to Treeland or Spider Lake Lodge feeling a bit burned from the sun's rays and windblown from cruising across open water. Practice the art of relaxation by laying out your towels or chairs at Treeland's outdoor swimming pool or down by the water on the sand beach, sunning deck or under the shade of a tree. Dive into the water and race each other to the raft. If you are staying at Spider Lake Lodge, walk down to the sandy beach and doze away the rest of the afternoon as you listen to the wind through the pine trees.

## ᠊ᡣᢌ EVENING

For dinner embark on another scenic drive north to **Garmisch USA**, a German-themed resort on Namakegon Lake. Have a seat in the restaurant overlooking the lake and watch the sun set while you dine on traditional German fare or dishes of scallops, veal, or pork. Fish entrées, such as the haddock almondine, are popular here. After your meal, take a stroll down Honeymoon Walk, a lakefront path made of stones that feature the names of couples married at the resort years ago.

Back at the resort, before you head back to your cabin or room, decompress from the day's activities in one of Treeland's saunas. If you are staying in Spider Lake Lodge's Murphy's Camp room, fill up that whirlpool bathtub, light some candles, and pop open that bottle of wine you purchased from Madeline's.

## *Day Three*

Don't leave the North Woods without feasting at the **Robin's Nest Café**, a local hot spot for breakfast. Chefs have put a new spin on some old favorites. Choose from appetizing concoctions such as blue cheese western omelet, seafood supreme omelet, thick potato pancakes, and biscuits and gravy. Indulge in the flowage combo, which consists of pancakes or a waffle with fruit, whipped cream, eggs, bacon, and sausage patties. Wash the food down with a mimosa or Bloody Mary.

Try to push aside your plates and force yourselves to leave Robin's Nest. This morning you will saddle up for a horseback ride at **Appa-Lolly Ranch** in Hayward. Or let someone else do the driving and arrange a carriage ride through the countryside with Appa-Lolly. (If you are visiting during the snowy months, the ranch offers sleigh rides, weather permitting.) The two of you will trek to

Digging the view at Copper Falls State Park. Photo courtesy of Wisconsin Department of Tourism.

the family's private lake, into the Chequamegon National Forest, and along the Namekagon River.

If horses are not your thing and you don't mind venturing a bit out of the area, make tracks to Copper Falls State Park, just north of Mellen. The park is one of the state's most beautiful recreational areas, and its highlight is—no surprise—40-foot Copper Falls. Along with Brownstone Falls, which features a convenient viewing platform, the two cascades make a great couple.

If you prefer that your last hours in Hayward be spent on the water, take a two-hour, 25-mile **narrated boat tour** on the *Chippewa Queen* pontoon boat for one last look at the scenic flowage. Tours depart from Treeland Resort.

### ☙ FOR MORE INFORMATION

**Cable Area Chamber of Commerce Visitor Center**
Highway 63 and County Road M
(P.O. Box 217), Cable
(800) 533-7454
www.cable4fun.com

**Chequamegon-Nicolet National Forest**
10650 Nyman Avenue, Hayward
(715) 634-4821, www.fs.fed.us

**Hayward Lakes Resort Association Information Center**
101 W. First Street,
Hayward
(715) 634-4801
www.haywardlakes.com

**Hayward Visitor Information Center**
Highways 63 and 27
(715) 634-8662
or (800) 72-HAYWARD

## ATTRACTIONS AND RECREATION

**Appa-Lolly Ranch**
501 E. River Road, Hayward
(715) 634-5059
Open daily year-round,
weather permitting.

**Chippewa Queen Boat Tours**
9630 N. Treeland Road, Hayward
(715) 462-3874

**Tremblay's Sweet Shop**
Main Street (P.O. Box 228), Hayward
(715) 634-2785

**Madeline's**
10576 Kansas Avenue,
Hayward
(715) 934-2525
Open for lunch and dinner daily.
Closed Sunday during the winter.

**Robins Nest Café**
11014 County Road B,
Hayward
(715) 462-3132
Open daily for breakfast and lunch.

## LODGING

**Spider Lake Lodge B&B**
10472 W. Murphy Boulevard, Hayward
(715) 462-3793
or (800) OLD-WISC (653-9472)
www.spiderlakelodge.com
Rooms are from $110.

**Treeland Resorts**
9630 Treeland Road, Hayward
(715) 462-3874
www.treelandresorts.com
Call for prices. Rates vary per
season and length of stay.

## DINING AND NIGHTLIFE

**Garmisch USA**
23040 Garmisch Road, Cable
(715) 794-2204
Open daily for dinner year-round,
except during March and April.

**The Hideout—Al Capone's
Northwoods Retreat**
12101W County Road CC,
Couderay
(715) 945-2746
www.alcaponehideout.com
Call for hours.

# CHAPTER EIGHTEEN

# Superior Pleasures:
# Bayfield and the Apostle Islands

The Bayfield peninsula and the Apostle Islands, the archipelago just north and east of the peninsula, are romantic lands that lend themselves to folklore. For example, Hermit Island is named after a man who lived there by himself supposedly because he suffered from unrequited love. The peninsula is a land of sandstone cliffs, sandy beaches, woodlands, and orchards. Here community activity tends to revolve around Lake Superior, the largest freshwater body on earth. On this getaway, the two of you will glide across the water in kayaks, a sailboat, or a schooner. You'll explore lighthouses and old fishing camps, and at night you'll cozy up on a private porch overlooking the water.

Base your vacation in the town of Bayfield, a waterfront community that feels more New England than Northern Wisconsin. The town's pier is home to boat rental companies, kayak outfitters, and coffee shops, and Bayfield has myriad bed and breakfasts and inns that are suitable for romantic couples, plus restaurants and sweet shops. The streets are bustling with friendly, sun-kissed faces. Tons of apples are harvested here every fall, and Bayfield's Apple Festival is hugely popular.

The suggested three-day itinerary may seem ambitious to some. But you can alter it according to your desired activity level. If the two of you love kayaking, you may want to spend the entire day paddling around the islands instead of embarking on a three-hour expedition. Or, if you would rather not exert that much energy, take a boat ride instead.

A bit of a forewarning: if you travel to Bayfield and the Apostle Islands during peak tourist weekends such as the Fourth of July or popular Apple Fest in October, be sure to book your room and cruises in advance. And don't rule out visiting during the winter. Although the winters are long and cold here, adventurous couples can take to the lake on skis to explore sea caves or spend the afternoon before a fireplace within your lakeside suite.

## Day One

### MORNING

Chances are, unless you already live in the northern tip of Wisconsin, it will take you quite a while to drive north to the Bayfield peninsula and to the little town of Bayfield. The good news is that you won't be following six-lane expressways but two-lane highways that wind through rolling hills and forests of birch and cedar trees. If you are driving from Superior along Highway 2, follow County Road G east of Iron River. This will eventually take you to the intersection of Highway 2 and 13. County G is especially romantic for its views of sloping farmland, creeks, and the occasional deer.

Follow Highway 2/13 into Ashland. A booming shipping town in the late 1800s, Ashland has become relatively subdued since then (although, with a population of nine thousand people, it is still the largest town in the area). One of the landmark buildings is the **Hotel Chequamegon** overlooking Chequamegon Bay. Have a seat in **Molly Cooper's Restaurant and Lounge** at a table overlooking the bay. Order anything from a bacon burger to seared salmon. After your lunch, meander around the hotel's terrace, and then head toward the marina, a five-minute walk from the hotel. There's a gazebo from which you can take in the beauty of Lake Superior. If you're not in too much of a hurry, stroll through Ashland's downtown area to view the collection of brownstone buildings, now filled with various antiques shops and cafés.

### AFTERNOON

Continue north on Highway 13 toward Bayfield and turn onto County Road J. This road will take you by most of the apple orchards and fruit farms located on the outskirts of Bayfield. Out here, you'll notice the sweet smell of purple lupine in June and brown-eyed Susans and daisies along the roadsides and in flower beds lining driveways. Depending on the time of year you visit, you can pick apples from late August through October and raspberries and cherries in July. Three favorite places to do so are the **Bayfield Apple Company, Good Earth Gardens,** and **Hauser's Superior View Farm**, all located about one mile from each other. At Good Earth Gardens pick blueberries or blackberries, and buy a bouquet of wildflowers for your traveling partner. At Hauser's, be sure to climb to the top of the rustic family barn for a glimpse of Lake Superior from 600 feet above the lake. You can also sample some mead (honey wine). At Bayfield Apple Company, share a slice of apple or raspberry pie. If you haven't had enough sweetness, just follow the signs to more orchards. There are more than 15 clustered in the area.

After your glorious afternoon in the country, drive into Bayfield and check in to your room at the Old Rittenhouse Inn or the Bayfield Inn. Like other waterfront resort towns, Bayfield contains a number of bed and breakfasts in restored older homes.

The Old Rittenhouse Inn, the epitome of Bayfield charm any time of the year. Photo courtesy of Wisconsin Department of Tourism.

Perhaps the most well-known B&B in the village is the **Old Rittenhouse Inn**, located near the top of the hill on Rittenhouse Avenue. Before booking your room, ask about special weekend getaways. The Rittenhouse frequently hosts couple-focused getaways such as wine-tasting weekends and Valentine's Day specials. Built in 1890 as a grand summer home for a Wisconsin general, the Rittenhouse houses 10 rooms in the main Queen Anne home, in the smaller Victorian home dubbed Le Chateau, and in a nearby cottage. The rooms are decorated in rich colors like purple and green and with antiques and reading chairs. Many come with whirlpool bathtubs and fireplaces. Splurge and book the Champagne suite. To give you an idea about how spacious this room is, know that this was formerly the house's ballroom.

For modern hotel-type accommodations and lakeside views, stay in the **Bayfield Inn**, located right by the waterfront and marina. This classy but not outrageously priced hotel offers 21 rooms in the inn and 10 in the guesthouses. The inn rooms, remodeled in 2002, are bright and breezy and feature down comforters. Book a suite with a private deck facing the lake.

After you check in, take a few moments to linger in your relaxing environs.

## EVENING

Next, walk to **Wild By Nature Market** in downtown Bayfield to create a picnic dinner for the two of you. Choose from sandwiches like portobello mushroom and wraps like chicken salad, Wisconsin cheese, and drinks such as iced tea and lemonade.

Then walk to the marina where you'll catch an evening sailboat ride. For about $20 per person, cruise the lake at sunset on a 30-foot sailboat with **Catchun-Sun Charter Co.** This route is probably the more romantic compared to other boat cruise options, because it will be just the two of you and a friendly, experienced captain on a 1969 Morgan sailboat. (Yes, you can help hoist the sails.) If you're in the mood for a longer evening cruise (one that lasts more than three hours) board an **Apostle Islands Cruise Service** boat for about $25 per person. These cruises shuttle visitors around various Apostle Islands, with some tours that focus on the lighthouses found on various islands. Whichever trip you choose, you will board your boat at the city dock.

After your boat cruise, stroll along the lakeshore path by the marina and behind the Bayfield Inn. Treat yourself to an ice cream cone at the Pier Plaza ice cream parlor right by the city dock and waterfront or a drink at the Bayfield Inn deck bar and grill overlooking the marina.

## Day Two

### ⌘ MORNING

Because today will be jam-packed with activities, fill up with a hearty breakfast at the **Egg Toss Bakery and Café**. This busy café, within walking distance

Enjoying Bayfield's scenic waterfront.

of the marina, has a country-porchlike atmosphere because of its open windows. It's tempting to stay here for a while with a cup of coffee. The Egg Toss has, not surprisingly, fluffy omelets and egg dishes, such as the Orchard Platter consisting of buckwheat pancakes, chicken apple sausage, and eggs. Or try the French Ecstasy with cinnamon bread and cream cheese. But don't overindulge on sticky buns; you'll need your energy for your kayaking tour of the Apostle Islands.

## BAYFIELD'S SPECIAL EVENTS

Bayfield hosts a variety of special events throughout the year that should appeal to romantic couples.

- Bundle up for the Snowshoe Social in January.
- Don vintage prom attire and dance to a 15-piece swing orchestra for the Blue Moon Ball at Bayfield Pavilion.
- Watch boats parade through the waters and attend music concerts during the Blessing of the Fleet in June.
- Purchase oil paintings at the Festival of the Arts in July.
- Watch Native American dances during Red Cliff Cultural Days in July.
- The Bayfield (Mostly) Schubert Festival consists of free chamber music concerts held in the beautiful Christ Episcopal Church every Thursday from mid-July to mid-August. The annual festival was begun in 1997 to honor Franz Schubert, but the musical offerings are not limited to those of the Austrian composer.
- The hugely popular Bayfield Apple Festival takes place annually during early October.

Fear not, kayak novices. Even if you are not an expert paddler or a triathlete but are in decent shape and not afraid of water, you should definitely give kayaking a shot. It is probably one of the best and most peaceful ways to explore the gorgeous Apostle Islands National Lakeshore. Join the folks at **Trek-n-Trail** for a morning cruise, such as the Basswood Island tour. Before leaving Bayfield, you will be taught basic kayaking techniques. Don't worry about buying kayaking equipment; all equipment is provided. On the Basswood Island tour you will paddle about an hour and a half to Basswood, located northeast of Bayfield and west of Madeline Island. As you paddle along the shoreline you'll pass over a shipwreck (the water is shallow and you can see the burnt ribbing of a ship), and by Honeymoon Rock. Steal a kiss here. Then, you'll take some time to dock and hike through the island's pine forests and by the brownstone quarry on the island. Don't worry about getting left behind in a crowd; the outfitter takes a maximum of 10 people on these trips.

## THE NEXT TIME AROUND

As the two of you will discover, three days will not be enough time for you to see and do everything in the Bayfield peninsula. If you have more time and are lucky enough to extend your trip to a week, or if you plan to return, here are a few more romantic excursions to consider.

The peninsula is beautiful beyond Bayfield. For a scenic drive to the north and west of the peninsula, drive west from Bayfield on Highway 13 to Meyers Beach, which is part of the Apostle Islands National Lakeshore. Here, away from the crowds, you can picnic, walk along a sandy beach, and view a stunning sunset. Not too far away, on the outskirts of Cornucopia, a little lakeside town to the west, you'll find Lazy Susan's Bed and Brunch hidden away amid birch and pine trees on the shore of Lake Superior. Built in 1998, the sprawling log home features three bedrooms, all with private baths, plus a heavenly Jacuzzi suite, which is ideal for longer stays on this side of the peninsula. In this second-floor suite you can unwind on the couch or soak in the Jacuzzi while watching the sun set. Don't forget to stop by Superior Letterpress Company in Cornucopia to buy handmade papers, on which you can write love letters to each other.

Back on shore, grab a casual lunch at the festive **Maggie's** or casual **Mama Get's**, two restaurants that serve supremely juicy hamburgers and whitefish fillets.

### AFTERNOON

After refueling, put on your walking shoes and have a look around Bayfield. The village of more than 600 people (although population doubles during the summer) is a walking town. Most shops are centered on Rittenhouse Avenue and its cross streets. Admire jewelry at Water Music on Second Street. Check out the indoor and outdoor sculptures at Kerr Studio on Front Street. Shop for nautical gifts, such as miniature ceramic lighthouses, at Keeper of the Light on Front Street. Get lost among the shelves at Bayfield Books on Second Street, which specializes in secondhand books. Take a break and enjoy a cup of coffee or tea in the bookstore's quaint cobblestone courtyard.

After shopping, take a leisurely hike along the Bayfield Brownstone Trail. Accessible from Washington Avenue, the wooded path will take you along a babbling brook called Pike's Creek and the old iron bridge, a town landmark.

Of course, if you are too tired and sunburned from your morning adventure, skip the afternoon of walking. Instead, head back to your room, mix a drink, grab a book, and recline on the expansive veranda of the Rittenhouse or your private deck at the Bayfield Inn.

## ✿ EVENING

Reward yourselves with an elegant multicourse dinner in the Old Ritten-house Inn dining room. The intimate room, filled with two-top tables and glowing candlelight, is an ideal spot for a classy, romantic dinner. Typically, the multicourse experience includes a soup, salad, entrée, and dessert. Dishes vary depending on the time of year you visit and what vegetables and fruits are in season locally. (One entrée example is pork loin served with an apple cider marmalade glaze.) Choose from a dizzying array of wines and spirits to com-plement your dinner.

If you're on a tight budget, don't despair. (Dinner can be a bit pricey for some at the Rittenhouse.) There are plenty of other restaurants in Bayfield. You can head to the Bayfield Inn's dining room for fresh whitefish fillets or pizza at **Greunke's Restaurant**. Both are located within a few yards of the shut-tle stop where buses carry folks to Big Top Chautauqua.

After dinner, drive or take the free shuttle from downtown Bayfield to **Big Top Chautauqua**, where the two of you will catch a music concert under a big, blue and white canvas tent. Erected at the bottom of Mount Ashwabay (a ski hill during the winter months), three miles south of Bayfield off Highway 13, Big Top is a throwback to the days of traveling tent shows and vaudeville acts. Big Top has welcomed performers such as the 1950s singing group the Letter-men, country singer Pam Tillis, and folk group Bela Fleck and the Flecktones. On some nights throughout the summer, a house band takes the stage with historical regional stories and anecdotes. With a casual, festive atmosphere, Big Top offers theater and bleacher seats. (You won't have to bring your own lawn chairs.) Most shows start at 7:30 p.m. or 8:15 p.m., so be sure you allow your-selves plenty of time for a relaxing dinner and for the drive to Mount Ash-wabay. Although tickets are available at the door, it is not uncommon for shows to sell out. Advance tickets are recommended.

## *Day Three*

### ✿ MORNING

Before boarding the shuttle to Madeline Island this morning, hang out in **Blue Horizons**, a café in downtown Bayfield, a short walk from the shuttle stop. It's a great spot to gather yourselves, review your itinerary for the day, and take in the Bayfield scene. Although you can drive your car to Madeline Island, you'll have more of a relaxing time on the island exploring via bicycle than navigat-ing through traffic. Be sure to bring a backpack with you on your day trip. Of course, if the weather isn't cooperating and it appears that it might rain all day, drive across. If you do decide to go this route, call the **Madeline Island Ferry Line** to reserve a spot for your car. If you walk onto the ferry, it'll cost about $16 for two round-trip tickets; if you drive, you'll pay about $35 for yourselves and the car for round-trip tickets. During the summer the earliest ferry departure

Strolling along Big Bay State Park on Madeleine Island. Photo courtesy of Wisconsin Department of Tourism.

to Madeline Island is at 7:00 a.m. The 20-minute ferry ride is a scenic little trip that provides you with a look at the grand resort homes lining Nebraska Row as you approach Madeline Island.

Named for Madeleine Cadotte, wife of French fur trader Michael Cadotte and daughter of Chief White Crane, the island was home to the Ojibway Indians from the 1400s through late 1800s. Through the seventeenth and eighteenth centuries, French fur traders and missionaries traveled to the island and set up trading posts and churches. Summer tourists started arriving in the late 1890s, particularly city dwellers seeking respite from hay fever during the region's cool summers. Part of the museum on the island consists of a warehouse building constructed by the American Fur Company in 1835. Madeline Island has a year-round population of 180 people that swells to 2,500 during the summer.

Once you are on the island, stop at **Mission Hill Coffee House** for sandwiches for your picnic. You'll also find a great selection of homemade goodies, wines, and microbrews.

You don't need to haul your bicycles with you on this trip if you don't want to. Call **Motion to Go** in La Pointe and rent bicycles or one tandem bicycle. If you're not in the mood for a workout, rent mopeds, which will allow you to see more of the 14-mile-long island in one day. Madeline Island is fairly bike-friendly. The speed limit for cars is 40 miles per hour throughout.

Once you're outfitted with bicycles, pedal northeastward on County Road H, following the signs to Hagen Road and **Big Bay State Park**, about seven miles from La Pointe. Once you arrive in the park, leave your bikes at the entrance to Barrier Beach, where you should walk hand in hand along the sandy shoreline, listening for loons and hunting for beach stones such as ruddy sand-

Madeleine Island's classy, yet laid-back Bell Street Tavern, a great place for dinner, drinks, and music.

stone, which was quarried in the Apostle Islands starting in 1869. Dip your toes in the cool, clear lake water. Big Bay is in a sheltered area and the water tends to be warmer than at other beaches in the area. But don't expect the offshore surface water to rise above 65 degrees Fahrenheit. You may encounter some brave children splashing in the water.

From the sand beach, walk along the boardwalk trail, which takes you by wetlands to the west and Lake Superior and the sand spit to the east. Admire the red pines, wild blueberries, and lichen growing on rocks and tree trunks. Keep walking until you reach the wildlife observation deck. Have a seat to watch the herons in the nearby lagoon, and listen to frogs singing and woodpeckers chattering.

After your walk you will probably be ready for a light lunch. Set up your picnic on the beach or on one of the tables located at the entrance to the beach area, where you parked your bicycles. Enjoy your sandwiches and each other's company, perhaps napping in the sun or shade as the wind breezes through the pines.

## ৬ AFTERNOON

Head back onto Hagen Road and go north on County Road H until you turn west onto Big Bay Road. Follow this quiet road back into La Pointe for another seven miles or so. All in all, you'll log about 14 miles on this loop.

Back in La Pointe, return your bicycles and stroll through the little town. The hub of the island, La Pointe is where you'll find a few restaurants, from casual pizza joints and ice cream shops to a coffee shop and a bar.

## ROUGHING IT (AND LOVING IT)

🐾 Although you'll find countless quaint and quiet bed and breakfasts in and around Bayfield, if the two of you are looking to spend time reacquainting not only with yourselves but with Mother Nature, rent a campsite for a night or two in one of the county parks or in Big Bay State Park on Madeline Island. If you're looking for serenity you might want to stay away from some of the campsites located along the Lake Superior shoreline during peak tourist season, unless you don't mind pitching a tent next to a family of eight. Try the Big Rock Park Campground, a 15-site campground northwest of Washburn off County Road C. Settle into a rustic site above the Sioux River, a Class A trout stream. If you decide to set up camp at Big Bay State Park, reserve a walk-in spot (sites 35–41), away from RVs and other vehicles coming and going in the campground. These sites, which tend to be occupied by couples, book weeks or even months in advance, so call early to reserve your spot.

### 🐾 EVENING

For dinner opt for the classy but casual Bell Street Tavern, located a block from the ferry dock. The **Bell Street Tavern** is part sports bar, part white-tablecloth restaurant, and part cocktail lounge. Dinners run the gamut, including vegetable Wellington, chicken marsala, and whitefish. Before or after your dinner have a seat by the stone hearth or at the expansive bar to listen to live music, from reggae to blues.

Return to Bayfield via the ferry. The last one leaves La Pointe at 11:30 p.m. on Friday and Saturday and at 10:30 p.m. on weekdays in the summer.

### 🐾 FOR MORE INFORMATION

**Ashland Area Chamber of Commerce**
805 Lake Shore Drive West, Ashland
(800) 284-9484
www.travelashlandcounty.com or
www.visitashland.com

**Bayfield Chamber of Commerce**
42 S. Broad Street, Bayfield
(715) 779-3335 or (800) 447-4094
www.bayfield.org

**Bayfield County Tourism
and Recreation**

(800) 472-6338
www.travelbayfieldcounty.com

**Madeline Island
Chamber of Commerce**
806 Main Street (P.O. Box 274),
La Pointe
(715) 747-2801 or (888) ISLE-FUN
www.madelineisland.com

**Northern Great Lakes Visitor Center**
Three miles west of Ashland on U.S.
Highway 2
(715) 685-9983

## ✆ ATTRACTIONS AND RECREATION

**Apostle Islands Cruise Service**
At the Bayfield City Dock
(715) 779-3925 or (800) 323-7619
www.apostleisland.com

**Bayfield Apple Company**
County Road J and Betzold Road, Bayfield
(800) 363-4JAM
www.bayfieldapple.com

**Big Bay State Park**
Hagen Road, Madeline Island
(715) 747-6425 or (888) 947-2757 for camping reservations
www.dnr.state.wi.us
Admission fee.

**Big Top Chautauqua**
Mailing address: 101 W. Bayfield Street, Washburn
Located at the foot of Mt. Ashwabay.
Follow signs from Highway 13 between Washburn and Bayfield.
(715) 373-5552 or (888) BIG-TENT (244-8368)
www.bigtop.org
Season runs June through September.

**Catchun-Sun Charter Co.**
P.O. Box 955, Bayfield
(715) 779-3111

**Good Earth Gardens**
87185 County Road J, Bayfield
(715) 779-5564

**Hauser's Superior View Farm**
County Road J, Bayfield
(715) 779-5404
www.superiorviewfarm.com

**Madeline Island Ferry Line**
Box 66MI, La Pointe
(715) 747-2051

www.madferry.com
Ferries run every 30 minutes daily during the summer months. The ferry will cross the bay during the winter until the lake freezes and will start service again once the ice breaks up in the spring. Call for a schedule.

**Motion to Go**
Lakeview Place, Middle Road, La Pointe
(715) 747-6585
Bicycles cost $7 per hour, $26 per day.
Mopeds are $17.50 an hour.

**Trek & Trail Adventure Outfitters**
Seven Washington Avenue, Bayfield
(800) 354-8735
www.trek-trail.com
Kayaking is offered on most days June through September.

## ✆ LODGING

**Bayfield Inn**
20 Rittenhouse Avenue, Bayfield
(715) 779-3363 or (800) 382-0995
www.bayfieldinn.com
Rooms are from $100.

**Old Rittenhouse Inn**
301 Rittenhouse Avenue, Bayfield
(715) 644-5438 or (888) 644-4667
www.rittenhouseinn.com
Rooms are from $99.

## ✆ DINING AND NIGHTLIFE

**Bell Street Tavern**
751 Bell Street, La Pointe
(715) 747-2700
www.bstavern.com
Open daily for lunch and dinner.

**Blue Horizons**
117 Rittenhouse Avenue, Bayfield
(715) 779-9619
Call for hours.

**Egg Toss Bakery and Café**
41 Maypenny Avenue, Bayfield
(715) 779-5181
www.eggtoss-bayfield.com
Open for breakfast and lunch.
Call for hours.

**Greunke's Restaurant**
17 Rittenhouse Ave., Bayfield
(715) 779-5480 or (800) 245-3072
Open for breakfast, lunch and dinner
April through October.
www.greunkesinn.com

**Hotel Chequamegon**
Molly Cooper's Restaurant and Lounge
101 Lake Shore Drive West, Ashland
(715) 682-9095 or (800) 946-5555
www.hotelc.com
Molly Cooper's is open daily for lunch
and dinner.

**Maggie's**
257 Maypenny Avenue, Bayfield
(715) 779-5641
www.maggies-bayfield.com
Open daily for lunch and dinner.

**Mama Get's Bistro and Brew**
200 Rittenhouse Avenue, Bayfield
(715) 779-7004
Open daily for lunch and dinner.

**Mission Hill Coffee House**
Lakeview Place, Middle Road and
County Road H, La Pointe
(715) 747-3100
Call for hours.

**Old Rittenhouse Inn**
See listing under lodging.

**Pier Plaza**
One Rittenhouse Avenue, Bayfield
(715) 779-3330
Open for breakfast, lunch, and dinner.
Call for hours.

**Wild By Nature Market**
100 Rittenhouse Avenue, Bayfield
(715) 779-5075

# CHAPTER NINETEEN

# Snow Fun in
# *Marathon County*

It's time to frolic together in the snow again (this time without your kids tossing snowballs at you). Strap on those snowshoes, dust off the ski boots, and sharpen the ice skates. During this getaway you'll save your cuddling time by the fire for the evenings and face the wind and snow during the sparkling days of a Wisconsin winter. After all, who can resist kissing a sweetheart with rosy cheeks made flush by a swoosh down a mountainside or a figure eight on the ice?

Just because the mercury is hovering below freezing and Old Man Winter recently unloaded six inches of snow onto the ground, couples vacationing in north-central Wisconsin will not be confined to a fireside love seat throughout the long winter months (although that would certainly be a pleasant way to pass an evening with your honey). In Marathon County, a dairy-, lumber-, and ginseng-producing county, couples have a number of options to prevent cabin fever from setting in during the white winters. Here you'll find numerous parks and nature preserves open for you to explore.

For this getaway set up home base in Wausau, a hilly town of about 40,000 situated along the rambling Wisconsin River. Wausau possesses a charming downtown and views of Rib Mountain in the distance. Expect to spend quite a lot of time outdoors on this vacation: snowshoeing in the secluded Dells of the Eau Claire Park, cross-country skiing through a forest, ice-skating under the stars in Wausau's historic downtown, and downhill skiing at Granite Peak. You will both get quite a workout during these few days, but in the evenings you will be rewarded with time to cozy up on the couch or curl into that mammoth bed and pull up the comforter.

## *Day One*
### ﹖ MORNING

Before you go: if you don't own snowshoes, rent them for about $10 per day at **Shepherd and Schaller Sporting Goods** in downtown Wausau or **The Sports**

**Den** in Marshfield. Also, pack a thermos of hot chocolate or cider for this morning's activity. After trekking through the chilly forest, you'll both be thankful for mugs full of warm liquid.

Although you can snowshoe along the groomed trails in Rib Mountain State Park in Wausau, the two of you should consider driving about 20 miles northeast of Wausau in rural Marathon County to the scenic and secluded Dells of the Eau Claire Park. Here you'll trek along bluffs, in river valleys, and past frozen waterfalls and other natural scenes that will make you stop in wonder and want to snap photographs. Winding through this park will be quite a peaceful outing; you may be the only couple there that morning. The 193-acre park includes a branch of the National Scenic Ice Age Trail, a thousand-mile trail through Wisconsin that follows the margin of the most recent continental glaciation. This trail is probably your best bet for snowshoeing, as it is wide enough for the two of you to shoe side by side and quite scenic as you make your way past white and red pines and birch and maple trees. You can also follow the Bluff Trail and the River Trail, which follow the Eau Claire River on the north and south sides past the rock outcroppings. However, these trails are a bit more hilly and rocky.

Snuggling up after a wintry walk at the Dells of the Eau Claire Park, near Wausau.

After you leave the park, and depending on how long you snowshoe, consider making another wintertime stop, this time at **Starwood Rides** near Ringle on Highway 29. There you and your sweetie can take a 30-minute horse-drawn sleigh ride. Request the Russian three-seater, which seats the two of you facing each other and the driver in the front. Your driver will stop at a fire circle, allowing you time to warm up with hot cider or chocolate.

As you bask in each other's company, drive back to Wausau and replenish yourselves with some luscious steaks or vegetarian burgers at **Hereford and Hops** restaurant. It's a good lunch spot and brewpub to rest from the morning's activities. The food is solid and the decor is polished, but the restaurant is not too fancy that you'll feel uncomfortable wearing your cold-weather sporting clothes. If you happen to be visiting Wausau during Valentine's weekend, order the chocolate-dipped strawberries for dessert.

## AFTERNOON

After lunch stop by **Cherisa's Wine and Gifts** to pick up a bottle of wine or bubbly and put together a gift basket of snacks for this evening.

Next, take about an hour to mosey through downtown Wausau along Third Street. You'll find a number of antiques shops, clothing boutiques, a coffeehouse, a bookstore, and more. If your feet aren't too tired and the wind isn't blowing too fiercely, stroll through the historic district surrounding downtown. (Of course, you can always drive through this area in the comfort of your heated car.) Admire the stately homes as you imagine your own dream house. The 10-block Andrew Warren Historic District consists of buildings constructed primarily between 1868 and 1934. You'll find Greek Revival, Italianate, Queen Anne, and Prairie-style houses designed by architects such as Frank Lloyd Wright, George Maher, and Alexander Erschweiler. For a map of the Warren District and the East Hill District, where the Leigh Yawkey Woodson Art Museum is located, call the Marathon County Historical Society at (715) 842-5750.

For a real treat, check in to the **Stewart Inn**, located in the Warren Historic District. Built in 1906 by Chicago architect George Maher, the Prairie school–style house has remained remarkably preserved over the years. Architectural enthusiasts will be impressed with the awesome fireplace made of fused glass, the shining white oak floors that don't creek, and the original pedestal sinks (you'll swear they just rolled off the assembly line in Kohler). Listed on the National Register of Historic Places, the house was converted to a bed and breakfast in 2001. It contains five spacious rooms, all with amenities frequent travelers will adore: high-thread-count cotton sheets, down comforters and pillows, flat-screen TVs, and DVD players. The owners, Paul and Jane Welter, hired an Amish firm from Plover to custom-build the oak tables, desks, and beds in every room. Try to reserve the Owner's Chamber, which is especially romantic with its king-size oak royal wrap bed, leather love seat, and double-steam spa.

If you want to be close to skiing at Granite Peak and Nine Mile Forest, consider the **Rib Mountain Inn**. Depending on how much space you want, and if you're interested in staying in a room with a kitchenette or kitchen, you can stay in a standard room in the lodge, in a townhouse, or in a villa. The rooms won't knock your socks off, but most of them have fireplaces and balconies. Instead of looking out onto Interstate 39, you can view a hardwood forest from your room.

After checking in, spend an hour or so relaxing in your room. If you're staying at the Stewart Inn, sink into one of those overstuffed couches in the great room in front of the fireplace or in the warm library and play a game of cards or Scrabble. At the Rib Mountain Inn, lounge in the lobby area by the wood stove with a cup of tea.

## ᥰ EVENING

For dinner, feast on some of the delightful dishes at **Back When Café**, a restaurant located in an intimate storefront on Third Street in downtown Wausau. Arrive early, take seats at the bar, and sip wine as a jazz band or piano player entertains. At your two-top table, relax over a dinner that may include entrées such as zucchini-filled ravioli or veal piccata with capers.

After dinner, if you're not too tired or cold, rent a pair of ice skates at Shepherd and Schaller Sporting Goods on Scott Street (just down the street from the rink and the restaurant) and walk over to the **Fourth Street Ice Rink** at Fourth Street Square. All lit up for night ice-skating, the square is the perfect spot for you to twirl your companion around (or keep him or her from sliding across the ice).

When your ankles have had enough, walk back to the Stewart Inn or drive back to Rib Mountain. You'll need a good night's sleep for another full day of activities. A pleasant surprise will await you if you stay at the Stewart Inn. The innkeeper will deliver warm cookies and milk to your room in the evening. So slide a compact disc into the stereo, give the steam bath a whirl, and tuck yourselves into that big bed.

## *Day Two*

## ᥰ MORNING

You and your companion can wake up to hot coffee delivered to your bedroom door in the Stewart Inn, followed by a hearty full breakfast in the dining room. (Unlike other B&Bs, at the Stewart Inn you can sit at your own little table for two rather than at a larger table where all guests sit together.) At Rib Mountain Inn, stop by the lobby for bagels and a bowl of cereal before making tracks to **Granite Peak at Rib Mountain State Park** for a morning of downhill skiing.

Following several years of expansion and renovation, Granite Peak (formerly called Rib Mountain) now boasts 72 ski runs, some with 60- to 70-degree grades. You can ski through wooded areas of aspen, maple, and oak trees and down freestyle runs. Bask in the moments of riding the chairlift together, viewing the surrounding area from atop Rib Mountain, and feeling the cool air embrace you as you swoosh down the slopes. And be sure to take a break every once in a while and indulge in a cup of hot chocolate or cider in the chalet.

If you like, brush up on your skiing skills by reserving a private lesson for the two of you. Or, have a go at snowboarding. The mountain is a popular spot for snowboarders, and you can rent a board if you wan to give it a shot.

If downhill skiing is a completely new sport to one of you and you're a bit intimidated by Granite Peak (and don't mind skiing with mostly children), spend the morning (and less money) at **Sylvan Hill Park** in Wausau. Sylvan Ski Hill has three runs for beginners and people they call "advanced beginner skiers." Instead of riding a chairlift to the top of the hill, you'll grab onto a rope tow. Because the hill does not produce its own snow, be sure to call in advance to find out if the runs are open. While you're at the park, relive your childhood and take a spin down the tubing hill (tubes are provided by the park).

Unless you plan on spending all sunlit hours skiing at Granite Peak, pack away those skis around 1:00 p.m. or 2:00 p.m. and grab a late lunch (a hot bowl of chili perhaps?) at the Granite Peak chalet.

## DAY SPA GETAWAY

As you drive Up North, take a break for a few hours at a secluded rest stop for couples. Spa in the Woods, located about 10 minutes north of Iola and 30 minutes east of Stevens Point, features a Hot Springs Therapeutic Spa set in a renovated silo surrounded by pine trees. Unwind in a milk bath marinade, or have your back rubbed in the barn's massage studio. For more information or to make an appointment, call (715) 445- 4720 or (920) 596-3643.

## AFTERNOON

Next, treat yourselves to a soak in a hot tub, followed by a Swedish massage at **The Hot Haus Spa**, located not far from Rib Mountain. Book an indoor or outdoor hot tub. Allow the jet streams to loosen those tense muscles as the steam rises above the two of you. Then, as if you thought you couldn't possibly be more relaxed, head to the treatment room for a massage. Sure, you enjoy giving each other massages, but you may be too exhausted from snowshoeing and skiing to do just that. Instead, treat both of yourselves to a massage, allowing the therapist to rub away the pain and instill some energy back into those muscles.

After lunch, drive back into Wausau for a delightful, inspiring visit to the **Leigh Yawkey Woodson Art Museum**. Housed in a 1931 English Tudor mansion on a hill above Wausau's downtown, the museum is best known for "Birds in Art," the annual juried art exhibition held in the fall. But the museum also showcases wildlife art oil paintings, watercolors, photographs, and sculpture throughout the year.

As you enter the museum, note the large bronze sculpture Rites of Spring, by Kent Ullberg, which depicts a pair of whooping cranes taking off for flight together. (This work of art was donated from a museum founder in memory of his wife.) Among the many pieces on view in the museum are freestanding male and female bird pairs created in porcelain by the late artist Dorothy Doughty and lithographs produced by naturalists such as John James Audubon and John and Elizabeth Gould.

## EVENING

For dinner, enjoy a hearty meal at **Carmelo's**, a casual Italian eatery with views of Granite Peak's ski runs. Carmelo's cooks traditional Italian fare such as ravioli, manicotti, and tortellini pasta, plus meat dishes such as Parmesan veal cutlets and tenderloin filets.

After dinner try to catch a musical or theatrical performance at the beautiful **Grand Theater**, a 1927 Greek Revival theater in downtown Wausau. The historic, renovated theater is a performance venue for a number of regional arts groups and visiting acts. You can view a musical presented by the Wausau Community Theatre, a Wausau Symphonic Band concert, or a show featuring visiting violinists, comedians, or troupes. Try to reserve box seats in the bal-

The Leigh Yawkey Woodson Art Museum in downtown Wausau.

cony so you and your companion can have a private little alcove in the theater.

Following the performance, back in your room, slip into the steamy hot tub for a warm bath before bedtime. Then, offer your companion a back massage to soothe any achy muscles. The favor will probably be returned.

## Day Three

### 🦢 MORNING

After breakfast at the inn, check out of your room and pack your car for one more outdoor wintertime activity. Cross-country skiing, a great cardiovascular workout, is also a perfect activity for companions. As you'll discover, the sport is quiet, allowing you to take in the surrounding wilderness of a park and hold conversations as you carve a path through the woods. At parks with double-lane trails, the two of you can ski side by side at a brisk or leisurely pace.

Cross-country skiing in the North Woods, a great way to feel alive in the dead of winter. Photo courtesy of Wisconsin Department of Tourism.

**Nine Mile Forest**, located just south of Rib Mountain, is a 4,800-acre preserve with four groomed cross-country trails, which range from 3.7 miles to 12.4 miles long. Depending on which route you choose (they are all scenic), you can spend anywhere from 45 minutes to hours upon hours in the forest. Glide along these trails and you'll pass stretches of Black Creek and Four-Mile Creek, swamp and forest areas with spruce, oak, and pine trees. Perhaps you will spot a rabbit or white-tailed deer.

You can change into your boots and bundle up in the chalet, and if you don't have your own cross-country skis, you can rent them at the chalet. Skiers will also have to pay a nominal trail fee. (Evening trail passes are less expensive.)

After your tour of the park, unwind with cups of hot chocolate or coffee by the wood stove in the cross-country ski lodge, and check out the vistas of the forest.

## AFTERNOON

For a hearty lunch, stop by **Water's Edge**, which overlooks the Wisconsin River and affords diners views of the river and downtown Wausau. The restaurant serves up mostly Italian food such as calzones and other pasta dishes in a casual environment. Try the wood-fired pizza. Topping options extend way beyond pepperoni and sausage. You can fix your pizza with shrimp, chicken, and blue cheese, among other ingredients.

As you savor this leisurely lunch, pat yourselves on the back for partaking in such an active weekend. Better yet, lean over the table and kiss your companion's ruddy cheeks.

## FOR MORE INFORMATION

**Wausau/Central Wisconsin Convention and Visitor Bureau**
10204 Park Plaza, Suite B, Mosinee
Information booth located off
I-39/Highway 51, Exit 185
(715) 355-8788
or (888) WI-VISIT (948-4748)
www.wausaucvb.com

## ATTRACTIONS AND RECREATION

**Cherisa's Wine and Gifts**
4520 Rib Moutain Drive,
Wausau
(715) 355-WINE (9463)
www.cherisaswine.com
Open Monday through Saturday, 10:00 a.m. to 7:00 p.m., and Sunday, 11:00 a.m. to 5:00 p.m.

**Fourth Street Ice Rink**
Located between Scott and Jefferson Streets
Call the visitor bureau for ice conditions and hours: (715) 355-8788
or (888) WI-VISIT (948-4748)

**Grand Theater**
415 Fourth Street, Wausau
(715) 842-0988 or (888) 2239-0421
www.grandtheater.org

**Granite Peak at Rib Mountain State Park**
3605 North Mountain Road, Wausau
(715) 845-2846
www.skigranitepeak.com
The ski hills are generally open from late November to early April, daily 9:00 a.m. to 9:00 p.m. Night skiing runs from 5:00 p.m. to 10:00 p.m. Adult tickets cost $38 per person for day skiing, $34 for afternoon skiing, and $20 for night skiing. Discounts are available if you plan to ski multiple days. Adult ski rentals are available for $25 per day.

**The Hot Haus Spa**
2110 Robin Lane,
Rib Mountain
(715) 849-TUBS (8827)
www.hothausspa.com
Open Sunday through Thursday, noon to 9:00 p.m., and Friday and Saturday, noon to 11:00 p.m.

**Leigh Yawkey Woodson Art Museum**
700 N. 12th Street, Wausau
(715) 845-7010
www.lywam.org
Open year-round, Tuesday through Friday, 9:00 a.m. to 4:00 p.m., and Saturday and Sunday, noon to 5:00 p.m. Closed Monday and holidays.
Free admission.

**Nine Mile Forest**
Entrance at County Road N and Red
Bud Road
Marathon County Forestry Department
chalet (715) 693-3001; forest
department (715) 261-1580
www.co.marathon.wi.us
Trails are open December through
March for cross-country skiing, Monday,
9:00 a.m. to 5:00 p.m., Tuesday through
Friday, 9:00 a.m. to 9:00 p.m., Saturday,
8:00 a.m. to 9:00 p.m., and Sunday, 8:00
a.m. to 5:00 p.m., and until 6:00 p.m. on
Sunday after the first weekend in
February. Skiers will be charged a trail
access fee.

**Shepherd and Schaller Sporting Goods
(snowshoe and ice skate rentals)**
324 Scott Street, Wausau
(715) 845-5432

**The Sports Den
(snowshoe and ski rentals)**
1202 S. Central Avenue, Marshfield
(715) 384-8313 or (800) 369-4734

**Starwood Rides (sleigh rides)**
R5271 Townhall Road, Ringle
(715) 446-2485
Rides are from $45. Reserve a time for
your sleigh ride in advance.

**Sylvan Hill Park (skiing for beginners)**
1329 Sylvan Street, Wausau
(715) 842-5411
Skiing will cost adults $7. The hill is
open on weekends through February.

## LODGING
**Rib Mountain Inn**
2900 Rib Mountain Way, Wausau
(715) 848-2802; (877) 960-8900
www.ribmtninn.com
Rooms are from $59; prices are higher
during ski season.

**Stewart Inn**
521 Grant Street, Wausau
(715) 849-5858
www.StewartInn.com.
Rooms are from $130.

## DINING AND NIGHTLIFE
**Back When Café**
606 Third Street, Wausau
(715) 848-5688
Open for lunch Tuesday through
Saturday and dinner Friday and
Saturday.

**Carmelo's**
3607 N. Mountain Drive,
Rib Mountain
(715) 845-5570
Open for dinner daily.

**Hereford & Hops**
2305 Sherman Street, Wausau
(715) 849-3700
Open for lunch and dinner daily.

**Water's Edge Café**
150 E. Stewart Avenue, Wausau
(715) 849-9022
Open for breakfast, lunch, and dinner
Monday through Saturday and for
breakfast and lunch Sunday.

# CHAPTER TWENTY

# Ruddy Cheeks and Warm Hearts:
# *Vilas and Oneida Counties*

Once hotbeds for logging and lumber during the 1800s, Vilas and Oneida Counties are now home to numerous vacation resorts that cater to folks looking for a little R & R in the woods or at the lakeside. Although a popular getaway during the summer for families, anglers and boaters, the North Woods is a superb spot for couples during the winter, when the snow cloaks the birch and pine trees and lodges and restaurants strike up the wood-burning fireplaces. During these months, when the snow-covered roads are crossed by families of deer instead of families in minivans, perhaps one of the best ways to explore the region is on the back of a snowmobile.

During this getaway, you will make your way through a region steeped in snowmobile history. It was here that the gas-powered sled originated and where top-notch racers compete every year at the World Championship Snowmobile Derby. Make your trip's headquarters in Saint Germain, home of the Snowmobile Hall of Fame. Saint Germain is surrounded by hundreds of miles of trails and countless lakes, with plenty of opportunities to view wildlife and to soak in a hot tub of a cozy lodge. Not all hotels and restaurants close for the season in September. In fact, many of them stay in business for the flocks of snowmobilers who head up here when the white stuff is fluffy and plentiful.

You don't have to be a seasoned snowmobiler to opt for this getaway. There are plenty of places to rent sleds, snowmobile suits, and helmets. Volunteers are always out marking and grooming trails; follow the signs and you shouldn't get lost. First timers might want to consider joining an organized snowmobile riding tour of the area. Inquire about these trips at the various outfitters in Saint Germain, Eagle River, and Minocqua.

## *Day One*

### ✎ MORNING

First off: gear up. If you don't already own a snowmobile you will need to rent two snowmobiles or a two-seat snowmobile (sometimes referred to as sleds). There are plenty of dealerships in and around the Saint Germain area that rent and sell sleds. Two businesses in Saint Germain that rent snowmobiles are **Paul's Rental** and **Saint Germain Sport Marine**, both located on Highway 70. Prices for one snowmobile start at $95 per day. If you don't already own helmets or snowmobile suits, you'll want to rent those, too. Both places rent accessories and two-seater snowmobiles. **Saint Germain Rentals and Tours**, also on Highway 70, offers weekend tour packages for full-day snowmobiling adventures through the North Woods. Purchase maps of regional snowmobiling trails at local visitor bureaus in Saint Germain, Eagle River, and Minocqua. If you are unfamiliar with the area and have questions, call the **Bo-Boen Snowmobile Club** in Saint Germain or visit the organization's Web site. The members groom more than 100 miles of trails in the region and know these trails inside and out. As they will tell you, trails are liable to change year to year. Be sure to follow the signs. Last, before you straddle that mobile, familiarize yourselves with snowmobiling safety. (For information on these matters, contact the **Association of Wisconsin Snowmobile Clubs** or the Wisconsin Department of Natural Resources.)

After suiting yourselves up, head over to the **International Snowmobile Hall of Fame**, located off Highway 70 on the west side of Saint Germain for a quick visit. Open since 1993, the museum contains a slew of sleds, from a 1964 Polaris snowmobile raced in the first snowmobile derby in Eagle River to the winning Black Magic Arctic Cat snowmobile Blair Morgan drove in the 2001 X Games. Also on hand are photos of Hall of Fame inductees and old jerseys from racers. Plus, you can have a seat and watch clips from previous world championship races.

---

## A TOWN BY ANY OTHER NAME

🐌 Here are some Wisconsin towns with romantic-sounding names: Romance, in Vernon County; Sweetheart City, in Marinette County; Heart Prairie, in Walworth County; Loveland Corners, in Barron County; and Honey Creek, in Racine County.

---

For lunch, make yourselves comfortable at the **Wolf Pack Café,** a cozy little restaurant located on Saint Germain's main drag (Highway 70) and across the street from the Bo-Boen snowmobile trail. This local spot has an especially friendly staff and serves meals with truly fresh ingredients. Expect real (not frozen) beef in those hand-patted burgers. Warm up with a cup of chili, and

Traveling in the fast lane via snowmobile near St. Germain.

top off your meal with a slice of homemade apple pie. Now the two of you are ready to face the chilly northern Wisconsin air.

## ✿ AFTERNOON

Hit the trails for an afternoon snowmobile ride through the North Woods. From Saint Germain, head in any direction and you won't be disappointed with the winter scenery. You can't go wrong with any of the trails: trail 70 takes you past Little and Big Saint Germain Lakes and the Wisconsin River, trails 70a and 70b wind around Pickeral Lake and the Rainbow Flowage, trail 6 weaves around the towns of Woodruff and Arbor Vitae, and trail 9 takes you west of Sayner.

After your ride, check in to your room for the next two nights. Snowmobiling couples looking for comfortable, romantic rooms that are close to trails will want to book at one of the following: Black Bear Lodge, Whitetail Lodge, or Hintz's North Star Lodge. You'll find **Black Bear Lodge** about one mile from Highway 70 in Saint Germain, with access to the Bo-Boen trail near the lodge. Lodge homes and cottages are located near Little Saint Germain Lake; many of the homes have scenic views from the living rooms. You can turn on the gas fireplace and curl up on the couch and look outside your window as the snow falls. Expect lodge-type decor such as forest green and plaids (no pastel pinks or purples in these suites). An economical option for couples is the Bear Trap Suite, a one-bedroom suite with a king bed. However, if you're looking to splurge on this getaway, or if you're planning to stay in town for a while and want more space, book the Jacuzzi Lodge Home, which boasts a double Jacuzzi tub and a stone fireplace. After riding the trails for hours, soothe your muscles by sliding into the jumbo tub.

**Whitetail Lodge** is located right of Highway 70 and County Road C, with access to trail 70. Perhaps the most romantic room at the lodge is the Luxury Getaway Dream Room, with a king bed, a gas fireplace, and an oversized whirlpool bathtub. Although the lodge's lobby is especially inviting, with its fieldstone fireplace and cupboard of games, if you stay in this room, chances are you may want to spend hours here. Request a woods-side room, so the two of you can lie in bed and watch the snow fall on cedar trees outside your window.

If you're looking for seclusion, make tracks to **Hintz's North Star Lodge**, located north of Saint Germain and Sayner on the lovely Star Lake and on snowmobile trail 11.

## EVENING

For dinner, make a reservation at **Hintz's North Star Lodge**. The rustic lodge, formerly called the Waldheim Hotel, was built in the 1890s for railroad and lumber executives before being transformed into a resort and restaurant. Request the romantic boat booth, where the two of you will take your meal in a hollowed-out canoe in the dining room. Otherwise, just about every table in the house offers you views of Star Lake through the restaurant's picture windows. In this restaurant you can savor fresh walleye, salmon, steak dishes, and traditional Wisconsin fare.

After dinner, unwind and cleanse your bodies in a wood-fired Finnish sauna at the Cranberry Inn in Eagle River. You won't want to leave this room on a cool, blustery Wisconsin evening.

Next, it's couple time. If you're at Whitetail Lodge, take a dip in the indoor pool and giant hot tub, or play a game of checkers in the comfy lobby. If you're staying at Black Bear Lodge rent a VCR and a movie from the lodge and snuggle up before the television. Watch how early snowmobiles performed in the home videos of snowmobile pioneer Carl Eliason. The lodge has a number of Eliason home videos for rent at the office.

## Day Two

### MORNING

Start your day by fueling yourselves with a hearty snowmobiler's breakfast at the **The Bear's Den** restaurant at Black Bear Lodge. For about $7 you'll be handed a steaming plate of eggs, bacon or sausage, deep-fried French toast, and American fries as well as coffee and orange juice.

From the Bear's Den, follow snowmobile trail 70 (not to be confused with Highway 70) across Little Saint Germain Lake, along the north shore of Big

Saint Germain Lake and north toward Sayner. For a quick detour, stop by Hug Road, a little windy road that leads to the shores of Little Saint Germain Lake. It's northwest across the lake from Black Bear Lodge. In Sayner stop by the birthplace of the snowmobile. It was in his Sayner garage that Carl Eliason built the first snowmobile over a period of about two years. It may not be the most romantic detour, but snowmobilers will get a kick out of seeing the 1924 model, which is on display during the winter at **Carl Eliason & Co. Lumber and Hardware** store on Main Street (Highway 155). Make this a short stop. (You want to have a lot of time to take the scenic route north.) During the summer and early fall, you can view the snowmobile at the Vilas County Historical Museum, also in downtown Sayner.

From Sayner, take a scenic drive toward Star Lake. If you want to check out the serene

Scenic and serene Rustic Road 60 (a.k.a. County Road K) near Boulder Junction.

sights around Star Lake, follow trail 7. From Star Lake follow 11 to Boulder Junction. These trails tend to be less crowded than those around the Eagle River area, allowing for good, solid couple time. No, you won't be able to have an intimate conversation over the running motors, but if you rent a two-seater, you'll be able to snuggle up close to each other during these rides as you pass by lofty conifers and birch trees and over frozen lakes that look especially stunning during the winter.

If you'd like to take a break from snowmobiling and prefer to drive your car to Sayner, Star Lake, and Boulder Junction, take the scenic route. Follow County Road C from Saint Germain to Sayner. From Sayner continue on County Road N to Star Lake and northwest on County Road K and County Road M to Boulder Junction. Be aware that you may not want to hit these county roads with your two-door, front-wheel-drive sports car after a snowstorm. If you do follow these roads, you'll be rewarded. Around the bend you may encounter white-tailed deer crossing the road. The 11.7-mile stretch on County Road K from Star Lake to Boulder Junction is state-designated Rustic Road 60. You'll also drive by Ballard Lake, White Birch Lake, and White Sand Lake.

When you enter Boulder Junction, you can't miss the giant sign welcoming you to the Muskie Capital of the World. (This is because more muskies reportedly are caught in the vicinity around Boulder Junction than anywhere else on earth.) Boulder Junction is a quaint, former railway town where logging companies shipped their products southward. Relax with your sweetheart over a scrumptious lunch in the **Outdoorsman Restaurant & Inn**, located on Main Street in a former house. (It will actually feel as if you are visiting someone's home and being waited upon.) You'll find lots of two-top tables tucked into various nooks of this restaurant; try to sit at a table by the crackling fireplace or wood-burning stove. Entrées on the menu include creations like the southwestern-style spring rolls, pepper-crusted duckling with shallots and a merlot demi-glace, or an eight-ounce Angus filet. As at the Wolf Pack Café, desserts here are homemade. Share a slice of strawberry shortcake or miniature cheesecake.

## STARGAZING

Here are some best bets for viewing the Big Dipper and Orion's Belt while in northern Wisconsin:

- While camping on Stockton Island in the Apostle Islands National Lakeshore
- On a rowboat in the middle of the Chippewa Flowage
- Near a cranberry bog in the Meadow Valley State Wildlife Area
- In the middle of a restored prairie in Crex Meadows Wildlife Area
- Alongside a waterfall in Copper Falls State Park

## AFTERNOON

Now both of you should take some time to stretch your legs and stroll hand in hand down Boulder Junction's Main Street and have a look at some of its shops. You may not be able to haul back home with you some of the lamps or rocking chairs for sale at The Hayloft, but you'll have fun wandering around the home decor shop, dreaming of your cabin in the woods. The Bear's Den is another stop for rustic, lodge-type decor. You can purchase wildlife photographs, carvings, or paintings at The Studio Gallery or Wiley Miller's Images. And you can choose books to cuddle up with at The Bookworm.

Hop back on your snowmobiles and drive south to Minocqua. You'll discover that numerous trails lead to Minocqua. Just follow the signs to the city. Depending on which trail you take, Minocqua is about 20 miles from Boulder Junction. Head to Lake Minocqua and follow the **Bearskin State Trail** for a few miles. This trail, a former railroad grade that travels south of Minocqua for about 18 miles, will take you across Minocqua Lake and past Baker and Bogler Lakes. For a break, drop by **Bosacki's Boat House** or the **Thirsty Whale** in Minocqua. These establishments are not exactly quiet, romantic places, but both will provide you with time to meet other snowmobiling couples. They are popular spots for snowmobilers and are community institutions. (Bosacki's has been family-run for four generations; the Thirsty Whale, right on Minocqua Lake, was once a livery and boathouse.) The Bearskin Trail runs near both these drink and food spots. While you're in downtown Minocqua stop by **Intimate Hours Lingerie and Gifts**. After your break, bundle up again and head back on the trails to Saint Germain.

## EVENING

Tonight you and your date will dine in downtown Saint Germain at **Golden Pines Restaurant and Lounge**, a relaxing spot for winter dining with a fireplace and hearty comfort food. The historic restaurant (the log building was built in 1931) attracts an adult crowd (few plastic booster seats are handed out here) and is primarily known for serving up rich German specialties; there's plenty of veal and schnitzel on the menu. It's a place where you can nibble on food and chat for as long as you like.

After your peaceful dinner, drive to Black Bear Lodge, which maintains a lighted ice-skating rink on Little Saint Germain Lake during winter months. Removed from the highway and the lights of Saint Germain and other surrounding towns, the frozen lake rink will provide you with yet another opportunity for together time and gazing into each other's eyes.

## Day Three

## MORNING

After rising with the sun in your cozy lodge room, pack your things, check out of your room, and return the rented snowmobiles. Once business is taken care of, stop by the **Saint Germain Bake Shoppe** for rich breakfast goodies. Yet another community institution (it's been churning out bear claws and crullers for decades), the bakery is a place for you to reward yourselves for all the activity you've done these past two days. Fill a bag with glazed doughnuts or blueberry muffins, or purchase butter cookies to nibble on during the drive home.

Settle into your car and drive eastward to Eagle River, the snowmobile capital of the world. Spend about an hour or two touring this town. Race fans will want to take a peek at the World Championship Snowmobile Derby Track, where races have been held in mid-January since 1966. (If you're in town during race weekend, be sure to buy a ticket to this popular event.) You'll also want to have a look at the Eagle River ice castle, erected near the train depot off Railroad Street every year between Christmas and New Year's Day. (Depending on weather conditions, the castle usually stands for about five to seven weeks after construction.) Built of about 3,000 pieces of 12-inch-thick ice cubes, the castle's design varies year to year. Have a picture taken of the two of you sitting on the throne.

Next, browse in downtown Eagle River, where plenty of shops and boutiques sell souvenirs. For a hearty lunch, sample the beef pasties or kielbasa at the **Four Seasons Café & Deli**. For more veggie-friendly options, have a seat at **Terra Nicole's**, a coffee and teahouse that also serves panini and pita sandwiches.

## AFTERNOON

Your next stop will be **Three Lakes Winery**, located in the former railroad depot in downtown Three Lakes, about 10 miles south of Eagle River. Started by John and Maureen McCain in 1972, the winery is now run by their sons and daughter-in-law. Primarily known for its cranberry wines made from locally grown cranberries, Three Lakes also produces a white wedding wine. (You can personalize the bottle with the groom and bride's name.) Spend a few moments sampling some of their wines and touring the facility.

Wrap up your getaway with a quick detour down a local Lover's Lane. Drive south on Highway 32 from Three Lakes for about 20 minutes. Lover's Lane is just south of the town of Hiles, just off the highway near the shores of Pine Lake.

## FOR MORE INFORMATION

**Boulder Junction**
**Chamber of Commerce**
Highway M (P.O. Box 286),
Boulder Junction
(715) 385-2400 or (800) GO-MUSKY
(466-8759), www.boulderjct.org

**Eagle River Area Chamber**
**of Commerce and Visitor Center**
201 North Railroad Street (P.O. Box 1917), Eagle River
(800) 359-6315, www.eagleriver.org

**Minocqua–Arbor Vitae–Woodruff**
**Area Chamber of Commerce**
P.O. Box 1006, Minocqua
(715) 356-5266 or (800) 446-6784
www.minocqua.org

**Sayner–Star Lake Area Chamber**
**of Commerce**
203 Main Street (P.O. Box 191), Sayner
(715) 542-3789 or (888) 722-3789
www.sayner-starlake.org

**Saint Germain Chamber of Commerce**
Info booth at intersection of Highways 70 and 155 (P.O. Box 155),
Saint Germain
(715) 477-2205 or (800) 727-7203
www.st-germain.com

## ATTRACTIONS AND RECREATION

**Association of Wisconsin**
**Snowmobile Clubs**
217 E. Pacific Street, Appleton
(920) 734-5530, www.awsc.org

**Bearskin State Trail**
Department of Natural Resources,
Trout Lake Forestry Headquarters
4125 County Road M, Boulder Junction
(715) 385-2727

**Bo-Boen Snowmobile Club**
P.O. Box 192, Street Germain
(715) 479-1419

**Carl Eliason & Company
Lumber and Hardware**
274 Main Street, Sayner
(715) 542-3233

**Cranberry Inn (Finnish sauna)**
1429 Silver Lake Road, Eagle River
(715) 479-2215
Call for rates.

**International Snowmobile
Hall of Fame**
8481 Highway 70, Saint Germain
(715) 542-4488
Open year-round, 10:00 a.m. to 5:00
p.m. Monday through Friday and 10:00
a.m. to 3:00 p.m. Saturday. Call ahead if
you plan to visit on a Saturday.
Free admission.

**Intimate Hours Lingerie and Gifts**
211 W. Milwaukee Street, Minocqua
(715) 356-9741

**Paul's Rental**
186 Highway 70, Saint Germain
(715) 479-5841
Snowmobiles rent from $95 per
weekday. Accessories are also available.

**Saint Germain Rentals and Tours**
6255 Highway 70 East, Saint Germain
(715) 479-8007 or (888) 479-8007

**Saint Germain Sport Marine**
Highway 70 (P.O. Box 399),
Saint Germain

(715) 479-4930
www.stgermainsportmarine.com
Rentals are from $95 per day. Accessories
are also available.

**Three Lakes Winery**
6971 Gogebic Street, Three Lakes
(715) 546-3080 or (800) 944-5434,
www.fruitwine.com
Open year-round 9:00 a.m. to 5:00 p.m.
daily. Closed major holidays.

## LODGING
**Black Bear Lodge**
1279 Halberstadt Road, Saint Germain
(715) 479-5778 or (800) 563-4340
www.blackbearlodge.com
A one-bedroom bear trap suite is from
$89 ($109 for Friday and Saturday
nights); a two-bedroom lodge home
with Jacuzzi and fireplace is $199 per
night ($249 for Friday and Saturday
nights).

**Hintz's North Star Lodge**
7919 County Road K, Star Lake
(715) 542-3600 or (800) 788-5215
www.hintznorthstar.com
Efficiency apartments rent from $65 per
night; villas rent from $125 per night.

**Whitetail Lodge & Whitetail Inn**
Highway 70 and County Road C, Saint
Germain
(715) 542-2578 or (800) 236-0460
www.whitetaillodge.com
Open year-round. Double rooms are
from $99.

## DINING AND NIGHTLIFE
**The Bear's Den restaurant**
Black Bear Lodge
1279 Halberstadt Road, Saint Germain
(715) 479-5778 or (800) 563-4340
www.blackbearlodge.com
Open year-round.

**Bosacki's Boat House**
305 W. Park Avenue, Minocqua
(715) 356-5292
www.bosackis.com
Open daily for lunch and dinner.

**Four Seasons Café and Deli**
107 Railroad Street, Eagle River
(715) 479-8499
Open year-round. Call for hours.

**Golden Pines Restaurant and Lounge**
8000 Highway 70, Saint Germain
(715) 479-7178
Open year-round for dinner, Monday
through Thursday, 4:00 p.m. to
9:00 p.m., and Friday and Saturday, 4:00
p.m. to 10:00 p.m.

**Hintz's North Star Lodge**
7919 County Road K, Star Lake
(715) 542-3600 or (800) 788-5215
www.hintznorthstar.com
During the winter, the restaurant is open
Thursday, Friday, and Saturday only. Call
for hours.

**Outdoorsman Restaurant & Inn**
Main Street (P.O. Box 319),
Boulder Junction
(715) 385-2826
Open for breakfast and lunch daily
and for dinner Thursday through
Monday.

**Saint Germain Bake Shoppe**
458 Highway 70, Saint Germain
(715) 479-9188
www.stgermainbakeshoppe.com
Hours vary per season. Call ahead.

**Terra Nicole's**
218 Wall Street,
Eagle River
(715) 479-8215
Open for breakfast and lunch.
Call for hours.

**Thirsty Whale**
453 Park Avenue, Minoqua
(715) 356-7108
Open year-round.
Hours vary per season.

**Wolf Pack Café**
426 Highway 70 East,
Saint Germain
(715) 479-8737
Open for breakfast and lunch Monday,
Wednesday, Thursday, Friday,
and Saturday.

# CHAPTER TWENTY-ONE

# Chutes and Bridges: Adventures in
# *Marinette County*

In Marinette County, a scenic, unspoiled region of Wisconsin that hugs Michigan's Upper Peninsula, the sounds of nature abound: water rushing over Precambrian rocks and wind rustling through red pines. Although it is home to numerous bicycling, hiking, and all-terrain vehicle trails; fishing spots; and parks, the county is not overrun by tourists. You and your honey won't be besieged by other visitors fighting for a picnic spot along the riverbank or under a tree. This is a getaway that offers plenty of one-on-one time, with hikes through the woods and time to explore the area's many waterfalls and opportunities to pause over the romantic stone and wooden bridges for a kiss.

Hydrophiles, rejoice. Marinette, dubbed the Waterfall Capital of Wisconsin, boasts anywhere from 13 to 17 waterfalls, primarily on the Peshtigo and Pike Rivers. Don't expect falls that resemble those at Niagara Falls, but count on seeing many miniwaterfalls surrounded by magnificent red pine and birch tree forests.

Thanks to efforts of a number of organizations (among them the Civilian Conservation Corps who planted trees and built park structures in the 1930s), the area contains many secluded spots for couples seeking quiet time with Mother Nature and each other. The area is gorgeous year-round, although you might want to consider visiting during the spring, when the melting winter snow causes the river waters to rush and churn under the bridges and over the rock formations, making quite a thrilling sight. Spend your nights at a bed and breakfast in or around Marinette. Outdoor enthusiasts might want to book a cozy, riverside cabin or campsite in the heart of the county where you can fall asleep to the sound of water rushing over rocks.

## *Day One*
### ☙ MORNING
Start your trip by visiting Twin Bridge Park and Veteran's Falls in Veteran's Memorial Park, located west of Highway 141 by the High Falls Flowage in the

west-central part of the county. (Entrance to each Marinette County Park will cost $2 per car. You might want to consider buying an annual pass for $10, which will allow access to all parks.) The 320-acre Veteran's Memorial Park has plenty of spots for you to relax and cuddle. Descend a hill and cross a bridge to admire the falls on the Thunder River. Then, watch the water pool at the bottom of Veteran's Falls.

---

## PACKERS FANS UNITE

It may not seem like the most romantic spot in the state, but many couples have chosen to hold wedding receptions at Lambeau Field in Green Bay, home to the professional football team the Green Bay Packers. The huge Lambeau Field Atrium, a multimillion-dollar addition to the renovated stadium, has three banquet rooms for receptions and other festivities. Die-hard fans can have their first dance together while looking out at the field through a glass window. More information is available by contacting the room rental staff at Lambeau Field, 2365 Lombardi Avenue, Green Bay, (920) 490-5962, www.packers.com

---

If you're visiting during the summer, chill out in the 90-acre Twin Bridge Park. You won't come upon any awesome waterfalls here compared to other county parks, but Twin Bridge is a quiet little haven where you can swim in the cool waters of the flowage and doze in the sun side by side. Take each other's hands and walk on one of the hiking trails.

Before exploring more waterfall parks, lounge over a lunch. Because most restaurants in the area are supper clubs and serve food in the evenings, you might be hard pressed to find a quaint restaurant or café near the parks. If you don't mind eating lunch in a bar, try **The Gateway Bar & Grill** in Crivitz. Order up hearty sandwiches served on homemade rolls (a local favorite). If the weather cooperates, stock up on gourmet picnic supplies at **Le Grappillion D'Ore**, a French bakery and café in Marinette, or one of the grocery stores in Crivitz or Wausaukee. You can savor your food at Twin Bridge or Dave's Falls Park.

### AFTERNOON

Named after a logger who died while trying to clear a logjam near the falls, **Dave's Falls** has two falls to admire and a few trails for you to wander along. The park, located along the Pike River, is accessible from Highway 141 north of Wausaukee. You won't have to hike for miles to view the falls. Walk down the stairs and hike a short distance through the woods. Pause on the footbridge over the river to watch the water rush over the rocks; the sight is almost mesmerizing.

Once you've had your fill of cascade admiration for the day, drive toward the city of Marinette along Highway 180, which follows the Menominee River. Be sure to stop at Lover's Lane about one mile west of Wausaukee.

If you and your sweetheart are looking for a truly secluded place to stay, book a room at **Shea-Dy Pines Log Home and Bed & Breakfast**, a spectacular, 6,500-square-foot country home built of white spruce logs in 1995. All five rooms in the log home were built with huge windows, affording spectacular views of the field in front of the house or the birch and pine woods surrounding the other sides of the house. The Wisconsin Room on the second floor is especially romantic with its four-poster, king-size bed, love seat, and high ceilings. Take note of the telescopes in the second-floor common room. You can peer through these tonight for stargazing.

After checking in to your room, put on some walking or hiking boots and explore some of the 800 acres the Sheas own. (During the winter, owners Lilli and Jim Shea provide snowshoes for guests.) Or, if you're in the mood to cuddle, recline in one of the lounge chairs on the porch and see how many deer you can count crossing the fields.

If you prefer to stay closer to town, check in to the **Lauerman Guest House**. Built in 1910, the Colonial Revival–style inn has seven rooms decorated with floral-pattern wallpaper and bedspreads and antique furniture. Stay in the Master Suite Room, which boasts its own private balcony looking out onto the Menominee River. After you unpack, feel free to wander back downstairs through the house, taking time to admire the black walnut and mahogany woodwork throughout, particularly the impressive staircase.

## DETOUR FOR LOVERS

Marinette County has a couple of places where you and your sweetie can re-create a love scene from a teen romance movie. Motor over to Lover's Lane, about one mile west of Wausaukee off Highway 180. Steal a kiss and snap a photograph of the street sign. Looking for another photo op or excuse to squeeze your companion? Pay a visit to Sweetheart City, a tiny town between Crivitz and Wausaukee, just north of County Road X, off Highway 141.

A sign of romance in Marinette County.

The **M&M Victorian Inn** also rents romantic rooms. For the more economical route, you can stay at the Best Western Riverfront Inn in Marinette, just down the street from the Lauerman Guest House.

Before the sun sets, walk along the Menominee River in downtown Marinette by Riverside Drive. Watch the occasional pair of swans gliding by. If you have time before dinner drive over to Stephenson Island, located in the middle of the river by Interstate Bridge. You'll find a small logging museum there with an exhibit on Queen Marinette (Marie Antoinette Chevalier), a local woman who managed a thriving trading post in the city during the mid-1800s.

## EVENING

Tonight treat yourselves to a three-course dinner at **La Grappe D'Ore**, an intimate French restaurant tucked into the M&M Victorian Inn on Marinette's Main Street. Call ahead to reserve the keyhole table, an almost-out-of-sight table for two or possibly four people located near the staircase and away from the dining room. La Grappe D'Ore's menu changes often, but you can expect innovative cuisine here (not just typical French food such as escargots). Choose from 2,000 bottles of wine in the cellar.

Before tucking yourselves into bed at Shea-Dy Pines, stop by the common room and peer out through the telescopes and into the dark Wisconsin night to search for stars and planets. If you are staying in the Lauerman mansion's master suite, pop open a bottle of wine (you can buy one at Le Grappillion D'Ore) and unwind on the balcony overlooking the Menominee River.

## Day Two

## MORNING

Whether you stay at Shea-Dy Pines or Lauerman Guest House, you'll be treated to full breakfasts, such as steaming Belgian waffles and ham omelets. Fill up on the breakfast. You'll need the energy this morning because the two of you will have a go at whitewater rafting down the Peshtigo River.

There are a number of outfitters in Marinette County that offer rafting tours of the Peshtigo River. Couples will especially enjoy a trip down the river arranged by **Wildman Whitewater Ranch**, which offers three-hour adventures down the longest continuous stretch of rapids in the Midwest. (Don't be put off by the name; it's run by Bill and Lisa Wildman.) Outfitted in lightweight ThrillKats (single, kayaklike rafts), the two of you will navigate over Class III rapids. Arrive early and take a short hike along the riverside trail to get a glimpse of some of the whitewater you'll be facing. But novice rafters need not fear: all trips are guided by a staff member from the ranch. Hardy souls can run the rapids in April and May suited up in cold-weather gear. Afterward, if

Challenging one of the Peshtigo River's many rapids. Photo courtesy of Wisconsin Department of Tourism.

you are sufficiently pumped to tackle the rapids again, you'll have the opportunity to rerun some of them.

After that heart-pounding adventure, you and your mate will love the idea of snuggling in front of a fire close to the rapids. If so, book a cabin or campsite at Wildman, a good stop for honeymooning campers. Also, if you want to spend a day at the ranch showing off more of your athletic prowess, reserve some time to tackle the alpine rope courses.

Also nearby is another outfitter, **Kosir's Rapid Rafts**, which offers trips on the Peshtigo's Class III and IV rapids. The facility also has individual campsites and RV sites. Lodging is available at the adjacent Rapids Resort in the form of log cabins overlooking the Peshtigo.

After your morning on the river, take some time to drive north about 10 miles from the ranch to McClintock Falls. McClintock Park is another gem of a park, with three bridges taking you over the Peshtigo River allowing you to get close to the rushing water. Have a seat under one of the hemlocks, and dip your toes in the cool water.

By lunchtime the two of you should have worked up strong appetites. Try the **Old Homestead Café** near Athelstane. Or drive back into Marinette. **Mickey-Lu Bar-B-Q** serves up meals that will please your taste buds and wallets. It's a tiny, homespun joint off the main drag where you can watch your ribs being smoked right in front of you. Choose from sandwiches such as the charbroiled hamburger or a bratwurst. Wash your meal down with a malted milkshake.

## ❧ AFTERNOON

From your lunch spot, drive to the far-eastern edge of Marinette to Red Arrow Park. Here take about 30 minutes to work off your lunch on the lakeside walking trails. Then, spread out a blanket on the sand and doze away the afternoon reading and talking as the cool Lake Michigan laps against the Seagull Bar, a sand spit perfect for couples looking for privacy.

If you are staying at Shea-Dy Pines, make an appointment for a massage therapist to visit both of you in your room. Have those aches and pains from your active morning eased away, and restore energy for this evening.

Oconto's elegant Oakwood Restaurant, a great place for that special someone.

## ❧ EVENING

Drive about 20 miles south of Marinette to the quaint town of Oconto for dinner at **The Oakwood Restaurant** located within the Governor Scofield Mansion Bed and Breakfast. With an expansive porch, formal gardens, and intimate dining rooms, the Oakwood is an ideal spot to celebrate anniversaries or birthdays or to pop the question. Before having a seat in the dining room or library, lounge on the elegant front porch and order an aperitif. The menu varies per season but can include salivation-inducing options such as lobster ravioli and grilled scallops. Complement your dinner with a bottle of wine or champagne, and top it off with a dessert such as chocolate croissant pudding with French-pressed coffee.

Although an evening at the Oakwood can be an all-night affair, if you are looking to take your companion to a show, check out the University of Wisconsin–Marinette's **Theatre on the Bay.** Past productions have included the musical *Hair* and the play *Our Town.*

If the two of you are visiting Marinette during the week in the summer, head over to Stephenson Island for the **Sunset Concert Series,** where you can listen to acoustic folk, rock, and country music bands perform in the pavilion for free.

## *Day Three*
### ⌘ MORNING

For breakfast, take a walk down memory lane at **Memories Restaurant**, a diner-style joint with nods to fifties music stars. The food, such as stuffed hash browns (eggs, cheese, and onions piled on top of pota-

Hiking amid radiant fall colors with someone you love . . . it doesn't get much better. Photo courtesy of Wisconsin Department of Tourism.

toes), is served quickly, though it tastes as if the chef has been preparing the meal for hours. Be sure to try some of the homemade bread.

Before leaving Marinette stock up on picnic supplies from Le Grappillion D'Ore. If you'd like to eat on your way Up North, stop by the **Crivitz Home Bakery** for coffee and doughnuts.

This morning you will drive north toward Niagara for visits to more waterfall parks and for a horse-drawn stagecoach ride at **Bjorkman's Horse Outings,** where he owners will organize a romantic one-hour ride through the fields and woods in a stagecoach driven by Belgian or Percheron horses. If this is your kind of outing, extend your visit with an overnight camping trip here or an evening cookout along the Menominee River.

Depending on which route you take homeward, stop by Smalley Falls or Long Slide Falls near Morgan Park, south of Niagara. Or, if you are heading westward, explore Eight Foot, Twelve Foot, and Eighteen Foot Falls. At Twelve Foot Falls County Park you can walk around the pond for a view of the Pike River falls. If you would like to see more falls, a trail leads you to Eight Foot Falls to the south. If you have time to explore more water parks, check out Strong Falls on the Pike River at Goodman Park. Get there by driving along Parkway Road, which passes by red pines, tamaracks, birch trees, and plenty of ponds and lakes. Built by the Civilian Conservation Corps, Goodman Park has lodges and plenty of picnic tables at which the two of you to can unwind. Stroll hand-in-hand along the trails and over the bridge, pausing every so often to embrace.

## FOR MORE INFORMATION

**Marinette Area Chamber of Commerce**
601 Marinette Avenue (P.O. Box 512), Marinette
(715) 735-6681 or (800) 236-6681

**Marinette County Parks and Outdoor Recreation Department**
For information on the waterfall parks
(715) 732-7530

**Marintte County Tourism Committee**
Marinette County UW-Extension Office
1926 Hall Avenue, Marinette
(800) 236-6681
www.marinettecounty.com

## ATTRACTIONS AND RECREATION

**Bjorkman's Horse Outings**
W5994 Chapman Road, Niagara
(715) 251-4408 or (888) 467-7367
www.horsefun.net

**Kosir's Rapid Rafts**
W14073 County Highway C, Athelstane
(715) 757-3431
www.kosirs.com

**Sunset Concert Series**
Stephenson Island
Highway 41 at the Menominee River
(715) 735-6681 or (800) 236-6681
Concerts begin at sunset on Tuesday evenings, June through August.

**Theatre on the Bay**
UW–Marinette
750 W. Bay Shore, Marinette
(715) 735-4313
www.marinette.uwc.edu

**Wildman Whitewater Ranch**
N12080 Allison Lane, Athelstane
(715) 757-2938
www.wildmanranch.com

## LODGING

**Lauerman Guest House Inn**
1975 Riverside Avenue, Marinette
(715) 732-7800
Rooms are from $85.

**M&M Victorian Inn**
See La Grappe D'Ore listing under "Lodging."

**Shea-Dy Pines Log Home and Bed & Breakfast**
W2844 Nettleton Road, Marinette
(715) 735-6600
www.shea-dypines.com
Rooms are from $80.

## DINING AND NIGHTLIFE

**Crivitz Home Bakery**
N6813 Highway 141, Crivitz
(715) 854-7944
Open daily.

**Gateway Bar & Grill**
607 N. Highway 141, Crivitz
(715) 854-7943
Open daily for breakfast,
lunch, and dinner.

**La Grappe D'Ore**
Located inside M&M Victorian Inn
1393 Main Street, Marinette
(715) 732-9531
Dinner served Tuesday through
Saturday; lunch served on request.

**Le Grappillion D'Ore bakery and café**
1701 Dunlap Square, Marinette
(715) 732-5390
Open Tuesday through Saturday.

**Memories Restaurant**
1378 Main Street, Marinette
(715) 735-3348
Open daily for breakfast and lunch.

**Mickey-Lu Bar-B-Q**
1710 Marinette Avenue, Marinette
(715) 735-7721
Open for lunch and dinner Tuesday
through Sunday.

**The Oakwood Restaurant**
In the Governor Scofield Mansion
610 Main Street, Oconto
(877) 357-6337
www.governorsmansionbb.com
Open for lunch and dinner Thursday
through Saturday and for brunch on
Sunday.

**Old Homestead Café**
W10869 County Road C, Athelstane
(715) 856-6860
Call for hours.

# Index

# MORE GREAT TITLES FROM TRAILS BOOKS & PRAIRIE OAK PRESS

## ACTIVITY GUIDES

Biking Wisconsin: 50 Great Road and Trail Rides, *Steve Johnson*

Great Cross-Country Ski Trails: Wisconsin, Minnesota, Michigan & Ontario,
*Wm. Chad McGrath*

Great Minnesota Walks: 49 Strolls, Rambles, Hikes, and Treks, *Wm. Chad McGrath*

Great Wisconsin Walks: 45 Strolls, Rambles, Hikes, and Treks, *Wm. Chad McGrath*

Minnesota Underground & the Best of the Black Hills, *Doris Green*

Paddling Illinois: 64 Great Trips by Canoe and Kayak, *Mike Svob*

Paddling Iowa: 96 Great Trips by Canoe and Kayak, *Nate Hoogeveen*

Paddling Northern Wisconsin: 82 Great Trips by Canoe and Kayak, *Mike Svob*

Paddling Southern Wisconsin: 82 Great Trips by Canoe and Kayak, *Mike Svob*

Walking Tours of Wisconsin's Historic Towns, *Lucy Rhodes,
Elizabeth McBride, Anita Matcha*

Wisconsin's Outdoor Treasures: A Guide to 150 Natural Destinations, *Tim Bewer*

Wisconsin Underground, *Doris Green*

## TRAVEL GUIDES

Classic Wisconsin Weekends, *Michael Bie*

County Parks of Wisconsin, Revised Edition, *Jeannette and Chet Bell*

Great Little Museums of the Midwest, *Christine des Garennes*

Great Minnesota Taverns, *David K. Wright & Monica G. Wright*

Great Minnesota Weekend Adventures, *Beth Gauper*

Great Weekend Adventures, *the Editors of Wisconsin Trails*

Great Wisconsin Taverns: 101 Distinctive Badger Bars, *Dennis Boyer*

Sacred Sites of Minnesota, *John-Brian Paprock & Teresa Peneguy Paprock*

Sacred Sites of Wisconsin, *John-Brian Paprock & Teresa Peneguy Paprock*

Tastes of Minnesota: A Food Lover's Tour, *Donna Tabbert Long*

The Great Iowa Touring Book: 27 Spectacular Auto Trips, *Mike Whye*

The Great Minnesota Touring Book: 30 Spectacular Auto Trips, *Thomas Huhti*

The Great Wisconsin Touring Book: 30 Spectacular Auto Tours, *Gary Knowles*

Wisconsin Family Weekends: 20 Fun Trips for You and the Kids,
*Susan Lampert Smith*

Wisconsin Golf Getaways, *Jeff Mayers and Jerry Poling*

Wisconsin Lighthouses: A Photographic and Historical Guide,
*Ken and Barb Wardius*

Wisconsin's Hometown Flavors, *Terese Allen*

Wisconsin Waterfalls, *Patrick Lisi*
Up North Wisconsin: A Region for All Seasons, *Sharyn Alden*

## HOME & GARDEN

Bountiful Wisconsin: 110 Favorite Recipes, *Terese Allen*
Codfather 2, *Jeff Hagen*
Creating a Perennial Garden in the Midwest, *Joan Severa*
Eating Well in Wisconsin, *Jerry Minnich*
Foods That Made Wisconsin Famous: 150 Great Recipes, *Richard J. Baumann*
Wisconsin Country Gourmet, *Marge Snyder & Suzanne Breckenridge*
Wisconsin Garden Guide, *Jerry Minnich*
Wisconsin Herb Cookbook, *Marge Snyder & Suzanne Breckenridge*

## HISTORICAL BOOKS

Barns of Wisconsin, *Jerry Apps*
Duck Hunting on the Fox: Hunting and Decoy-Carving Traditions,
*Stephen M. Miller*
Portrait of the Past: A Photographic Journey Through Wisconsin 1865-1920,
*Howard Mead, Jill Dean, and Susan Smith*
Prairie Whistles: Tales of Midwest Railroading, *Dennis Boyer*
Shipwrecks of Lake Michigan, *Benjamin J. Shelak*
Wisconsin At War: 20th Century Conflicts Through the Eyes of Veterans, *Dr.
James F. McIntosh, M.D.*
Wisconsin's Historic Houses & Living History Museums, *Krista Finstad Hanson*
Wisconsin: The Story of the Badger State, *Norman K. Risjord*

## GIFT BOOKS

Celebrating Door County's Wild Places, *The Ridges Sanctuary*
Fairlawn: Restoring the Splendor, *Tom Davis*
Madison, *Photography by Brent Nicastro*
Milwaukee, *Photography by Todd Dacquisto*
Milwaukee Architecture: A Guide to Notable Buildings, *Joseph Korom*
Spirit of the North: A Photographic Journey Through Northern Wisconsin,
*Richard Hamilton Smith*
The Spirit of Door County: A Photographic Essay, *Darryl R. Beers*
Uncommon Sense: The Life Of Marshall Erdman, *Doug Moe & Alice D'Alessio*

## LEGENDS & LORE

Driftless Spirits: Ghosts of Southwest Wisconsin, *Dennis Boyer*
Haunted Wisconsin, *Michael Norman and Beth Scott*

The Beast of Bray Road: Tailing Wisconsin's Werewolf, *Linda S. Godfrey*
The Eagle's Voice: Tales Told by Indian Effigy Mounds, *Gary J. Maier, M.D.*
The Poison Widow: A True Story of Sin, Strychnine, & Murder, *Linda S. Godfrey*
The W-Files: True Reports of Wisconsin's Unexplained Phenomena, *Jay Rath*

## YOUNG READERS

ABCs Naturally, *Lynne Smith Diebel & Jann Faust Kalscheur*
ABCs of Wisconsin, *Dori Hillestad Butler, Illustrated by Alison Relyea*
H is for Hawkeye, *Jay Wagner, Illustrated by Eileen Potts Dawson*
H is for Hoosier, *Dori Hillestad Butler, Illustrated by Eileen Potts Dawson*
Wisconsin Portraits, *Martin Hintz*
Wisconsin Sports Heroes, *Martin Hintz*
W is for Wisconsin, *Dori Hillestad Butler, Illustrated by Eileen Potts Dawson*

## SPORTS

Cold Wars: 40+ Years of Packer-Viking Rivalry, *Todd Mishler*
Downfield: Untold Stories of the Green Bay Packers, *Jerry Poling*
Green Bay Packers Titletown Trivia Teasers, *Don Davenport*
Mean on Sunday: The Autobiography of Ray Nitschke, *Robert W. Wells*
Mudbaths and Bloodbaths: The Inside Story of the Bears-Packers Rivalry, *Gary D'Amato & Cliff Christl*
Packers By the Numbers: Jersey Numbers and the Players Who Wore Them, *John Maxymuk*

## OTHER

Driftless Stories, *John Motoviloff*
River Stories: Growing Up on the Wisconsin, *Delores Chamberlain*
The Wisconsin Father's Guide to Divorce, *James Novak*
Travels With Sophie: The Journal of Louise E. Wegner,
*Edited by Gene L. LaBerge & Michelle L. Maurer*
Trout Friends, *Bill Stokes*
Wild Wisconsin Notebook, *James Buchholz*

For a free catalog, phone, write, or e-mail us.

### Trails Books
P.O. Box 317, Black Earth, WI 53515
(800) 236-8088 • e-mail: books@wistrails.com